Shanghai Quartet

Emerging Writers in Creative Nonfiction

General Editor: Lee Gutkind

Editorial Board:

Robert Atwan
Madeleine Blais
James Boylan
Annie Dillard
P. J. Dempsey
Laurie Graham
Tracy Kidder
Francine Ringold
Ilena Silverman
Lea Simonds
Michael P. Weber

SHANGHAI QUARTET

the crossings of four women of china

MIN-ZHAN LU

Duquesne University Press
Pittsburgh, Pennsylvania

This book is published by
DUQUESNE UNIVERSITY PRESS
600 Forbes Avenue
Pittsburgh, Pennsylvania 15282

Library of Congress Cataloging-in-Publication Data

Lu, Min-Zhan, 1946 –
    Shanghai quartet: the crossings of four women of China/by Min-Zhan Lu.
        p. cm.
    ISBN 0-8207-0322-2 (hardcover: alk. paper)
    1. Women — China — Shanghai — Case studies.   2. Families — China — Shanghai — Case studies.   3. Lu, Min-Zhan, 1946 — Family.   4. Lu family.   5. Mothers and daughters — China — Shanghai — Case studies.   6. Intergenerational relations — China — Shanghai — Case studies.   7. Chinese American women — Family — Case studies.   8. Women immigrants — United States — Case studies.   I. Title: Crossings of four women of china.   II. Emerging writers in creative nonfiction.
    HQ1770.S47 L8 2001
    305.47'0951'132 — dc21

                                                                        2001002339

This book is printed on acid-free paper.
Published in the United States of America.

In some instances, names have been changed and composites devised so as to respect and protect the privacy of individuals depicted in this book.

Contents

For Yvonne, Anne, Johnny, and Bruce

Acknowledgments

For support during the writing of this book, I would like to thank the Drake University Center for the Humanities and my department chair, Joseph Lenz. I am also grateful to my editor, Susan Wadsworth-Booth, for her prompt and insightful feedback.

My thanks to all those who have read and commented on different versions of this manuscript and especially to Joanne Brown, Nien Cheng, Francis W. Feng, Pat Harris, Cynthia Lewis, Donald Morrill, David Mura, Anne Tan Piazza, Norah Robertson, Nancy St. Clair, Susan Smith, Jody Swilky, Thom Swiss, David Wolfe, and Jerry Zhu.

To Phil and Susan Smith and to David Bartholomae for making me believe from the beginning that there is a book somewhere and for reminding me through the years to get started.

I thank Elizabeth Robertson and Bruce Horner for the many mornings, afternoons, and late nights they've spent poring over every line of the manuscript through its multiple versions, for their ever gentle but equally witty and probing comments, questions, and suggestions, and for what each has taught me about my life, my writing, and this book.

My thanks to Dr. Evelyn Sun for making my new life in the United States possible. Thanks as well to Shirley Gao for helping me pursue my education.

My deepest gratitude to Robert and Shirley Horner for their steady love and support across the cultural gaps from the first day their son brought my daughter and me home.

Thanks to Derek and Jerry for the brothers each has been to me during the past 30 years and for the standing welcome they've extended to me and my family.

I want to thank Elizabeth and Margaret for the woman and sister each has been. Thanks for the trip to Shanghai on my 50th birthday, for sensing my need to go back to move forward and for yet once again sensing it long before I myself had. In the interest of privacy, I've tried to keep you out of the pages to follow. But you know you are everywhere, in the stories told here and in me, as I have worked on these stories. I know these stories are as much yours as mine. Each of us remembers and lives them differently. I also know that both of you will take my version seriously. As always, you'll weigh it in the context of your sense of me and my needs. You'll tell me up front exactly where you disagree. But you'll love me no less in spite of our differences. And I thank you for letting me know all this through 50 years of words and deeds. Without you this book would never have been written.

And, for everything, always, Yvonne and Bruce.

Prologue

A Few Words To My Daughter

I wrote these family stories hoping that you will someday want to read them. I offer them to you as beginnings: notes on a lifeline of crossings for you to take over and work on.

In Chinese, we call immigrants *yi min*. The literal translation for *yimin* is people (*min*) who have moved (*yi*). But the word *yi* is often used in combination with other words to mean a variety of actions, not just the act of moving to or from a place. *Yi* could mean the effort to change, shift, transplant, influence, transfer, or give. *Yi* appears in literary idioms, such as to *graft* flowers and plants to one another, to *remove* mountains and seas, or to *transform* customs and traditions. I like to think of you and me as a certain type of immigrant: people who move on because we can't keep ourselves from wanting to *yi* — fuse, confuse, and diffuse — set ways of doing things. And I ask you to think of us as the descendants of immigrants working on the art of *yi* at life's crossings.

To claim such an immigrant heritage might appear absurd, since you know as well as I do that neither my grandmother, my mother, nor my and my sisters' nanny ever traveled outside China. In fact, two of them have never lived a single day outside Shanghai, the city of their (and our) birth. Nevertheless, think of them as immigrants on at least two counts. According to both my English and Chinese dictionaries, immigrants are people who move from one country to another for permanent residency. History has forced our elders to move from one China to another, as Shanghai became a treaty city in 1843 after China lost the first Opium War to Western gunboats; as it was "returned" in 1945 to the Chinese Nationalist Republic under Chiang Kai-shek; as it was taken over by the Communist Revolution of 1949; as it underwent the Cultural Revolution in 1966; and finally, as it was swept by a "great leap Westward" in the mid-1980s. In the city of Shanghai, our elders truly lived "everywhere" and in "all times" — *Gu Jin Zhong Wai* (the ancient, modern, Chinese, and foreign).

Of course, the specific details of their lives in China often differed from those you and I now face in the United States. Yet, the experience of standing at a crossroads and being pulled in a confusing array of directions remains familiar. They too seemed to share an unwillingness to trust official designations: reluctant to settle into any of the ever-changing roles assigned them by the forces warring over China, by the China they had had to leave behind and by the China into which they were being naturalized. They are the sort of immigrants who couldn't help but ask themselves: "Why not?" "What if?" "How about if I . . .?" As a result, they often seemed to have voluntarily exiled themselves from relatives and friends who, finding them difficult to classify, labeled them the Not Three, Nor Fours (as we say in Shanghai of people lacking cultural authenticity). This makes me see our elders as not only immigrants by virtue of circumstances — compelled to move across regimes and cultures — but also *immigrants* in spirit, yearning to *yi* — to fuse, confuse, and diffuse — traditions.

Immigrant yearning is something I knew firsthand and long before I crossed the Pacific Ocean. But I would not recognize it as such until I received my official designation as a Chinese Immigrant at the end of my ten-year passage from being a Foreign Student in 1981 to becoming an Alien Resident and then, a naturalized citizen of the United States of America. You will not find this yearning documented in passports or certificates. It is a lifeline spun more often by actions immigrants refrained from taking than actions taken, more in the attempts they made than in the results of such attempts, and more by a collage of mundane efforts than by isolated, dramatic moves.

Memories of our elders' yearning haunt me. They filled me with fear, guilt, hope, pain, and joy when I weighed the risk of pursuing a doctorate in English at the age of 36. They made me act "weird," as you like to say when you're frustrated by my contradictory reactions to the slightest turn in either of our lives. New questions and new explanations emerged as I deliberated in 1981 over whether to break my ten-year marriage with your father and thus risk losing custody of you at the tender age of eight, or in 1984 over whether to remarry, this time to "a foreigner 11 years younger!" (as one family friend said of my second husband). Time and again, I have lost track of my elders' yearning to *yi* because I was simply viewing their lives through the lens of only one or two of the regimes they had crossed. Every phase in your life — entering teenage years, graduating from medical school, or moving in with the man you love — has brought changes in my understanding of our elders' yearning.

I have wanted for years to write about this lifeline so elusive and yet so tenacious that it remains unbroken by the deaths of my grandmother and mother or by the expanse of the Pacific Ocean now separating my nanny from me.

In the spring of 1996, when my sisters gave me a paid trip to Shanghai for my 50th birthday, I found a new impetus for writing about our elders' yearning to *yi*. As you know, during my first return in 15 years, I had the opportunity to spend a night with my and my sisters' nanny, Ahfen, at her place. That night, Ahfen recited for me an entire Buddhist scripture, pausing to parse the classic Chinese to show me that she had learned to recognize the characters and grasp their traditional meanings. "A part of my lessons," she explained, for earning her certificate, at age 80, as a disciple of a master monk at the big temple.

Amazed by the new turns in Ahfen's life, I was struck by the fact that I had just reached the age at which she and my mother were uprooted by the Cultural Revolution. In fact, if I were to live as long and fully as Ahfen, I had just reached the beginning of the second half of my life. No more excuses for delay. Writing about my elders' yearning can help me grasp how I have lived this lifeline in the past, and how I might try to use it differently in the future, if I were to take my past in new and unexpected directions in the years to come, as my grandmother certainly had until the end of her 94 years, as Ahfen was still trying to, and as my mother would have undoubtedly wanted to, had cancer not taken her away at age 60.

During that night in 1996, as Ahfen and I reminisced over your little antics before leaving China at the age of eight, she kept on muttering: "Twenty-three and a medical student!"

"Your mother would have been so proud!" she added with a pat on my knee.

This, I understood, was Ahfen's way of letting me know that she remembered how bleak life had been for me at 23. I followed Nanny back to 1969. I saw again my mother's bony back as she stood, hunched over a cup of hot water, in front of the windows: working the evening air to waft her love across the city to my father behind prison bars. I felt again the weight of memory on my mother and, through her, on me, as I watched her cope with the upheavals of the Cultural Revolution. I recalled my longing to understand how she was reliving her past and why. How much I still resented my mother's reticence! Thinking about myself at 23 made me wonder what you might be thinking about me at that very moment. What you would say at 50, if I did not try harder to let you in? It was as if Ahfen had somehow tapped open a floodgate I did not know was there until I felt her hand on my knee and let myself remember how much I had missed her touch during the last 15 years. In her eight-by-eight room on top of a rickety stairway, I experienced a sudden convergence of thoughts.

The silence of immigrants about their past has become a well-established topic in the writings of their children. Immigrant children have mostly traced that silence to the physical exhaustion resulting from their parents' need to learn English, get a job, feed the family, educate the children. Many have written about immigrants' psychological unwillingness to relive past pain and suffering, their refusal to burden their children with stories of gruesome circumstances from which they had strived so hard to remove their children. Others have pointed to the cultural difference between the immigrants' "old country" sense of what can be (or must never be) told and their children's "American," "new world" expectations. What I know about some immigrants suggests yet another possible reason for this collective silence.

It seems that immigrants like our elders often measure their present according to the changes in how they have remembered, understood, and made use of a past event during different points of their immigration. They have found it hard to separate "what happened" during a past event from their migrating views of that event. Some of their reticence might have been compounded by the split they notice between their desire to talk about their changing memories and the eagerness they sense in some of their listeners for a straight story of that past event. Most immigrants know how to package their life according to standard expectations for a straight story. Many of them have indeed told, have had to tell, some version of such stories during immigration or job interviews. But their reluctance to tell more might stem from a conviction that some — themselves as well as those listeners who care about them and about the people populating our past — deserve more; more about why they have clung so desperately to the past; more about why they have not always taken the same route in and out of that event; more about why they have not always remembered a past event in the same way others involved in it have understood or recounted it; more about how they have fed that past and have fed off of it; more than they know how to convey; more than their listeners know how to hear.

In the post-Mao Shanghai of 1996 and with the slightest touch, Ahfen prodded me to place both my frustration toward my mother's reticence concerning her past and my desire to tell you more about my elders' beyond the realm of our immediate family. I realized that I might scavenge my family's past for stories on how some immigrants have talked about their yearning, how and why they've found some crossings more difficult to recount than others, how they have improvised with words, gestures, and silences when dealing with these difficulties, and how they have used these improvisations to sustain one another's yearning as they remember the past, cope with the present, and envision the future. I might begin with the hope of compiling a family manual — a book of "how to's" — for recounting life at crossings, in the *yi*. I might proceed with the hope of reaching others besides you, immigrants in spirit or according to government legislation, who would treat my stories as tools to be tested — assessed and reshaped — through their own hands-on experience in new and drastically different crossings. I might continue with the hope that they, as well as you, would add their own accounts to my stories, helping me to come up with new ways of living in the flux of *yi*.

To keep hope in sight, I smuggled the feel of my nanny's pat through customs back to my home in the U.S. The following pages embody where it has taken me.

I

Haopo

(1889–1983)

A Woman of Good Fortune

An Exception

I grew up knowing it was rare to have grandmothers who could read and write. It was even more unusual to have grandmothers who worked outside the house long after getting married and having children. My *Haopo*, meaning "Good Granny" in Chinese, was an exception.

Of the stories she told, I liked best the story of how Haopo got her school name. In my mind, this story is sealed in two scenes, one from my own childhood in the early 1950s under Mao's communism, and the other a composite of images I had gleaned from movies and novels set in the last decades of the Chin dynasty, the China of Haopo's girlhood.

To recall this story is, first, to long to be eight years old again. My father was hosting a party for his Western diplomat and banker patients on the first floor of our home. This meant that all the servants, including our nanny, Ahfen, would be busy in the pantry, so my sisters and I could hang around all evening in Haopo's suite on the second floor, which was to the right of my parents' suite, across the hall from the upstairs small dining room, which was itself connected to the back staircase leading to the pantry and the servants' quarters, and directly underneath my bedroom on the third floor. This also meant that we could sample the hors d'oeuvres, the 12 main courses, and the desserts Cook would send up in the same sequence they were served to the guests, while we savored the fact that we might ask Haopo for as many stories as we managed to stay awake to hear. We might even talk Haopo into letting us fall asleep in her bed before Ahfen could free herself from downstairs duties to move us back to our bedrooms.

"Tell us about when you got your school name!" I'd beg as I slid deeper into the countless featherweight pillows and silk-fiber padded blankets piled on Haopo's queen-sized bed.

Slowly, I rubbed my cheeks and toes against the cotton bedding so finely woven that — as Ahfen had showed me when ironing — it felt smoother than damask and warmed to the skin faster than flannel. And

I let my imagination roam through a household Haopo had helped us conceive with picture-book illustrations of her two favorite classic novels, *The Dream of the Red Chamber* and Pa Chin's *The Family*. I pictured a huge compound of buildings linked together by courtyards and corridors. I housed my four-year-old grandmother, her eight-year-old No-Good Brother, and her elderly parents in the main quarter. In more quarters to both sides, I placed Haopo's three grown stepbrothers with their wives and children. I envisioned a household where everything one said or did was known to everyone else; because the doors between chambers were always left open, leaving only the ten-inch-high wooden door ledges in between to keep people in their rightful places; because servants and slave girls were in waiting day and night and regularly bribed to share their knowledge of things they were supposed to have been both too dumb and too loyal to take note of; because Haopo's mother — a Nobody Wanted Spinster until her late 30s — was supposed to preside over three stepdaughters-in-law, each with sons of their own, and sons much more diligent and intelligent than the No-Good Brother Haopo's mother had surprised everyone by delivering in her early 40s.

Armed with the warmth of Haopo's queen-sized bed and my script for what we might call the *Sepia Chambers of Haopo's Family*, I was ready for Haopo's vibrant coloratura voice:

> *Every night, my father would get very upset at my No Good Brother: "Wrath of heaven, what evil deed did I commit in my previous life to deserve you! Eight years old and still hasn't learned the Family Register."*
>
> *From the antechamber where my mother embroidered and I played on the lap of my nanny, we could hear everything from the study, down to my father's trembling fingers when he turned the rice paper pages.*

Haopo knew how to tell a story with sound and color. She made us hear her four-year-old self chanting a nursery rhyme as she and her nanny clap-clapped in keeping with the beat and between elaborate hand movements. We registered the shock on her mother's face when, without missing a beat with her clapping, Haopo suddenly switched from the nursery rhyme to chanting the Family Register, which her No-Good Brother was supposed to be reciting for her father in the study but had once again stumbled over and completely lost track of. We watched as Haopo's mother, too startled to immediately put a stop to Haopo's undaughterly behavior — learning was for sons, not daughters, and children spoke only when ordered to by their elders — waited for the father's wrath to descend. We sighed with relief for mother and daughter when Haopo's father merely cleared his throat and called Haopo into the study to test her on the Family Register, this time from the beginning to the end. And we cheered as our four-year-old grandmother spun verse after verse of the family genealogy and family rules her father had been trying in vain to instill in his No-Good Son. We waited impatiently for Haopo to finish reciting her family register, which, at 65, she could still sail through without having to pause and catch her breath more than once every four lines. We waited for her recitation to end, so that we could once again be both grateful and angry at her father for saying to her mother, "If only you'd borne this one a son!"

We knew exactly how the story would end: from that evening on, Haopo's father let her hang around the study and watch as he went over the classics with her brother. She thus became her brother's study companion, like those boy servants you see in *The Dream of the Red Chamber*. During the day, when her mother tried to make sure that the No-Good Brother reviewed his lessons, Haopo would give her mother a little nudge every time the brother messed up or skipped a line. About a year later, Haopo's father found out that she'd taught herself more characters than her brother had learned from the nightly sessions. So, her father told her mother that, next year, Haopo could accompany the No-Good Brother to the family school.

We knew this ending line by line. Nevertheless, we patiently let the cadence and sonority of Haopo's voice guide us through, so that, in conclusion, we could all join her to announce with her father: "Her school name will be *Xi Ying* (Exceptionally Outstanding)!"

I begin with this story because of its impact on my sisters and me: it turned us into the granddaughters of an Exception, a fact I took great comfort in.

When my sisters and I made our public appearances, relatives dutifully cooed: "What good fortune! Three beautiful *Qian Jin* (1,000 pieces of gold)!" I sensed the undertones even before I understood that a girl from an upperclass family was called a *Qian Jin* because 1,000 pieces of gold was all the parents should expect in return for raising her for her future husband's family. The fortune of having three beautiful daughters could never compare to the fortune of having one son, especially if he turned out to be like my father: "Filial, famous surgeon with a thriving practice for Western diplomats and bankers, husband to a beautiful wife from a rich Catholic family, owner of a mansion in the priciest section of the former French Concession, . . .!" This fortune seemed all the more stunning since it kept pouring in after 1949, under the Dictatorship of the Proletariat, The Great Helmsman Mao Zedong, the People's Liberation Army, and the Glorious Communist Party, and in a city learning to sever all attachments to things labeled Imperialistic or Bourgeois. A fortune blemished only by the fact that my father had failed to produce a son to continue the family line and pass down the fortune.

Unless. . . .

By the time I turned eight, I knew full well the remedies other grandmothers would have pressed upon my parents. In first grade, three girls in my classroom alone were named Brother to Follow. This taught me to appreciate the fact that my Haopo had named me with the character "profound" combined with the character meaning "agile, sensitive, clever, or diligent." Other grandmothers would also expect my parents to adopt, as our nanny Ahfen had been advised to adopt the second boy of her dead husband's brother. This, I understood, was the reason someone had once left a newborn boy outside our garden gate. Other grandmothers would later insist that our parents scout for sons-in-law willing to let their sons bear our family name in return for inheriting the family fortune.

Luckily, our grandmother was Exceptional. In a Chinese laced with literary expressions, Haopo always maintained: "We do not value sons over daughters." She assured all that Dada, my grandfather, had always practiced this principle in all decisions concerning their children, my father and his sister. This was our family tradition long before it had become a political slogan under the People's Government.

Being the true son of an Exceptional woman, my father would chime in with an English steeped in 18 years of missionary schools and gilded by postdoctoral work at Johns Hopkins: "What is this bloody nonsense about family name? Ignorant, local superstition. It's the genes that count!"

I dreaded to think of our fate in the hands of any other grandmother.

At eight, I had other reasons for loving the story of Haopo's school name. I saw in it my grandmother's first success in distinguishing herself from her stepsisters, sisters-in-law, and the daughters of her stepbrothers.

I understood this was not what the story was supposed to mean to me. To begin with, it was supposed to illustrate my grandmother's exceptional intelligence. My grandmother herself never made the point directly. Nevertheless, it was driven home every time we heard the story of my father's first spoken words. As the story went, my father did not talk even after he turned three. Others were beginning to assume he was born dumb. Then, one day, out of the blue, he just broke out with verse after verse of a classic poem my grandmother had been teaching the women she tutored at home.

"Super intelligent from the day he was born!" Haopo always concluded.

"Like mother, like son!" My elders always cut in before Haopo could go on to enumerate all the first prizes her son had won from the best missionary elementary school, secondary school, and university in Shanghai.

Aside from Haopo's exceptional intelligence, the story of her school name was also supposed to demonstrate her good fortune in having been born to parents with foresight about her needs and potential. We had heard other stories concerning her mother's wisdom: "I was so puny and limp that the midwife was going to take me straight to the trash. But my mother had me wrapped instead against her bare chest for four days and four nights until she felt me twitch. I was her last hope. She already knew how my brother was going to turn out." We had been repeatedly cautioned not to mistake her father's decision to send Haopo to school as a reward for my four-year-old grandmother's undaughterly behavior. Rather, we were made to understand it as an act of precaution, an indication of the father's ability to anticipate No-Good Brother's failure to take proper care of her after their father's eventual death. And we were taught to appreciate the magnitude of a child's fortune in having parents with such foresight: we grew up hearing others raving over my father's fortune in having a mother with the wisdom to send him to the British-run public school in the International Settlement long before any of her peers had realized that such an investment was to be indispensable for "anyone hoping to be anyone in Shanghai."

However, at eight, I was not particularly interested in stories of either my elders' outstanding intelligence or parental foresight. I had simply presumed both to be my birthright. I wanted leads on how to distinguish myself from my sisters. I wanted my elders to treat me as an exception, as Haopo seemed to have managed in the story of her school name.

Ironically, my wish to be an exception originated from my chagrin over not inheriting my mother's well-known beauty, unlike my sisters. Instead, I'd been taught by my elders to recognize — in the only photo of my teenage Haopo, where her bound feet were still swathed in three-inch brocade slippers rather than having been let loose into the size four leather shoes I grew up seeing her wear — my own broad forehead, faint eyebrows, bulbous nose, and long chin. At eight, it was no consolation to notice that the same — so ugly! — features which had caused endless teasing when in my possession had, when appearing on my grandmother's face, been often lauded by the believers of physiognomy as signatures of her exceptional good fortune. (Great fortune was another entitlement I expected for me and all members of my family.) However, our much noted facial resemblance did give me secret hope that it might somehow lead my elders to perceive me as also being exceptional like my grandmother.

Anxious to impress this lineage on others, I tried to "look smart," as others were always saying in praise of Haopo's demeanor and wardrobe. I spent hours in front of the mirror trying to coax my eyes to speak and listen with the intensity I noticed in Haopo when she sat for a photo or conversed with a guest. I watched my grandmother as she put together an outfit, playing with the subtle differences between myriad shades of blue, brown or gray — the only colors she wore — and between an array of silk, linen, and wool of varying textures and weight. I emulated the way she turned around to examine how her robe caressed her shoulders or hugged her hip, unconsciously learning not to let the look of a particular color, fabric or fashion on someone else tell me how I should dress.

Besides looking smart, I wanted to appear *guai* like Haopo. A tricky concept in Shanghai dialect. Children are called *guai* when they are well-behaved and obedient, like my sisters. But to call a grownup *guai*, I soon noticed, could mean a variety of things, from being ingenious or artful to being cunning, shrewd, or crafty. I could tell from listening to stories that, even as a child, Haopo was cunning-obedient in grown-up ways. She had an uncanny ability to get away with doing things unimaginable for other daughters. She knew how to get what she wanted. As the saying went, she was quick to figure out which direction the wind blows and how to steer the boat with the current.

I coveted Haopo's cunning obedience. For I was the child who wanted — Too much! — fun, gifts, and attention. I was always doing things to make my elders ask: why can't you be *guai* like your sisters?

My mother believed in the saying that one's personality was sealed by the time one turned three. She illustrated the differences between me and my elder sister by repeating two stories from our earlier childhood:

> *I told Number One to put her tiny hand over her eyebrow to shade herself from the sun, and she'd still have that hand up when we turned around and the sun was coming from the back. Guai from the beginning!*
>
> *Not Number Two. The year she turned four, I told her not to tell anyone about her birthday. The next thing I knew, she'd told all our neighbors: "My mom said I'm not to tell you tomorrow is my birthday." It was so embarrassing when all those presents started coming in.*

I understood this story was supposed to illustrate my lack of *guai*: my constant disregard for the instructions of my elders and my need to become more obedient like my sisters. Yet, when I listened really carefully to the story, as my mother was always telling me to, I noticed instead the cacophony of rules floating around our household. I saw myself lacking in Haopo's cunning obedience — her knack at figuring out which of these rules could be broken, when, and where.

Birthdays were crazy times in our family. There was the Chinese way. You celebrate only when you are considered important. Like Haopo. Your guests said: *A little token, not good.* You said as you casually handed the gift to the servant standing behind: *You are too polite, I don't deserve it.* All cheered when the longevity noodles were brought in after the 14-course meal.

There was the Western way. Your guests said: *I got this gift specially for you.* You said *I love it* as you tore open the wrappings. You wore the gift the next time you saw the person, to show your appreciation. (*Never do that with Chinese relatives and friends. They'll think you are desperate, have nothing else to wear.*) All sang Happy Birthday to you when the cake came in. You blew out the candles with Nanny's help and made a wish, which you should never tell anyone.

Haopo had her birthday celebrations big, the Chinese way. With her good fortune, one expected that. Being filial children, my parents would not dream of doing any less for her. There would be several cakes (chestnut cream, her favorite) to hold all those candles. Papa got two celebrations, a 14-course feast in June of the lunar calendar and then a party in July of the solar calendar. Gifts would arrive from patients and other doctors (with names he couldn't always match with faces) and "those Chinese," his name for "old-fashioned" relatives and friends.

Mmma did not want hers either way. Her people were weird. They observed the birthdays of their patron saints. They fasted and then went to midnight mass on Christmas Eve because it was a birthday. "Bloody nuisance," Papa complained. For Christmas, he liked a lot of guests, food, champagne, dancing, and gifts under the tree. Midnight mass meant extra waiting for us kids, anxious to open the presents as soon as midnight struck.

When it came to us girls, things really got out of hand. Haopo would never fail us. Whatever trinket we wanted, drop a hint and she'd deliver. Papa surprised us with the big ones — gold watches, imported toys, and once, a three-story doll house, an exact replica of our house on HengShan Road. Call in the magicians. Noodles and dinner for the relatives and friends. Cake and tea for kids from the club, from the ballet classes (with their mothers and nannies, of course). Why not? We had the money, the space, the servants, and everyone wanted to stay on good terms with the doctor. Mmma wasn't so sure. A modern upbringing was what she wanted for her daughters. But how could any child deserve so much attention, and gifts which easily cost more than what most people made in a month? Mmma did not believe in material manifestations of love: shallow, wasteful.

I wanted to please Mmma. But I wanted ever so much one of those paper doll books my sister got, a tall, blue-eyed blonde in three postures, accompanied by a wardrobe of fur-lined evening gowns, lacy lingerie, crystal slippers. Knowing that my mother's "do not tell" was not the only rule for birthdays, I did some selective listening. Instead of telling about my birthday (as my mother had instructed me not to), I gave away information on what my mother had said (which she had not directly told me not to tell). I hadn't completely disobeyed, which, I explained to myself, was why Mmma always chuckled when mimicking my "my mother said I'm not to tell you." I got what I wanted, tons of presents. But I couldn't get my elders to call me *guai*, as Haopo seemed to have managed when she got her elders to send her to school. I could not get my elders to consider me an exception.

I decided I needed to grab some of my grandmother's cunning obedience, fast! Just a small portion of it, since I had fewer people lording over me. For Haopo, there had been her father, No-Good Brother, her mother, the nuns at the convent school, and later, her husband — my Dada — and eventually her son, Eddie — my father. Not to mention that child Emperor and then Sun Yat-sen, whom she admired, or Chiang Kai-shek, whom she didn't much care for, or Mao Zedong, whom she was cautious never to criticize. And then, of course, there were the Sikhs brought by the British to police the International Settlement, the Annamese guarding the French Concession, the Japanese during the occupation, the National Army, the People's Liberation Army. . . . There were so many of them that I soon lost track. Big People, I called them, so that I could concentrate on what interested me most: how Haopo managed to please them all yet still get what she wanted. To trick Haopo into giving away her secret, I made her repeat her stories.

"Tell me about when they sent you to boarding school," I'd beg as I settled deeper into the soft bedding of her queen-sized bed.

"Well, the year I turned 14, my mother called together my brothers to settle my whole life. . . ." At eight, I no longer needed Haopo's asides to follow the grid of traditions enmeshed in this historical family meeting. I knew about the custom of settling a girl's whole life (*ding zhong sheng*): hiring a matchmaker to convince prospective in-laws that the girl's *bazi* — eight letters signifying the year, month, date, and time of a person's birth and therefore, that person's fortune — would not clash with the *bazi* of their son. The classics taught: upon growing up, every daughter should take a husband. So most girls had their lives settled as early as age two or three. I was also old enough to know that being a widow, Haopo's mother had to rely on the support of her stepsons to pressure her No-Good Son to take this appropriate action. Kong Fuzi (Confucius) says: the eldest brother acts as father. Haopo had been under the charge of her No-Good Brother ever since her father's death and after her brothers had divided the family property to set up separate households. However, her brother had been too busy parading his bird cages in tea houses to fulfill his fatherly duty. Instead, his "business" had significantly drained the share allotted to their household, making it less likely that Haopo would have sufficient dowry to attract a good match.

Such background knowledge allowed me simply to luxuriate in the smooth warmth of Haopo's bed and her coloratura voice. Gently kneading the soft inside of Haopo's right elbow, I half-listened as she described her mother's rapidly deteriorating health and anxiety to see Haopo's whole life settled right away. Her mother had sought the backings of her stepsons because of their excellent standing in the City: one was a cotton merchant like Haopo's father, and the other two were respected scholars. Besides, although the stepsons were themselves progressive scholars, they were known for having married women trained by and capable of raising daughters strictly according to classic teachings on female virtues.

My interest in the story did not begin until Haopo reached the point where her stepbrothers suggested that, after a matchmaker had been hired and while Haopo was waiting to be betrothed, she be sent to a boarding school run by the Catholic nuns on the western outskirts of Shanghai. Believing that there could be no worse fate than becoming a Nobody-Wanted Spinster living under the roof of a No-Good Brother, her stepbrothers hinted that, if the matchmakers were to fail to find Haopo a suitable husband, a convent school education might at least give Haopo the dreadful but nevertheless necessary option of earning her own living as a private tutor.

I loved it when Haopo impersonated her four brothers by shifting the register of her voice to capture their speech patterns:

"More schooling? She has already eaten too much ink for her own good. Everyone knows that book learning can only breed trouble, not sons and grandsons! I'll never find her a husband."

"In my humble opinion, Xiyin has never neglected her female virtues. She can sew, embroider, and wait on her elders better than most in this family."

"She is modest and circumspect."

I had always been extra careful that no one could say that I put my book learning in front of my female duties: I knew not to shame my parents for letting me study the books. I would not do anything to give other parents reason to keep their daughters from school.

"I'm not going to let these foreign devils put ideas in her already puffy head. What if she turns into one of those female students shaming their families by running around in public and disobeying their elders?"

"In my humble opinion, the nuns at the convent school are very discreet. They will prepare Xiyin to be a good daughter-in-law for any respectable family. Besides, we can ask Xiyin to make a promise, right now, that she'll come home as soon as a match is set or whenever she is needed at home."

My eldest brother paused and looked towards me. I'd been standing behind my mother with my eyes carefully lowered to the ground. But I quickly nudged my mother, ever so slightly, to let my mother know I gave my promise if she so desired.

My mother liked the double solution Big Brother offered. This way, if she were to die before I was betrothed, she could go with her eyes closed.

Even my No-Good Brother couldn't object to the plan. It wouldn't cost him any extra, since my Big Brother had offered to foot the tuition. And if, as he predicted, no good family would want me because of my book learning, it might help clear me off his hands.

So a year later, I entered Morning Star.

"And you got what you wanted, right?" I'd ask.

But I could never get a straight answer from Haopo. She would claim that she was thankful for her good fortune. She had Chinese composition, English, arithmetic, geography, and history, and she learned to paint, knit, cross-stitch, needlepoint and crochet. The skills came in handy later when she had to help Dada out with the children's education: by teaching in the daytime and taking in handicraft work from the department stores at night. Then, she'd remind me that if she had not been sent to school, her No-Good Brother might have found her a younger husband in the Chinese City from a family more comparable in standing to her own.

"And you," Haopo would tease, "might never exist."

That alone convinced me that attending Morning Star was what Haopo had wanted. Simple logic: what turned out best for Papa and therefore, me, had to be what was best for her — what she really wanted. Yet all I could ever get my grandmother to admit was that she was fortunate. The road was open. She moved along, made use of it.

But I felt I knew better: It had to take something, a lot, to figure out which road would be open and for how long under the laws of the many Big Persons running the city and one's life. Haopo just wouldn't admit that to me because she too believed that I needed more patience and obedience like my sisters, not more ideas about how to make my elders let me have what I wanted. So I kept on begging her to repeat the story, listening for the slightest change in her script, for an opening to trick her into revealing the secret to her cunning obedience. But she never did.

A Maker of Bargains

"A woman of good fortune!" People always said of my grand-mother, with a mixture of admiration, envy, perplexity, and resigna-tion. I thus learned to see Fortune as the god of all gods, of all those human or supernatural but equally fickle and mysterious forces orches-trating the accidents of our lives. And I learned to admire Haopo's ability to gain fortune in spite of the fact that Fortune had not always been as kind to her as he had been to other Good Fortune women of her generation.

By the time I turned 11 and entered junior high, I had begun to chronicle the turning points in Haopo's life as a series of bargaining sessions with the god of Fortune. I accordingly assessed Haopo's cun-ning obedience in terms of her ingenuity as a bargainer — her quick-ness in spotting a bargain and in figuring out how to barter for it. For instance, Fortune had given Haopo parents who cared about her well being. But he had also made them so old that she was left in the charge of her No-Good Brother. Haopo, however, was quick to see as a bargain the education No-Good Brother was too dumb and lazy to seize and her stepsisters were too dumb and timid to desire. And she was *guai* enough to know that the only way to get Fortune to grant her this bargain was to prove to the world that she could be both the kind of student her father and scholarly stepbrothers had wanted out of her No-Good Brother and the kind of virtuous woman they had expected from their own wives and daughters — the only kind Fortune was sup-posed to favor. This, I concluded, was why my 60-something grand-mother could still recite the family register backward and forward: from having taken care to act as if she was obeying every single rule prescribed for both Good Sons and Good Daughters.

Haopo had to bargain just as hard and astutely for a good marriage as she had for her education. Although Fortune had granted Haopo the opportunity to study uninterruptedly until graduation from the convent school, he also granted her No-Good Brother the pleasure of seeing his predictions turn true: no Good Family in the Chinese City wanted an Old Maid (at 19, 20, and then, 21) with so little dowry and so much schooling. In the end, the matchmaker found a 36-year-old widower with a struggling jewelry business.

"I'm not afraid of a woman who has eaten ink. Just let me have a look at her!" My late grandfather was reported to have said when approached by the matchmaker.

A viewing was arranged. On a certain date, a rickshaw carrying Haopo (chaperoned by her nanny, of course) passed by a street corner where Dada and the matchmaker waited. Dada liked what he saw. So did Nanny. Haopo had to keep her eyes lowered. "Not that it mattered," Haopo always added for us children. It would have been too forward for a daughter to form any opinion concerning her marriage arrangement. So Haopo wisely left things to Fortune.

I imagined Haopo holding a session with Fortune then and there. Haopo promised to be the kind of virtuous wife and good mother that begged Fortune's pleasure and favor. In return, she asked that Fortune make sure that the widower was a Good Person like her father and scholarly stepbrothers. Haopo cajoled: "Let my life be your instrument for showing the world that it indeed pays to be good in ways which please you, so more will be ready to obey and worship you."

Then, Haopo put all her energy into crocheting the most intricate counterpane anyone had ever seen. Haopo always said that she crocheted the counterpane to show her mother she was content with the marriage arrangement: "So that my poor mother might die with both her eyes and mouth closed!" And she wanted to thank the widower for not holding her book learning against her: repay him with the envy and admiration she wanted her counterpane to bring from the wedding guests.

Again, Fortune granted Haopo more than she had bargained for.

"Poor Dada," people always said of my grandfather, because he did not live to see his son prosper. My grandfather died four years before I was born. So I only knew Dada through photos and stories. In the family photo Haopo kept on her dresser, Dada looked to me more like he was Haopo's father: his floor-length robe, silk vest, and cotton shoes looked out of place beside my ten-year-old father's three-piece suits, my aunt's missionary school uniform, and Haopo's high-heeled pumps and lacy parasols. I remember being struck by the sight of my grandfather's moon-shaped, (thickly) bespectacled head toppling over a slight torso, with its round shoulders and protruding stomach. And I was amazed by the resemblance I saw between my Dada in the photo and that drawing of Oz in the hardback *Wizard of Oz* Papa had bought us. I hadn't come across the term *orientalism* yet. But, having noticed this resemblance, I automatically housed my grandfather on the side of the Chinese and the ancient in my scheme of "ancient, modern, Chinese, and foreign" — the Chinese literary expression for "everywhere" or "all the time."

In my early adolescent understanding of Haopo's dealings with Fortune, my grandfather was a mixed bag of good and bad bargains. Gathering from the Dada stories Haopo told, Dada was more than the Good Person Haopo had bargained for. He was an Old Good Person, which in Shanghai dialect meant he was easygoing and soft-hearted to a fault. That had its virtues in matters inside the stone-framed gates of the rowhouse my grandfather rented. Like Haopo's scholarly stepbrothers, my grandfather never raised his voice, nor raised a hand toward her or the children. Furthermore, he always consulted Haopo on matters inside or outside the household and in ways most of their contemporaries did not know how to imagine. This made it easy for Haopo to model her relations with Dada after the teachings of the classics: respect one another as one would an honored guest.

Yet, being an Old Good Person, Dada couldn't hold his own in outside affairs like Haopo's Good Person stepbrothers. He was too gentle in his dealings to make a steady living as a pearl and precious stone merchant. Even when Fortune beckoned under Haopo's pleading and plodding, Dada had trouble following:

One day, right after we moved from the Chinese City into the International Settlement, my third brother stopped by with good news. The father of a boy attending my brother's school, an established Ombudsman, had agreed to give Dada a try at his bank. Dada would have to wear Western suits. He also needed to learn a few phrases in English for when a foreigner came in and the English-speaking clerk was not around.

"Do you suppose Brother-in-law could manage?" my brother asked.

"Sure!" I answered.

I knew Western suits made Dada feel half-dressed: he was used to having his trousers covered by the floor length robe. But I also knew that he would consider this a small sacrifice for the children's education.

That afternoon, Dada went out to the department store and bought a suit. At night, I went over the English phrases with him. We practiced and practiced, me acting as the foreigner and he trying to greet me. Even the kids learned to chant good-morning-sir, this-way-please, just-a-moment while imitating Dada's gestures. He hoped the gestures might help in case the foreigner couldn't get through Dada's thick Suzhou accent or when Dada ran out of his list of phrases.

Yet, no matter how we practiced in the evenings, Dada got tongue-tied as soon as a foreign-looking person walked into the bank. Bless his gentle soul, your Dada was afraid to step on an ant when he walked.

"Father, you'll get used to it," I assured him. And he promised to keep on trying. But it got to be so bad that he would have cramps as soon as he walked into the bank. So he stopped going. He didn't tell me right away. Didn't know how to, thought he'd break my heart. So I had to find out from my brother.

Dada later explained that he just couldn't get used to the suits. He'd be thinking about his naked trouser legs all the time. And when he tried to get rid of the thought, the English phrases seemed to take off with it. But I told him not to worry: we'd manage. So Dada went back to his jewelry business in the City. And my third brother found me a position teaching Chinese and art at a school sponsored by Chinese merchants.

We understood from this story that Haopo had taken the teaching position only because she wanted to emulate the mother of Mencius.

In the picture books Haopo bought us after Sunday school, Mencius became the scholar he was because his virtuous mother had changed the family abode three times during his childhood to ensure that he had the appropriate environment for his learning. Likewise, Haopo had persuaded Dada to move the family from the Chinese City into the International Settlement so that my father could attend the British-run public school — "the best and a soon-to-be must for everyone aspiring to be anyone in Shanghai," even though most of Haopo's contemporaries would take many more years to recognize the bargain.

Like the mother of Mencius, who wove night and day by the side of her son to support his studies, Haopo labored to raise funds for the children's education. Yet, to earn the reputation of "A modern day mother of Mencius," the epithet Haopo's school principal third stepbrother would eventually offer Haopo on her seventieth birthday, Haopo had to do things which would seem unimaginable to other Good Mothers. Haopo had explained to me why people like her scholar brothers and the German-trained doctor who treated my sinuses always referred to their wives as the *inside person*. According to the classics, the wife was to apply her virtues — wisdom, capacity, versatility, talent — within the family. Yet, because of Dada's Old Good Person's heart and thus, his inability to come up with the necessary funding for the children's education, Haopo had to take her virtues far outside the stone-framed gates to their home. To supplement Dada's income, Haopo not only took in knitting, crochet, and needlepoint work from the department stores but went out to teach school and offer private tutoring.

"I always told your father that so long as he made the grades to keep his scholarship, I'd crochet until my eyes went blind and my fingers locked into a knot to find money for all the things other kids in his school had," Haopo would recall and sigh as she carefully spread her ointment — ordered by her son from abroad! — around the swollen joints on her thumb and forefinger. From what I could tell, my father needed a lot of things: movie tickets, toys, ice cream coupons. . . .

He went to school with the children of Shanghai's Best Families, and Haopo didn't want him to feel left out.

The stories Haopo told suggested that she only worked outside the house to raise funds for the children's education. However, when I listened to her reciting from the classics, from books by Hardy, Hugo, Tolstoy, Austen, or from *The Dream of the Red Chamber, Three Kingdoms, Waterbogs,* and when I watched her reminiscing with her former colleagues and students over old photos, I could not help but notice a real passion for learning and teaching seeping through her face and voice. This convinced me that my grandmother had always had her heart set on a teaching career. But she knew this was a bargain she could only secure on Fortune's terms. So she persuaded Fortune to help rather than punish her for pursuing it with the same *guai* she used to nudge him to grant her her schooling: by never complaining about the Old Good Man Fortune had sent her. She always reminded others that being Dada's inside person was all she'd ever wanted, if circumstances had allowed. She never gave anyone reasons to think that working outside the house had kept her from treating Dada with proper modesty and circumspection in private and public. She impressed on others that even though Haopo was the one who had to gather information and report to Dada on the children's education, she dutifully sought and honored Dada's decisions. And Fortune rewarded Haopo for acting as if she had been given the husband she had asked for: it granted her the opportunities to be an outside as well as an inside person.

"A modern day Hua Mu-lan!" This was the other part of the epithet Haopo earned on her 70th birthday from her school principal third stepbrother. At a very young age, I had come across the story of Hua Mu-lan from reading picture books and watching local operas. During those early years, I saw the story as beginning with the summons to war of Mu-lan's old, frail father, progressing with Mu-lan leaving her weaving looms to dress up as a man and set off to war in her father's stead, and ending with her rise through the ranks to become a general by the end of the war without anyone realizing she was a woman. At 12, when I heard Haopo's stepbrother compare Haopo to Hua Mu-lan, I thought he was praising Haopo for being the Exception her father had named her: venturing outside the house in Dada's stead for the good of the family.

Several years later, I was assigned in high school literature class to recite the Ode of Hua Mu-lan, a classic verse in rhyming five-character lines. I noticed then, as a result of my irritation over having two extra verses to memorize, that the Ode did not end where I thought the story ended. The Ode ended with a detailed description of Hua Mu-lan's return, after the war, to her female duties. We were told of her joy in changing back to female attire, of her virtues in marriage and mother-hood. I realized then that Hua Mu-lan had earned her legendary status not simply because she had fooled the outside world about her sex but also because she remained true to her gender in spite of her adven-tures. To the author of the Ode and, presumably, to Haopo's school principal brother, what made Hua Mu-lan so marvelous was her ability to step back into her female duties as quickly and deftly after the war as she had earlier stepped into those of a male warrior.

This realization reinforced my conviction that the essence of Haopo's cunning obedience resided in her ability to convince the world that she could handle outside matters in ways my grandfather had failed and still remain the inside person expected of all virtuous women, the only kind Fortune was supposed to favor. Haopo, who could recite the Ode backward and forward, had probably realized from the beginning that this was her only bargaining chip with Fortune for a teaching career. In fact, being the modern-day version, Haopo did Mu-lan one better. Haopo often managed to ease back to her mother-wife duties several times each day, as she shuttled in and out of the stone-framed doors of the family home; the mansions of her tutees in the City, the International Settlement, or the French Concession;

the various gates of (her son's British-run) public school, (her daughter's American) missionary school, or the Chinese-sponsored school (where Haopo taught); and the revolving doors of the department stores which bought her handiwork.

By 16, I took pride in but was never entirely satisfied with my own interpretation of Haopo's bargaining skills. I liked the fact that I was finally able to explain to myself how Haopo might have gotten others to let her do what she had wanted. But I was also aware that my interpretation had taught me little about how Haopo managed to figure out long before her peers what she had wanted — what was or was not going to be a bargain for her and her family. At 16, I was much more interested in Haopo's knack for spotting bargains. It seemed that, as my desires expanded beyond my four-year-old hunger for birthday gifts, the forces twirling around me had become infinitely more elusive and complex than the tug of war between my elders over birthday rituals. Trying to figure out what I wanted had become much more taxing and daunting.

What had it been like for my grandmother to try to land on a bargain in a city like Shanghai?

In fifth grade history, I learned to call Modern China the years between 1843 (the signing of the Treaty of Nanking at the close of the Opium War, which opened Shanghai as one of the five ports for foreign trade) and 1949 (the founding of the People's Republic of China under Mao's Communist Party.) And I memorized Mao's diagnosis of modern China as a semi-feudal, semi-capitalist, and semi-colonized society. I did my arithmetic. Born in 1889, my grandmother matured with modern Shanghai. So, even before I learned the official definitions of a feudal, capitalist, colonial, or socialist society, I had this vague sense that Haopo's well-known cunning obedience had something to do with the way she dealt with the criss-crossing of these historical forces.

All agreed that Haopo was truly a woman of good fortune. The literal translation of the Chinese expression for fortune is: *road of transportation*. What was the secret to Haopo's knack for picking the right road of transportation in a city taken over and over and over again by British gunboats, the French Consulate, American missionaries, the Catholic Church, the gang bosses of the Red/Green Dragon, the Japanese army and any of the ever-changing governments holding the fort long enough to collect its infamous opium revenue? A city known by its *Three Shanghais*: the Shanghai of foreigners, the Shanghai of Westernized Chinese, and the Shanghai of the Chinese. A city of four cities separated often by a mere alleyway: the International Settlement, the French Concession, the Chinese Cities to the south and north. Some counted five, if you considered that section of the International Settlement called Little Tokyo with a population of over 30,000 Japanese and under the rule of a Japanese (*not* the British and American!) consul-general.

How did Haopo figure out what was a bargain for herself and her children in a city where, as they said, if you were smart you would turn all cash, as soon as you received it, into rice, oil, toilet paper or whatever you might need to live on. For even as it changed hands, a new government or warlord could be moving into Shanghai and making those dollar bills useful only for wallpapering your attic. They'd also warn you never to buy more than you'd need for the week with that cash. Put what was left in gold or diamonds. For before the day was over you could be running from the calamities of war with nothing on your back.

Through the years, as I became more interested in knowing my grandmother as not only a daughter and student but also as a lover, wife, educator, friend, mother, and immigrant, I realized that, for Haopo, bargaining for an opportunity to attend Morning Star or marry Dada or send her children to missionary schools was much like trying to put a price on an item carrying multiple price tags while knowing that none of those tags were put there by people you were totally willing to trust.

In 1996, when I took my first trip home after 15 years in the United States, I got a taste of what life could have been like for Haopo back then. The post-Mao Shanghai was once again opened to the West. Friends and relatives found themselves suddenly facing a maze of three-pronged cross sections at every move. Listening to them, I sensed that bargaining, a Chinese propensity according to a popular guide I picked up at a U.S. bookstore, took on different meanings when it was conducted at such crossings.

On my first Sunday back home, my high school friend Jing took me shopping at the antique mall outside the Old Chinese City.

"One hundred yuan!" The vendor quoted on a wooden jewelry box while sizing up Jing and me.

"Incredible bargain!" I thought to myself (100 yuan was the equivalent of 12 U.S. dollars and one third of what I'd pay for a comparable item from the Pottery Barn catalog).

"Twenty," Jing countered.

"Seventy-five."

"Thirty-five."

In a hurry to move on, I kept on nudging Jing — our code for signaling my eagerness for the item.

"Forty."

"What a bargain," I exclaimed as we walked away with the box. "Forty yuan! I couldn't even get a decent tee shirt for five bucks in the States."

Jing's response: *You Americans.*

Jing pointed out that we, Americans, tend to assess the value of things according to the price tag existing back home, in the First World. We buy only things we know would cost more where we came from. This type of bargain hunting would only work when you wanted to (and could) rely on and reaffirm the established value of things. People like Jing, on the other hand, had to put their energy elsewhere. When your life is punctuated by the constant fluctuations of the price of things — in Jing's case, education, marriage, children, career, houses,

and jewelry boxes before, during, and after the Cultural Revolution —
you learn to distrust all price tags. So you've got nothing to rely on but
your own sense of why you wanted something at which cost.

In 1966, during the height of the Cultural Revolution, Jing, along
with many other Society Youths from Rotten Nine Category Anti-
Revolutionary Families, had "answered" the government's call to settle
into isolated villages as farmers in the outer regions of China. For 15
years, she had to first obtain a leave from the village leader and then
hike some ten hours through rocky mountains to get to the nearest
station to catch a bus to begin her three-day journey home. Marrying a
local cadre was thus considered the best protection she could get from
unfair labor assignments and sexual harassment. Then, in the early
1980s, after her father was rehabilitated, women who had survived the
ordeal of farm work without any "local attachments" were called the
smart ones, the only ones "free" to take advantage of the newly opened
opportunity for regaining residency in Shanghai or obtaining a permit to go abroad. Assessing what was best for her — whether to seek
marriage with a local farmer during the first 15 years of her "settlement" or, having been married, to break the marriage following
her father's rehabilitation — involved more than learning the market
value of such a marriage or divorce. It required an ability to assess what
the alleged bargain meant for her, measure the gap between the
market price and its worth for her, and live with the consequences of
her decisions.

"I come here every Sunday," Jing went on, "just to see if I can still
do it." It doesn't matter what she takes home. She keeps everything she
buys, especially the things she regrets having bought. To remind herself
of the consequences. To help her figure out what she wants.

A form of exercise, a test of some sort of necessary life skill.

Standing there with Jing in the middle of ten blocks of antique
vendors, I remembered again Haopo's refusal to give a straight answer

to my childish probing on how she got her elders to let her do what she had wanted. By 1996, I had long since realized that Haopo was using her roundabout answers to remind me that all she had to work with both before and after the school deal was her sense of the should-, could-, and might-have-beens. She had wanted to shift my curiosity from how she got what she wanted to how she learned to put her price on things and live with the consequences. She had wanted to prepare me for a life where the market value of things seemed designed to render most of my aspirations and efforts irrelevant.

It struck me as ironic that I had to wait until my return to Shanghai after 15 years of naturalization in the U.S. and a trip to the antique mall with Jing to find the language for framing my adult view of Haopo's cunning obedience: it resides in her understanding that good bargains were made, not found, through disciplined deliberation over why one wanted something, at what price. Every time she recited her family register when telling the story of how she got her school name, Haopo was probably also silently reviewing the rules she had subtly broken as well as the rules she had chosen to obey through the years. She was weighing the consequences of each act to prepare herself for further crossings.

My grandmother saw herself as a maker, not a spotter, of bargains. A maker of bargains at life's crossings.

I had been tracking what I now call my grandmother's bargain-making principles ever since the outbreak of the Cultural Revolution in 1966. The vertical descent of my father's fortune during the movement made me extremely envious of a recent upturn in the life of his *less fortunate* elder sister, my aunt. I was anxious to figure out how and why she was able to pull it off. Coincidentally, I found a series of lessons on the art of bargain-making embedded in Haopo's well-known devotion to her children's education.

"True good fortune!" People exclaimed during the height of the

Cultural Revolution, whenever Haopo showed the postcard-sized colored family photos her daughter — my aunt — sent from Hong Kong with her monthly check. All previous symbols of Haopo's old-age fortune had disappeared following one sultry August afternoon in 1966, when the Cultural Revolutionary Red Guards marched into my parents' house on HengShan Road. By 1968, Haopo's Good Fortune son had been locked behind prison bars for two years, serving time for a six-year prison sentence and on charges he would not be shown until his release in 1972, on the afternoon of Nixon's visit to Shanghai. Her *good-looking daughter-in-law from a rich Catholic family* was providing 24-hour care to an infant for 25 yuan a month, the same wage her former servants were earning from their new, revolutionary cadre employers. Like many other Anti-Revolutionary Rotten Nine Categories families, we had been "swept out" of our house and installed by the Cultural Revolutionary Housing Bureau in a one-and-a-half-room suite on the second floor of a rowhouse with three beds, a table, a few chairs, and a 12-yuan per-person monthly subsistence fee. Meanwhile, Haopo's *less fortunate daughter*, having finally obtained her exit permit and having reunited with her husband just two years prior to the Cultural Revolution, had found work at the University of Hong Kong — *the best in the colony* — and was making dozens of times more than she had ever earned back in China.

By 1968, people readily attributed my aunt's success in securing such a lucrative job abroad to the very-best-education Haopo was known for having helped Dada give to both their children. All conveniently brushed from their minds the many times during the previous 40-some years when they had questioned, behind her back, Haopo's *foolish investment in the education of her ill-fortuned daughter.* All unequivocally proceeded to congratulate Haopo on her great foresight. Everyone knew the saying: raise sons as insurance against the insecurity of old age. Haopo alone had the premonition to know the insurance policy she could take out on her daughter, even though this one would take 25 years longer to mature than the one she took out on her son.

Up until 1966, my understanding of Haopo's devotion to my aunt's education had been swayed by the stories Haopo and my father told. Haopo always traced her resolution to invest in my aunt's education to a dream she had had just a few weeks before she went into labor for her firstborn. When napping, Haopo saw an old hag walking up and tossing a bundle into her lap. "Treasure it, even though it may not appear much to look at right now," the old woman whispered before the shock of an object hitting Haopo's stomach woke her. When Haopo relayed the dream to Dada, he agreed with her that it portended the coming of their first-born. And yes, girl or boy, they would treasure it as they had been instructed to by the old hag in Haopo's dream.

While growing up, I took the story as yet another proof of Haopo's *guai* in getting others to grant her what she wanted. Haopo had always said that her nanny had predicted from the shape of her stomach that her firstborn was going to be a girl. My grandmother had obviously wanted to make sure that her daughter would be given the same educational opportunities her elderly father had granted her. Yet, being a mere wife and mother, it was not Haopo's place to proclaim and seal her daughter's fate as her father had hers. So my smart grandmother conjured up a fairy godmother — the old hag — to caution Dada and the rest of the world against devaluing her "not much to look at" baby girl.

From my father, I gathered an entirely different explanation for Haopo's devotion to my aunt's education. Papa had a load of my-mother-always-favored-my-sister-over-me stories. Most days, the only time we saw Papa was around seven or eight o'clock in the evening when we loitered around my parents' suite, watching them get dressed for their evening functions. As my mother studied herself in the mirror to make sure she had painted her two eyebrows level (no small task, since the left bone arched higher, as in all us girls, she'd remind us), she would relay through the open bathroom door what she had heard that morning from Haopo: my aunt was having financial difficulties again. My cousin (the only one of the five girls — me, my two sisters, and my aunt's two daughters — talented and conscientious enough in my mother's mind to really deserve such costly lessons) might have to give up piano.

"Maybe we ought to help out," Mmma would conclude quietly.

Papa usually gave in, but not until after a long sigh followed by some stories illustrating the unfairness of it all. My father prefaced all his stories with the reminder that, since his excellent grades had earned him all sorts of scholarships, it had not been his education but his sister's which had compelled Haopo to teach, knit, crochet, and tutor to raise funds. He would go on to detail Haopo's efforts to move his sister from the Chinese school to the more expensive convent school, after Haopo had noticed that my aunt (in third grade) was not getting the kind of homework my father took home (from first grade) at the British public school. He told of how, after noticing his sister's difficulty with following the English captions on the silent movies, Haopo promptly enrolled my aunt in the best — meaning most expensive — American-run school for girls.

We could all tell that even after close to 40 years, Papa was still pining for every single ice cream or tin toy soldier which he believed his sister's education had cheated him out of from the fund Haopo raised for "the children." With his knack for storytelling, Papa made us fume with his preteen self as he computed the hours his sister's education had robbed from his play time, when he was forced by his mother to go — twice a week and all the way across the city — to tutor his sister at her American boarding school so that she could catch up with the school work which was now being assigned and had to be completed — as his had always been at the British public school — in English.

In his rich baritone, my father would entice us to conclude with and for him: it had obviously cost much more for Haopo to give his sister a first-rate education than to give the same to him, so why should he alone be held responsible for paying back, for supporting his mother and easing his sister's financial stress? By 1968, I would have given anything to hear, once again and live, my father's baritone raving against Haopo's favoritism. I knew my mother longed for the same as she kept nightly vigil in front of the window: huddled over a cup of hot water and staring into that thin sliver of starlit sky wedged between the rowhouses. It was almost as if my mother was daring everything separating her from my father — the police, Red Guards, barbed wire, prison gates — to sever this wedge of sky from the sky he could be looking at from his cell window. She believed that, if he was still alive and well enough, he would be straining to catch a glimpse of the same sky at that very moment.

Yearning for the return of my father, I found it hard to move past Papa's complaints of Haopo's favoritism whenever I noticed Haopo's excitement over her daughter's adventures abroad. Nevertheless, I felt compelled to try. The Cultural Revolution had taught me to wonder if Haopo's devotion to her daughter had its origin not so much in her preference for one child over another, as my father had claimed, but rather in her identification with people the world had deemed "not much to look at." This, I was beginning to suspect, was at the heart of Haopo's well-known foresight (what I would today call the source of her cunning obedience as a maker of bargains): my grandmother had not fought for the best education for her daughter because she had spotted before others the bargain her daughter would turn out to be, but because she distrusted the world's view of who were and were not worthy of an opportunity to improve themselves and their lives. She believed in the right of that opportunity to all, her firstborn daughter or her second-born son, her children or the children of the Best of Shanghai Families, her newly labeled Anti-Revolutionary son or Patriotic Overseas Chinese daughter.

I learned this in the summer of 1966. The morning after the Red Guards took off, Haopo rose at dawn and fumbled her way through the empty house down to the kitchen, with its shattered windows and walls with football-sized holes in them, to make a pot of congee. The Red Guards had taken away from her all the symbols of her good fortune: her filial son, his practice, all his savings, and her burial clothes. Yet she made congee and served her newly-titled Parasites of Anti-Revolutionary Rotten Nine Category daughter-in-law and granddaughter.

"Too thick. I'll try with more water and less rice tomorrow," she muttered after tasting it, announcing her plan to serve as the family breakfast maker. She thus stated without words: she would not let the Red Guards take her (and our) spirit away. We were as worthy of her love as we had ever been, her congee reassured us.

My grandmother's congee taught me to trust that she would have put the same energy into my father's education as she had in my aunt's if she had had to raise them in a world where girls were valued over boys. My grandmother had not "forced" my father to travel across the city to tutor his sister because she favored her daughter over her son, but because she did not believe — as others did — that her daughter was slower than her son. She understood that it would take her daughter longer to catch up with her studies simply because her daughter had not been deemed worthy of a seat at the boys-only British public school which had offered her son a scholarship.

Having experienced firsthand my grandmother's determination to side with those deemed by the world *not much to look at*, a determination I now take to be a first principle in Haopo's bargain making, I realized that Haopo had probably given Papa the same vote of confidence she had given his *less fortunate* sister. He just couldn't have experienced it with the same intensity because, until the Cultural Revolution, breaks had always seemed to come his way so easily. As I watched my mother keep her nightly vigil in front of the window, working the air with her taut back to send my father her love, I secretly sent along my hope that my Rotten Anti-Revolutionary Nine Category father would know to bathe himself daily with memories of Haopo's face and voice when, taunted by his classmates from the Best of Shanghai Families for being merely a Poor Scholarship Boy, his mother had reassured him that he was every bit as worthy and deserving of the best education only some parents could afford to buy their children.

Throughout the years of the Cultural Revolution, my mother regularly fasted on rice and pickled vegetables, a reminder of the fact that this was the diet we feared my diabetic father had been subjected to in his prison cell — and the only diet we knew we would have been able to afford if our 12-yuan-per-person monthly subsistence fee had not been supplemented by checks my aunt sent from Hong Kong. So it was hard for me to not join others in viewing my aunt's checks as the primary returns for my grandmother's investment in her education. However, it was also during this period that I first perceived a different kind of return from this investment of Haopo's, one which had materialized long before the checks began arriving. The return I have in mind was much less tangible than money or prestige but also much more precious: the knowledge that you are just as worthy and capable as anyone else if given the same opportunity. It is the will to improve yourself and life in circumstances — and this to me is the most important part — which seem designed to remind you of the folly and futility of your efforts.

The Haopo spirit, I called it back then. The backbone of Haopo's bargain-making endeavors, is how I put it now.

I came to this realization when, during the years of the Cultural Revolution, I pondered my father's and my own chances for eventually turning our lives around. My anxiety over such possibilities compelled me to comb my aunt's life for insights on how she had managed to survive and then rise above her misfortunes. A subplot began to emerge from my father's my-mother-favored-my-sister-over-me stories: a story of my aunt's efforts to work, slowly but surely, against the odds miring her life. Within my father's story of Haopo forcing him to tutor his sister was the story of my aunt catching up with her school work to graduate among the top five in her class. His story of Haopo's obsession over a cure for the illness which had forced my aunt to quit college for a full year also detailed what my aunt had to go through to eventually complete her degree in bio-chemistry. Stories of Haopo's stress over my aunt's financial situation and her baby-sitting needs also illustrated the work my aunt put into learning a new trade after the Communist Revolution of 1949, when she was assigned to work in a science library.

As I traced the Haopo spirit in my aunt's endeavors, one side of me wanted to believe that if she could manage, then both my father and I might also eventually manage to turn our lives around. Another side of me feared that neither of us had enough of that spirit to sustain us. This, in turn, led me to wonder if my father had always known that his sister's will to improve her self and her life in all circumstances was the real return she had gained from Haopo's investment in her education, a return which could not be measured, nor matched, by the exorbitant income he had managed to earn in return for his education. Maybe this return was what had been riling Papa all those years, although he had been too proud to admit what he was too smart not to have noticed: Haopo's fights for his sister's education — at his expense, he believed — had endowed his sister with a confidence and tenacity he did not trust himself to have.

When "forced" to tutor his sister, my father had probably witnessed his sister's determination and patience to excel in her studies. He had noticed that his sister might be slow to catch up but when she did, she was rewarded with the confidence that she had earned her success against all odds, and that she could do it again when necessary. I wondered if her confidence had frightened my father, making him question if he would have been as determined and worked as hard if the world had not been so quick to pronounce him bright and deserving of his mother's devotion to his education. His sister had proven herself a maker of bargains. He, my father might have worried, had merely been a lucky receiver of bargains. And he begrudged his sister their mother's favors, believing that she had passed on to his sister and not, he feared, to him the will to improve his self and life in circumstances designed to remind him of the futility of his efforts.

My speculations made me fear with and for my father behind prison bars, for I understood that, more than any other time in his life, my father would need the Haopo spirit to keep him going. Fearing for his life, I found it harder and harder not to wonder how my family would have fared if my father had also managed to leave China before 1966. I was old enough to remember the long discussions behind closed doors about what Haopo afterwards referred to as *the risk of leaving* taken when my aunt was in her mid-40s. At 12, even I knew, from the fate of numerous relatives, about the risks involved: if my uncle was lucky enough to be the one-in-100 to get his permit to go to Hong Kong, there would be the inevitable long separation between husband and wife, parents and children. If the permit was denied, he might be labeled an Anti-Socialist for the rest of his life. When debating whether my father should apply for an exit visa, I had often heard him remind my mother that, even if he were lucky enough to get his exit visa, the risk of leaving, for him and for us, would also involve losing the impressive income he alone had managed to earn from his Western diplomat and banker patients in spite of the Communist Revolution of 1949. It would involve years of hardship in Hong Kong when starting a practice from scratch.

In 1968, fearing for my father's life behind prison bars, I often found myself wishing he had worked harder to leave China. I wondered if he would have tried harder if he had been more confident in his (and our) ability to survive the hardship he anticipated from his need to start all over again, from the bottom, in a strange city, so late in life. I wondered if he was right in concluding that we simply did not have enough of the Haopo spirit in us. Of all the color photos my aunt sent from Hong Kong, the one which left the deepest impression had my 50-something aunt proudly holding a diploma she had just earned through correspondence courses, a degree she needed to secure her job at *the best university in the colony.* The photo made me wonder if, as my father watched his sister tackle one hurdle after another in her education and career, he, like me, had become more and more impressed by and envious of my aunt's clear possession of the Haopo spirit. I wondered if he too had coveted his sister's tenacity in testing and exercising her potential.

My aunt's tenacity made me fear for my father and with him, for me. I feared the Cultural Revolution would never end. I feared that neither my father nor I would have enough of the Haopo spirit to survive its turmoil. I feared we would not have enough of the Haopo spirit to turn our lives around if and when the movement did end. I feared for him every time I recalled the vehemence with which he had stressed to my mother the hardship of starting all over again, when they weighed the pros and cons of his pursuing an exit visa. I feared for myself when I remembered the disappointment in his eyes when, in 1963, I was classified a Society Youth after the national school board pronounced me unworthy for any of the colleges I'd applied to. I feared when I recollected his hesitation when my mother suggested that they try to send me abroad to continue my education.

"Why a Ph.D. in English?" Others kept asking in 1981 after I survived my first term in the U.S. It was easier simply to maintain that I had became an English major by default: having had no undergraduate training but fair exposure to English language and literature through home life, my best chance of getting an advanced education was to apply to the English graduate program in the Shanghai Language Institute when the national entrance examinations were reinstituted in 1978. Two years of study at the Institute had in turn helped me to build up credentials to obtain admission to an English graduate program in the U.S. — the only way I could get out of China. I knew I had other reasons for wanting to remain in the field. I enjoyed playing with ideas and words. I understood the power of language from having seen it used and abused. I believed that, if book-burning was a ritual observed by both Hitler's Nazis and Mao's Red Guards, then a life devoted to the reading and writing of books was worth considering. I had noticed that non-native speaking readers and writers often open unexpected possibilities for English. For someone in my situation, however, none of these reasons appeared particularly relevant.

I was 35, had a daughter to raise, and planned to remain in the States. Everywhere I turned, I found more reasons to explore other career options than to remain in English: the market was oversaturated with English Ph.Ds (the handbook to the graduate program I entered dutifully warned), academics are the worst paid professionals in the U.S. (get an MBA — takes only two years and pays really well, relatives and friends advised), foreign students never do well in English courses (cautioned others who had successfully survived graduate school and established themselves), the surest way to turn a foreign student visa to a green card was to get certified as a math teacher or a male nurse (the whisper went among fellow foreign students).

Why pursue a Ph.D. in English when, for the first time in my life, I could explore other possibilities? I would have to work just as hard coping with the different challenges each option might pose, but I would have a better chance of securing what my daughter and I most urgently needed: steady income and a green card. I found it ironic that trying to sustain my interest in English literature and teaching turned out to be just as taxing in this land of opportunity and freedom as it had been back home, where a Bureau of Higher Education dictated when, where, or whether I was (not) fit for further learning. To stay on course, I retrieved a series of mini-lessons my grandmother had left me on how to deliberate over why I wanted something, at what price, when it appeared to have no immediate market value.

One cluster of lessons took place betweeen 1963 and 1966, after I was classified a Society Youth, along with millions of high school graduates also deemed by the government to be unworthy of further education. To fill time (while waiting along with other Society Youth for a job assignment which might eventually materialize for a tiny percentage of us and for an opportunity to continue my education abroad, if and when my family and I had figured out a good excuse to secure me an exit visa), I took up Chinese brush painting and French in addition to furthering my readings in English literature. Haopo offered me the mahogany table stationed at the center of her suite (where she entertained her visitors) as my daily work desk because her room had French Windows on two sides and was brighter and airier than mine on the third floor. Sitting at the opposite end from where I painted, Haopo talked about the ivory crocheting hooks my grandfather had fashioned when keeping her company, at this very table, as she tried out more varieties of figure-sized dolls from the finest of silk threads. She recalled the street model which had taken my teenaged father years to build out of construction paper, bought with money he saved from his allowance, to let me know that it was not his capacity to earn high scores at tests alone which had made him the fine surgeon he was. She traced the different stages in my aunt's growth as an amateur painter, first picking up charcoal drawing when convalescing from the illness that had forced her to quit college and, years later, water-color and oil when waiting for the government to issue her passport to join her husband in Hong Kong. Haopo took note of every new move I made, whether I was trying to capture the flow of the leaf of a chrysanthemum with six tones of green in a single brush stroke or convey in black ink the parched tips of bamboo leaves rustling against the autumn wind. Whether I appeared happy or disappointed at the result, she lured me to talk about what I was aiming at and why, to figure out where I might have fallen short and how to try again with my next project.

Trying to recall our conversations during those afternoons, I wondered if Haopo had paid extra attention to my paintings not simply because she was herself once an amateur painter but also because she understood long before I did that the real return for my dabbling with painting would lie not in the actual paintings I produced but in the memories of my endeavors, of what I might learn from these memories about myself and about the nature of learning. She wanted me to know myself as having once tried to question a verdict from the Bureau of Higher Education pronouncing me unfit for further learning. She wanted me to think of learning as involving disciplined self-probing as well as access to good teachers and learning facilities. She kept me company as I learned Chinese brush painting between 1963 and 1966, so that I had an opportunity to take part in the very spirit I was to envy so much in her and my aunt throughout the Cultural Revolution.

To remind me that I indeed had, Haopo made sure that I kept with me one of my paintings from that period. In 1966, the Red Guards came to search our house for Anti-Revolutionary Four Old Elements and left afterwards with almost all our possessions, leaving only a layer of ankle-deep paper scraps from books and photos they had destroyed. When Haopo scavenged through the debris and retrieved from it a few crumpled Chinese paintings of mine, my reaction had been: "Why bother!" My reasoning: What was the point in holding on to pieces of paper which even the Red Guards had not deemed worthy of destroying or confiscating? Why waste the energy when the three of us — my grandmother, my mother, and I — had to wear our few daily yuan of grocery money in secret pockets sewn into the waistbands of our one change of pants? When every time a group of Red Guards came to demand money to "support" their Cultural Revolutionary activities, we had to pray that they would not notice the slight bulges around our waists. Or that if they did, they would leave us with enough money to survive the week, not just welts and cuts on our bodies — our rightful punishment for hiding our *stinky money* from the Revolution. I refused to touch the paintings Haopo had retrieved from the debris. It puzzled me even more to see my grandmother carefully tucking them away among the few changes of clothing left her by the Red Guards. Being the experienced teacher, Haopo knew I was not yet ready to hear (what I later realized to be) her reasons for "bothering" with the paintings: to help me remember that I had not given up on myself during my life as a Society Youth, and to stimulate me into using this experience to figure out how not to give up in my new life as a Parasite of Rotten Nine Categories. She merely said: "Who knows, they might come in handy some day."

When I got married in 1971, Haopo took the paintings from under her winter blanket and put them by the side of my two bags of personal belongings. My dowry. I thought my grandmother had given me back the paintings so that I might finally get them framed and displayed in my new home at the Overseas Apartment, a place which my first husband's father had bought with Patriotic Overseas currency, a place where I hoped life might resume from the point it had left me that hot summer afternoon in 1966 when the Red Guards marched into my parents' house. So I did. And I hung one of them, a horizontal panel of bamboo shoots in black ink, on the wall facing my bed.

In 1972, after my father's political rehabilitation, the possibility of seeking work as a substitute middle school teacher opened up. My effort to seek work was met with caution and consternation from well-meaning relatives and friends: "Why bother? With the rehabilitation of both your father and your father-in-law, you don't need the money anymore!" "Who will take care of your daughter?" "You might become a target in the next political movement!" During both periods, head-aches and breathing difficulties (due to depression?) would keep me in bed for days at a stretch. I passed many hours staring at the painting on the wall facing my bed and accidentally found a new use for it. The painting brought back memories of the conversations I had with my grandmother as she kept me company while I tried out new brush strokes. It brought back the image of Haopo balancing her 77-year-old body over her three inches let-loose bound-feet, as she retrieved it from the debris left by the Red Guards. I wondered if my grandmother had sent it along as part of my dowry to remind me that I had once believed that I wouldn't, couldn't, settle for a life assigned to me. I got a job teaching middle school and in 1978, studied for the entrance exam-ination for graduate school.

In 1981, when an opportunity came up to leave China on a student visa, it seemed a matter of course that I took the painting out of the frame and carefully packed it in one of the two suitcases I was allowed to bring across the border. "I am taking with me one of the paintings you saved from the Red Guards," I told my 92-year-old grandmother on parting. "Good," she said as she squeezed my hand.

Ten months later, my daughter joined me in the U.S. After the rent, groceries, and busfare, we would have barely enough left from my graduate assistant stipend for me to debate over whether I should be selfish — spend it on a babysitter so I could attend a poetry reading — or be good and buy my daughter the 64 colored crayons I saw at the art supply store. My daughter had been drawing so beautifully with the material we dug out of a box a friend had left after she cleaned up her five-year-old daughter's room. It made me think about all those art supplies with which parents like my own all over the world were smothering their kids while other parents like myself couldn't afford them. I had, as one family friend put it, "broken a good marriage for a degree and a career." I had uprooted my daughter from the material comfort she had enjoyed in China. Time and again, I had to return to the painting my Haopo had preserved from my Society Youth days.

Struggling to remain on track, I realized that no one, not even Haopo herself nor my aunt, ever "had" Haopo's spirit in the sense my father or myself imagined it during the Cultural Revolution. It was not a thing to be *had* but a series of moves to be deliberately exercised. Without always realizing it, all of us whose lives had been touched by Haopo had in one way or another partaken in it. To continue to take part in it was where my father and I should have put our energy: to retrieve our memories of the times when, with the help of Haopo, we had attempted not to let the predictions of others — government policies or well-meaning friends and relatives in the land of freedom and opportunities or of scarcity and totalitarianism — confine our aspirations and efforts. Instead, we needed to look for new opportunities for testing and improvising on our previous attempts.

But I never got around to sharing my realization with my father. He died in 1983 in a car accident one week after he was finally permitted to leave China and enter the States.

The summer following my father's death, I lay for hours at a stretch on the floor, staring into the ceiling dry-eyed while waiting for the grief that refused to come. It wasn't the abrupt ending of my father's life that rankled me. I knew he was in a good mood when it happened. He was still new enough in the States to be carrying with him that sense of elation one feels when facing a long-awaited (potential) upward turn in life. I was angry at fate for having put him through the Cultural Revolution and then robbing him of this chance to find out that he was every bit as much Haopo's child as his sister. He need not have feared that Haopo had favored only his sister with her spirit. I wanted fate to bring my father back, to give him what it owed him: a few years of life as a nobody-immigrant to prove his fears wrong.

As I lay there in the summer heat staring at the ceiling, I longed for my Papa to have a chance to rework his memories. I wanted him to recognize what I had been too dumb to realize until lately and too proud to admit to him before it was too late: he had partaken in the Haopo spirit when he methodically sponge-bathed every part of his body (every day of the year in his three-by-six cement prison cell without heat, air, or light) out of the daily ration of less than one quart cold water for all purposes. So, in spite of his severe diabetes, he had returned without having developed a single sore on his body. Haopo had not needed to wait for Papa's eventual release to find out that the government could take away 80 pounds in weight and six years in lifespan from her son, but not the spirit she had planted. She had trusted him to plot and strive, to make use of the little gestures, words, and deeds she had left him when his classmates from the Best of Shanghai Families had derided him for being a mere Poor Scholarship Boy.

I wanted for my father that chance to tell me what he never did: Haopo had left us enough to try living as makers of bargains rather than as chance receivers of bargains. But most of all, I wanted an opportunity to tell him the same, which I, being his daughter, never did tell him either. What I did was worse. When he wrote to tell me of his desire to come to the States, I fed his fear with mine. I advised him to wait until his newly arrived daughters had had a chance to establish themselves and be in better positions to support him. I detailed the hardships awaiting him if he came before we got established: the dreary life of a live-in nurse-housekeeper for some wealthy old couple — the only job open for Chinese MDs without work permits. I withheld my vote of confidence for his right and ability to improve his life, whenever and in whatever way he desired.

I wanted my father back to tell him I was wrong to fear for and with him. I rehearsed in my mind the things I could have said to prove our fear wrong, what I would have said if he were still alive to hear them. I gradually recollected one little act after another my father had done for and with me to keep me in touch with the Haopo spirit, things I had been too wrapped up in our fear to take full note of when they took place. I remembered the rapture in his eyes as he pored over the photographs illustrating the new surgical procedures and equipment in the books he had ordered from England to keep himself updated, just in case he decided to *take the risk of leaving China*. I had watched him teach himself to paint in oil — spending hours to perfect the highlight on an apple he was trying to capture on canvas — throughout the early 1960s, after his deft surgeon's hands were idled by a government policy and his work as a family physician for Western diplomats and bankers left him more leisure in the afternoons. I recalled the ways in which he had unwittingly baited my curiosity in the literature he collected in his library through his refusal to put a book down when using the toilet and the gravity with which he pronounced me too young to fully appreciate a piece of good writing.

Waiting for the grief which refused to come following my father's accidental death, I realized that these, too, were the memories I had intuitively drawn upon when I did what I could during my Society Youth days and the Cultural Revolution years to keep alive my desire to know, to learn, more. I wanted my father back to thank him. I wanted a chance to rework our relations and memories, so that we might stop feeding one another's fear, so I could be more to my daughter than what he had been to me. So my daughter might be more to me than what I had been to him.

Then I saw in my mind's eyes my grandmother balancing her 77-year-old body over her three inches of let-loose bound-feet as she rummaged through the debris for my paintings. I heard her say: death might take your father away, as the Red Guards took my son from me during the Cultural Revolution. But nothing can take away the memories connecting our fears and our acts of daring. Nothing can keep you from finding new uses for them. Love for the father my grandmother had given me seeped through my chagrin over all those discussions my father and I should have had, never got around to and could no longer have. Tears came as I rose to find a place on the wall for my painting.

A Maker of Love

For a long time, I thought romantic love was an art exclusive to the Modern and Western parts of my world. It was not something about which I would turn to Victims of Arranged Marriages like my grand-parents for insights. The closest picture I could ever get of the type of lover my grandmother was capable of being, therefore, would have to come from Haopo's passion for her two small sisters, my Wong Haopo and Jen Haopo.

From the way my elders said Small Sisters, I sensed something was out of the ordinary long before I learned that the prefix "small" predicates sisterhood established among women in the workplace, which, during Haopo's time, usually meant among cotton mill work-ers, prostitutes, entertainers, dancing hall companions, shop assist-ants, and servants. Upstairs, Haopo's Small Sisters were introduced as her former students. Downstairs, they were called two courtesans turned concubines.

As soon as we were old enough to understand, Haopo told of the evil deeds — the flood (Wong family) and addiction (Jen family) leading the families to sell her Small Sisters, at the age of six, to a famous brothel in Shanghai. The sisters were both in their early 20s when Haopo was hired by the two men who had redeemed the sisters. Since the trend at the time was to have high school graduates as concubines, the men wanted Haopo to make their new acquisitions more Female Student-like. Three times a week, Haopo worked with the two on their reading and writing skills.

"And before we knew it," Haopo always said, "we had become inseparable."

Then, one day, her students asked if Haopo would take offense if they invited her to become their sworn sister. Haopo replied she'd be honored to. "Without even consulting Dada," Haopo would add. Haopo knew that Dada would never want her to hurt anyone's feelings, although most husbands would surely have forbidden it.

Haopo told of the story of my father coming home upset because the son of the big wife of the Jen household had spread the rumor at school about Haopo's shameful background. The logic was simple: the Small Sister of a redeemed courtesan had to be one herself.

"Nothing to be ashamed of even if this had been true," Haopo reassured my father: "Shame only to the ones who sold and bought my sisters."

"I suppose I should have felt flattered," Haopo always added when she came to this part: "Anyone who had seen my face ought to have known that if I had been sold into a brothel as a child, they would only have made a chambermaid of me." (This story always makes me think Haopo would have liked the story my daughter told me. A male friend in college said to her one day that he was relieved to find out from a friend that my daughter was not a lesbian. He just assumed she was since she seemed so close with "those people." My daughter's reply: "Why relieved, for you or me?")

By the early 1950s, one of Haopo's Small Sisters, my Wong Haopo, had moved to a city three hours' train ride from Shanghai. Every spring, Haopo would get a letter from Wong Haopo announcing the date of her arrival for a two-week stay with us. Immediately, Haopo would get on the phone with Jen Haopo to make arrangements for two overnights so the three of them could play mahjong (with my mother making up the foursome) and then chat into the early hours in the privacy of Haopo's suite.

From my father's complaints in response to my mother's prompting to go and welcome his house guests, I picked up words to nickname one of Haopo's small sisters as the Fanatic Haopo and the other, the Superstitious Haopo. My Fanatic (Wong) Haopo, they said, was the luckier of the two. Grandpa Wong's big wife was a peasant woman whom he had abandoned as soon as he came to Shanghai. He was an enlightened man (who visited brothels?): a school administrator swept off his feet by Fanatic Haopo's vivacity. He was determined to make an honest wife of her and a mother to his two sons by his country Big Wife. And she did not let him down, they agreed: you would have hardly guessed her brothel background if you hadn't seen the amount of rice wine she could drink or heard her sing.

I remember a woman in her early 60s. Always dressed in liberation style: white or gray shirts with open collars buttoned in the front like those worn by party cadres, instead of the Chinese-style tops and gowns with frog buttons running down the side, like those worn by my grandmother. I understood what my elders meant by Fanatic Haopo's vivacity. Her eyebrows danced, keeping cadence with her descriptions of the goings-on at the Patriotic Religious Organization. Then, she'd tilt her head slightly back to the right, daring her listeners, with the smile in her eyes, to question her. A young girl with an old face, I called her.

It was from a conversation between her and my grandmother that I first heard about denominations and got the idea that Christians didn't always agree with one another: some considered the Baptists, what Wong Haopo called *my church*, more authentic than the Methodist church my grandmother attended. My Fanatic Haopo was also the only person frequenting our house who would say *our Chairman Mao* this and *our Great Leader Chairman Mao* that, like the Revolutionary Enthusiasts at school, on the radio, and in the newspapers.

I remember the flower baskets Fanatic Haopo carved out of the rinds of tangerines, fashioned so that you could pick out the sections, one at a time, from the space left in between the handle and the body of the basket. And I would ask for an apple, even though bananas were my favorite, just so she could peel the skin into one long spiraling half-inch ribbon, which she then taught me to gradually unwrap from the top as I ate my way down the fruit. They said she was taught all these tricks, and opera singing, at the brothel to charm her clients. She was a quick learner, which probably spared her many beatings.

Most of all, I remember my delight at finding an adult other than the servants up, dressed, and at work at 6:30 in the morning, after my nanny had dragged me down from my bed to the no longer fresh-looking toast and egg waiting for me in the small dining room on the second floor. At the other end of the oval dining table, left from our days in the smaller house I was born into, Fanatic Haopo sat every morning to practice her shorthand, which she hoped to perfect, she explained to me, so that she could serve one day as the secretary at her Patriotic People's Church.

They called her "the crazy one" when she was sent to represent the local Patriotic Religious Organization at the regional conference, just before she got cancer. I imagined her frantically jotting down every word spoken by the Party cadres, and I was ashamed to admit to my parents that I took pride in having a relative who would have been considered a Revolutionary Enthusiast by even my teachers and classmates. "Pathetic!" my father concluded on Wong Haopo's fanaticism. Haopo sent her congratulations. She recalled that Wong Haopo's enthusiasm as a student was what had initially drawn her to the Small Sister.

I think Haopo never forgot that she could only imagine what it would be like to have been sold into a brothel at six. She knew never to proclaim what she herself would have done (or not done) in Wong Haopo's place. My grandmother would not judge, instead trusting her Small Sister to work through how and where to apply her enthusiasm when physical survival was no longer the only driving force for learning to serve. That was the kind of lover my grandmother felt her Small Sister deserved.

That was also the kind of lover my grandmother tried to be for her other Small Sister. Upstairs and downstairs, all agreed that my Super-stitious (Jen) Haopo would have fared much better if she'd not been so stubborn. The prettier of the two, she was bought by a rich merchant to be his third wife. As soon as she felt she could trust my grandmother, Jen Haopo had announced in her quiet way that she was not too dumb to learn her lessons but simply not interested in doing what old man Jen wanted of her. She had seen through the red dust of this world. Men, the kind she was destined for, would always be men: today, the fad was to acquire a female student. Tomorrow, there would be something else. She would not stoop to vie for his favor. Come what may, the sooner the better.

They said she was lucky. He found her high, arrogant spirit novel, so he kept returning to her whenever he got tired of the number four and five he brought home after her, even though she had not even borne him any sons. But most of all, she was lucky to live under a Big Wife who was only interested in eating vegetarian and chanting cate-chism, to accumulate good deeds for her children to counter the evil deeds her own father and husband had committed. Big Wife was also deemed lucky, since Old Man Jen never forgot his debt to her rich cotton merchant ancestors, and he was willing to leave her alone with the Buddha hall she had built on the third floor of his house after, of course, she had borne him two sons. Big Wife took a liking to my Jen Haopo when she showed more interest in the Buddha than in pleasing the master of the house. "A younger sister sent to me by my ancestors," Big Wife was heard to have said when Old Man Jen complained about the amount of time his concubine was spending with Big Wife in her Buddha hall.

I remember a soft-spoken woman with jet-black hair swept into a bun held by a 24-karat gold pin with a jade top. A classic beauty, as we called women with cherry shaped mouths, deep dimples, round dark eyes, and thin arched eyebrows in an oval face. A serene face: statuesque like the Madonna in my mother's study and the Goddess of Mercy to whom my Nanny burned incense. Jen Haopo's "backwardness" disturbed me. (Because some of her facial expressions reminded me so much of Mmma?) I wanted her to cut her hair so that it would wash and dry more easily, as Haopo was always saying to the servants when explaining the advantages of getting rid of their buns, as she had done long ago. I was ashamed to see my Superstitious Haopo's three-inch small feet still not let loose as they rested side by side with my grandmother's size-four leather pumps stuffed with cotton wool to fill the empty space left by her unbound three inch feet. And I wondered what the three Small Sisters could possibly have found to say to one another after we'd all gone to bed.

I understood too little about the sexual politics of brothels and concubinage to sense the radicalness of my Superstitious Haopo. Because I had heard more about the lucky ending to her denunciation of the red dust of this mortal world, I couldn't grasp the scope of the risk she took, but Haopo must have understood the day her stubborn Small Sister confided in Haopo her determination to be too dumb to become Old Man Jen's Female Student. Ironically, because I had failed to fathom the foundation of the love binding my grandmother and her fanatic and superstitious Small Sisters, I was all the more impressed by the depth of their affection for one another.

"Love at first sight" was the classic Chinese saying Haopo and her Small Sisters had always used to describe their relationship. That's the kind of lovers they would have been and deserved to have, I concluded, if they had been free to choose their mates.

The stories my grandmother told of her third stepbrother, my Third Grandpa, was another place to which I went in search of lessons on love. We had all heard Haopo admit that her third brother, the one who went to Japan in search of knowledge for reform, was the kind of Good Man she had once daydreamed of marrying. So, as a child, I was always watching Third Grandpa to figure out if it was bad or good fortune for Haopo that none of his scholar contemporaries had wanted to marry her: Why wouldn't they marry Haopo? How would they have treated Haopo if they had married her?

Third Grandpa was one of the few people I knew who wore the kind of robe my grandfather had on in his photos, although, when Third Grandpa sat down, you could see that underneath he wore Western-style pants (with creases and cuffs) and shoes with leather tops and soles. From his conversation with Haopo, I first heard the names of Rousseau, Peter the Great, Emperor Meiji, Tolstoy, Chekhov, Hugo, Ibsen, Darwin . . . pronounced in Chinese. The two of them also made references to Ba Jin, Lu Xun, Lao She and books and plays which I would later run across in high school literature courses. To Third Grandpa, Haopo told us to bring the one-page-a-day calligraphy we did during summer vacation (to earn the end-of-the-break reward, a five-dollar per person spending spree at the bead store in the Old City Temple district).

This stroke shows strength, he'd say, putting a red circle on it with the Parker fountain pen he carried between the second and third frog-buttons on the curve cutting across the upper left of his robe. *Be always sure to lift your wrist!* He'd warn when he came to another stroke. Like Haopo, he could tell just from looking at your strokes that you'd been lazy, resting your wrist on the desk.

I don't know how much English Third Grandpa knew. But I am certain he was fluent in Japanese. However, I had never heard him pronounce any of the foreign concepts which filled his conversation with Haopo — "romanticism," "enlightenment," "Darwinism," "le Bastille," "democracy," etc. — in any tongue other than Chinese. I didn't fully appreciate its significance until I learned from history books of the radicalism of Chinese scholars like Third Grandpa, who were schooled in the tradition of civil service examinations but determined to build a curriculum which offered mathematics, foreign languages, geography, historical studies, and physical education.

Haopo said Third Grandpa turned to "saving the nation through book learning" after he had grown disillusioned by the outcome of the Republican Revolution during the 1910s. He founded a prestigious (boys only) high school in the Chinese City and devoted his energy to arming his students with authentic learning inquiry which, as the saying goes, could be hidden in your stomach and never be taken away by anyone, warlords or foreign invaders. People called him pure and high, which everyone in Shanghai knows also meant poor and foolish. He seemed indifferent to the material profit his knowledge could bring him from the Shanghais of the foreigners and the Westernized Chinese. "A true Chinese scholar," Haopo called him, adding with a sigh: "He could afford to be one." And we understood she was referring to the money left him by Haopo's merchant father.

The thing that most intrigued me about my Third Grandpa was, of course, his *romance* (this is the exact word Haopo used in its Chinese pronunciation, *longmanshi*). I loved to hear the story of Third Grandpa Lin and Plum Blossom, the 12-year-old slave girl his wife brought to the household as a part of her dowry. "A pretty and quiet child, deep dimples and almond fair skin," Haopo always said:

> *It all started when my sister-in-law first got pregnant and couldn't wait on your Third Grandpa during those long nights he spent on his studies, so she sent Plum Blossom in her stead. A quick learner, Plum Blossom intuited without his ever having to say a word how he liked his ink ground, his favorite Dragon-well tea brewed, his midnight lotus-seed soup sweetened, and his charcoal-filled copper hand-warmer heated in the winter. To help her kill time while waiting through the long nights quietly on a stool at the foot of his desk, he gave her square-blocks of characters to learn. My brother always said: The mind is a terrible thing to waste.*
>
> *Pretty soon, Plum Blossom knew enough words to fetch him the books*

he was looking for from the shelves and file his lectures. She learned to do calligraphy by copying his notes for him. A sensible girl, she was always respectful, never neglecting her household chores in the daytime, even though she had to know that in some ways, she had become more special to your great uncle than his wife. My poor third sister-in-law was a gentle and understanding woman, like the big sister-in-law in Ba Jin's book The Family. *My sister-in-law could barely read. Besides, the eight children — four girls and four boys — kept her busy with household duties. So she was grateful that Plum Blossom was there to take care of the study.*

When my sister-in-law died, I told your Dada it was time to make complete the other two. A good deed, Dada agreed. So I acted as their matchmaker. My third-brother liked the idea, and Plum Blossom said she'd obey his decision. So your Dada and I made arrangements for a wedding feast, one appropriate for a wife, not a concubine, to do justice to Plum Blossom for all those years. His older children were not too pleased. But they seem to have come around since.

I noticed, though, that his sons referred to her as *Young Girl Plum Blossom,* the way they called slaves in novels. We, however, were told to call her Third Grandma.

"What a waste!" Haopo always said of the threesome, in spite of her open admiration for her brother's scholarship. My grandmother thus taught me to remember that Plum Blossom was 12 when she was first sent by her mistress to Third Grandpa's study and in her mid-30s by the time Haopo arranged for him to marry her. Not having yet read *The Family,* a novel greatly admired by Haopo and Third Grandpa, I could not fully follow Haopo's analysis of the parallel between the novel and the situation involving the three. Yet, being an expert in half-listening, I retained just enough to piece together the connections Haopo had been making after I read the novel in high school.

Haopo wanted us to ask: what was happening with her brother, his wife, and his wife's slave during the over two dozen years, besides the birth of eight children? Were attempts ever made, as was the custom, to find Plum Blossom a husband able to come up with the money to redeem her? Like the slave girl in *The Family*, Plum Blossom would have no recourse but to hint of those attempts to her master, with the hope that he'd intervene. Did he intervene upon hearing the news? How did he explain to his wife why her slave should remain with his household?

Haopo taught me to wonder if any of that was necessary. His wife, being understanding like the wife of the eldest brother in the novel, would have intuited his affection for her slave before he did and accordingly arranged for Plum Blossom to be there, whenever he might need her, without his ever having to breathe a word. In fact, his wife might even have offered her slave to him as a concubine (as wise wives were supposed to). If so, what words would he use to turn down the proposal, explaining to both mistress and slave his views on monogamy?

Or maybe, he, being liberal, had encouraged her slave to read (his favorite) *The Family*. In the novel, a young revolutionary-minded master courts his aunt's slave girl and then fails to save her from committing suicide in defiance of her owners' decision to give her as a concubine to the master's friend, who was 40 years the slave's senior. What did Plum Blossom think when she came to this part of the novel? Yet again, maybe he did not deem it appropriate for his slave to read novels. Most probably, master and slave kept their feelings for one another pent up, as proper for men and women of virtue, as did the eldest brother in the novel and the love of his heart.

Haopo would go on and on. I had the impression that if Haopo were the author of these three lives, she'd make sure that Third Grandpa cried with his wife on her death bed, and with his slave girl on their wedding night, over the 20-year tangle involving the threesome. And she would want him to know to thank both wife and slave girl for making him the scholar he was known and respected for being.

I can therefore guess how my Haopo would want me to think about the father-in-law of a family friend — China's first and most renowned petroleum research scientist, who married, on the same day, two of his most promising students. One to take care of his lab and the other, his home, as was agreed upon by the three before the wedding. It makes my brain hurt (as my students put it) to think about how the 50-something professor worked out his deal with his 20-something promising students. A solid marriage, according to their daughter-in-law, one which had sustained them through one world war and two revolutions.

How could those two agree to it and stay content with it? I am, once again, being harder on the ones I care more about. I hope they did not do it because they believed that good lab-wife does not good house-wife make and vice versa. In my more optimistic days, I picture them sharing a dorm room through their promising college years, poring over their books across from one another, night after night, at their narrow desk in the dorm, with the tops of their heads almost touching, looking up to exchange encouraging smiles over the books, talking late into the nights from their bunk beds about their dreams of love, family, excelling as research scientists. I want to believe (although I sometimes have difficulty convincing myself) that they accepted his proposal because it became clear that only one of them would be allowed into his lab, with the support of the other.

In my version, he had his ideas about which one would be more suitable for the lab, and which, for the house. But they insisted that they draw lots, knowing that either one could have excelled in the lab with the support of the other, and neither without. And this was what I hope sustained them through the next 50 years, the knowledge that they were in it for each other. They were only saved from despairing over their truncated lives because they knew that, at the end of each day, both would be there to appreciate the different trials this deal had imposed, and to rejoice, vicariously, at the different rewards of which each had been robbed. But did he ever understand that without either to run his house and his lab, he would never have been the first and most renowned? I doubt it. I can only hope instead that they knew that both of them could have been first and most renowned if either had partners as competent and dedicated as themselves.

I knew this was the conviction my grandmother wanted me to have when she left me her version of Third Grandpa's *romance*. I know because she had also left me enough to imagine a different kind of partnership by a husband and wife.

They said my Dada had told the matchmaker he was not afraid to marry a woman who had eaten too much ink. Haopo left me stories to believe neither was he afraid to fall in love with such a woman.

We often remember things we didn't know we had stored in our memory until we are ready for them. Lately, I've been recalling stories of Dada I was not so interested in when growing up. The Dada in these tales is much more complex than the Old Good Man in the Dada-at-the-bank story. This man seemed to share Haopo's passion for the not-much-to-look-ats. Not just because he didn't have the heart to hurt anyone. But also because his old good heart seemed willing to labor at letting his wife love him as his equal and loving her back as her equal. An ambitious attempt in a world determined to remind him of how superior he ought to have been and yet how inferior he had become to her.

The world would not let him forget that he was a failure in outside affairs. She was a success, but she was supposed to have been merely his inside person. Hen-pecked, they would say of him here. She would be called a woman who wears the pants in the house. We called him a man who is afraid of his wife, and her, a she-tiger. I know the tyranny of such words. I can imagine the quagmire in which my grandparents trod. I've seen the unsolicited sympathy lavished on my husband in this postmodern U.S. and have occasionally caught myself doing the same to the husbands of friends. I have come across too many husbands in this land of freedom who, unable to forgive themselves for needing their wives to help out, become experts in verbal and psychological abuse. And I know enough about the shame and anger of feeling ugly (from seeing it reflected in the mirror of social expectations) and how they can deaden one's response to the soft, white-hot search of a lover's fingertips. Nevertheless, my grandparents waded on, as Haopo's stories indicate.

One story Haopo liked to tell took us back to the end of the Qing dynasty. "I've got a surprise for you," Dada announced one afternoon. Haopo opened the brown paper parcel to find his knee-length pony tail coiled inside. "One of the first men in the City to cut it off," she told me proudly. The Republican Revolution took place in 1911, so my grandparents couldn't have been married for more than six months. A first declaration of love?

She said he did it because he knew she would have wanted him to. She liked it even more because she knew the pride he took in his tail. *So full and lush*, people had said of it. The beam on his face told her such comments made him feel young and virile. She understood the depth of her middle-aged Old Good Person's effort to match her more modern outlook. To illustrate the love she felt without having to use the word, she told of the O'Henry story in which the couple sold what was most precious to each (she, her long blonde hair and he, his gold watch) to buy a gift for the other (she, a gold chain for his watch and he, a comb for her hair).

The story of Dada's surprise gift brings back memories of my pride when, at 12, Haopo offered to let me use *Dada's hooks* when crocheting a pair of gloves for my mother's birthday. I recall two hooks: one with a fat, round tip for working with wool yarn and the other, with a nose so fine and sharply angled that it could be eased into the tightest loop to bring through the finest of the silk threads. Haopo told me both were hand-shaped by Dada out of quality ivory. "Feel the difference?" She always asked me. (She never let anyone use the hooks outside her sight.)

As I recall the feel of Dada's hooks, I picture him keeping Haopo company in the long, winter evenings as she experimented with the finger-sized dolls which would make her so popular with the department store buyers. He carved and sanded away under a lamp across the mahogany table from his wife. Then he passed his hook over to her to try out. His eyes followed the movements of her hands until he felt his own throbbing in rhythm with hers. And he sensed how he would recontour the tip so his hook would writhe in and out of the loops she made, gentle but firm.

She said he made new and better ones whenever the old ones broke, developing an eye for ivory as he improved on his craftsmanship along where her experiments were taking them. Because of this image of Dada — of a husband helping his wife help him out, I was able intuitively to sense the hunger of a lover in Haopo's voice when she talked about her loneliness, and I tucked it away in my memory. I had to wait until turning 50 to recognize that Haopo was merely 45 when a stroke paralyzed Dada from the waist down. She was 52 when he died. For years, I bowdlerized my grandmother's lament over that empty spot in her queen-sized bed which no one else could fill after Dada's stroke. (I reassured myself she meant to say *after Dada's death*.)

Like most adolescents, I found any reminder of the sexuality of my elders grossly embarrassing. Furthermore, I grew up believing that though women have sexual organs, only men have sexual desires and gratification. I reserved the word "love" strictly for spiritual and emotional relations. And I had been trained by books and movies to perceive "romantic love" as an irrelevant topic for the kinds of Old-Fashioned Arranged Marriages my grandparents had. Like other speakers of the Shanghai dialect, I usually switched to written, standard Chinese or to English when I used the term "love." "Sex," a word I didn't use in any of these languages, was a more complicated story. In some English novels, men and women made love. Upstairs, we talked about men and women falling in love, getting married, sharing a bedroom (where they kiss and hug, activities which, I assumed for a long time, led people to give birth to babies). Downstairs, they talked of women who had (or had not) been slept with by men. Men made love to women, it seemed, because it made them feel good and gave them sons. Women endured being made love to because we had to: a marital duty for people like Haopo's Small Sisters, a sacrifice for love in my mother's case. If the idea of Haopo and Dada falling in love with each other was already so radical that it would take me years to even consider it a possibility, the idea of Haopo (missing) making love to Dada was simply unthinkable. It would be like calling your grandmother an unnatural woman.

But Haopo wanted me to know the unnatural as natural. Her loneliness, she announced in spite of my busy mental remodification, began with his paralysis seven years before his death. Once I heard this conversation concerning the husband of my godmother, who was known for always fooling around with his nurses. "What do you expect," the others said. I understood what they meant. My godmother had been paralyzed from the chest down since catching meningitis when touring India with her husband on their second wedding anniversary. "Cannot satisfy his needs," they whispered. "What about hers?" Haopo asked. Strange idea: expecting a woman to suffer from lack of lovemaking, as if it were something she rightly desired and deserved. Yet my grandmother had wanted it in my mind, for when I'd be ready for it.

It takes two to love: to love and make love.

What kind of lover would either of them have had to become so that they could love with body, heart, and mind? Haopo left me the story of Dada's misstep to mull over the question I had yet to pose.

Haopo always talked of Dada's dalliance with the other woman, Ah Kai, with this opener: "It was, once again, Dada's good heart which got him into trouble." Had to be fate, all agreed, that out of all the places in the Chinese City, Ah Kai's father should choose to sell his 16-year-old daughter right in front of the jewelry store Dada was managing after his failed try at the bank.

Ah Kai's family had run away from calamities — a famine following a flood — to Shanghai the year earlier, and they were trying to raise the fare to return home. Days went by, but no transaction took place. In the meantime, Dada was haunted by the shame and fear he saw in the girl's eyes. It pained him to hear the onlookers assess her (plain) features and (young, able) body. After the third day, Dada gave the father what he was asking and trainfare for the girl to go home with the family. A good deed, Haopo agreed when he told her that evening. To repair the dent this deed would put on their budget, she offered to make one more doll each night. He said he could learn to do the stuffing so they could turn in at the usual time. And both assumed that would be the last they'd hear from the family.

Two days later, when Dada arrived at work, there was Ah Kai huddled by the door with a note from her father someone had written for him. It said that the family had left Ah Kai behind because they had four boys to feed and couldn't afford another mouth. They were sending Ah Kai to Dada since he had already paid for her. Dada could do what he saw fit with the girl. Later, Ah Kai was to tell Haopo that her father had reassured her in parting that Dada looked like a man with a good heart, she'd be all right *in his hands.*

Businessmen on the block knew that Dada, being the Old Good Man, had never kept another woman and would need them to render ideas and lend strength. No one took seriously Dada's protest that he didn't plan to keep her. Someone mentioned a furnished room for rent where he had just set up house for his paramour. Another offered a loan to tide Dada over until he figured out a way to account to Wife for the expenses he'd need for his Small Household.

Dada said: "Maybe I should take the girl to my inside person. She would know how to help this girl out."

They took him to be saying: "I have to get permission from Big Wife until I dare to acquire a concubine."

What's the point, they asked. Tell Wife afterwards. Wives always come around faster after the fact.

Remember, they added, fate delivered this girl right into your lap. Pushing your boat against the tide would bring bad luck.

So they took charge: a deposit was put down for the room, word was sent home that Dada would be detained by business engagements that evening, and money was collected to order a 14-course feast so all present could help Dada celebrate his new acquisition.

"Poor Dada," Haopo always said when she came to this part:

> *Didn't know how to say no, didn't want to hurt anyone's feelings. You know, these people thought they were doing him a favor, to return some of*

the favors he was always doing them. Poor Ah Kai, she was so scared by what could be waiting for her out there that she, too, begged him to keep her. So Dada set up house with Ah Kai with the money he usually spent on lunch and at the tea house. They say a proud rabbit has three dwellings. That didn't turn out true for Dada. What man could ask for more from either of Dada's dwellings? In one, he found an obedient, grateful, frugal concubine, always anxious to please. In the other, he found his favorite dishes waiting, with me and the children eager as ever to share the day's happenings.

Dada's remorse was hollowing his heart like a sharp-edged spoon, scooping out all the joy and tenderness he once felt. And his own good conscience was what was doing the scraping. So Dada decided to ask for help. He tried for days to bring up the subject but could never seem to get past "Mother, I've been feeling out of sorts lately." I told him I didn't need him to point that out. But I didn't bother to ask why. I thought he was still recovering from the bank trial. The idea of another woman simply never crossed my mind. I thought he was different.

Then Dada made sure some of Ah Kai's hair would remain on his woolen robe when he returned home. He knew I'd notice when brushing it. Your aunt and I wore our hair short, and Nanny's had gone gray. He needed my question to help him open up. Your Dada was a shy man but also an honest man. He never lied.

The hair strategy worked. When Haopo asked, Dada readily recounted the leading causes and final results of his misstep.

What now, he asked.

She said she needed a few days to think the matter over.

When Haopo told her nanny, Nanny reminded her of the story of why-men-need-the-other-women:

One day, a big wife asked her husband why he was always hanging around his courtesan concubines. Wasn't Wife much more beautiful, intelligent, and loyal to him than any of them?

As he answered in the affirmative, he knocked off a vase sitting on the side table by his chair.

"Oh, look at what you've just done. That was a valuable antique," the wife cried.

"Well," the husband said, "if I had done the same at one of my concubines', I am sure she would have said — oh, did the noise scare you? How stupid of me to put the vase so close to the chair."

Haopo heard Nanny: men were all the same. Good wives had to be generous wives. She should rejoice that her husband could afford to buy the attention he needed from the other woman. Good wives were also smart wives. They understood that content husbands were more easily managed husbands.

Reason told Haopo not to ask for the impossible. Look around you. Do you see another man as willing to ask and listen to his wife's ideas on outside affairs as yours? Let the other woman take care of his personal needs to free you to better take care of your and the children's needs. Ah Kai could offer Dada something neither Haopo nor the children could: she would never remind Dada of the Westernized Shanghai, the very thought of which gave him cramps. Wasn't it enough that he had to let go of his children, watching them learn to talk about things and in words he could barely grasp and only through her mediation? Why not leave him Ah Kai, who was nobody's child, to keep and to make him feel important and safe?

Reason said, All men needed that.

But Haopo's heart and body told her otherwise: he could be different.

Reason said, No woman could be housewife, bread earner, and lover all at the same time.

Her heart and body said she was willing to give it a try.

She liked where they were going before all this.

So she asked him if he, too, wanted their old way of life back.

He did.

And they talked deep into the night, and night after night, to figure out how to help each other heal the wound left by Dada's misstep.

The rest was history, Haopo always said in conclusion. Ah Kai was freed from her bondage to Dada with the promise that she could expect the same financial support for as long as she needed it. Haopo and Ah Kai adopted one another as sisters. Ah Kai learned to knit and crochet and support herself within a year. When she turned 19, a marriage was arranged, with Ah Kai's consent, between her and a widower who had been told her history to make sure that he understood she had done nothing shameful.

What did my grandparents talk about night after night to leave Haopo such fond memories of a man who had committed such an atrocity against her and another woman? Because Haopo did not leave any details, I can only guess.

When I imagine Haopo and Dada talking night after night, I see my 30-something grandmother lying in bed, waiting for the touch of Dada's long, deft, jeweler's fingers. When it came, she burnt under it. She couldn't help wondering if the same caress had been shared by another woman. And she could not forgive herself for having believed that wives and husbands could be more than what the book said: respect each other as one does one's most honored guest. So now she had to pay for the intimacy she had come to expect and treasure. I think this is how I would have felt.

I wish my grandmother had left me more than an image of the two of them talking, night after night. I want to know how she let him help her speak her anger and pain. How she helped him tell his shame and regret. How they worked together to salvage from the ashes that ember of trust to fire up the desire to give and take all of each other. Who was the first to bring up their fear over what others would think and say about the actions they took to rectify Dada's misstep? It should not require much imagination to fill in the world's reaction: so typical of him, so afraid of his wife, to surrender so helplessly to her ways. A typical Wangxifeng of the *Dream of the Red Chamber* would be her title, as they call all conniving wives. Did he, the shy one, ever learn to talk (without the help of her question) about the burden of bearing such labels? Did he learn to help her talk about hers and afterwards make her laugh with the quiet irony they said he shared with my mother? I hope he did, although I have trouble convincing myself.

My husband and I bear enough labels in this postmodern United States to make me wish Haopo had left me more details. I am the woman who broke a marriage for a degree and career. A Chinese divorcee with a Caucasian husband 11 years her junior. It does not require much to figure out his tags. How to feel loveable in spite of the tyranny of such labels is something my husband and I are still fumbling with after 15 years together. I wish my Haopo had left me more clues to how she and Dada had talked, night after night. I want to know what they said with their words and bodies to make her remember him the way she did.

I hope they spent as much time talking about the injuries done to Ah Kai as about one another's sufferings and worries. What about Ah Kai's heart? Had his good heart also led her to trust and love him? Did my grandparents expect to release her heart as quickly and unequivocally as they severed her bondage? I want my grandfather to have felt and admitted his guilt to Ah Kai when Haopo accompanied him to release her. Can I trust my grandmother to have helped him understand that until he learned to respect all women she would not be able to love herself, without which she would be too numb to love him back?

Haopo was a tough storyteller to follow. She fed me with the picture of a man and woman talking with open hearts, minds, and bodies, night after night. Yet she withheld the details of their trippings and tripping-overs so that I had to take that image where I could, when and where I needed it. She expected me to form my own questions. And she would never want to let her life take over how I filled in the answers. My grandparents began with an arranged marriage divided by the ancient and modern, the middle (kingdom) and the foreign. Yet they dreamt of no less than this image of two partners in the making of love. A family heirloom for me and my daughter no one, Red Guards or customs officers, can confiscate wherever we migrate.

Hers was a brave and hardworking heart. Haopo silently rewrote the family register as she kept adding more and more chairs to her annual feast for the dead. One slave girl, two ex-courtesans, an other-woman. . . . She would have added more, gay or straight, black or white, if she had met and survived them. Her dictum seems to have run something like this: (kindred)-spirits are thicker than blood. She revised this ritual of ancestor worship because she did not fear the power of the dead to curse us. Rather, she believed in the power of the (loving) dead in us. She wanted to thank the dead for having helped us love and let love. An annual exercise of heart.

How should my daughter and I keep up this tradition?

I think Haopo would say what she always said: "Times have changed."

Keep up the exercise but improvise on the format. Think about them, talk about them, write about them, living and dead. But don't let anyone tell you who belongs and who doesn't.

I will try.

Farewells

When news of Haopo's passing came in 1983, my first thought was, she did not live to be 100. My second thought: she went the way she had wanted to go — she had passed away peacefully in her sleep, at night.

I made myself a cup of Dragon-Well tea (*two pinches of tender green tips with water still bubbling,* the way Haopo drank hers) and kept vigil in my room in the attic of a three-story house on the east coast of the

United States. The story of Haopo's great-grandmother came to mind. "Healthy till the end," I heard Haopo say. One morning, Haopo's great-grandmother woke up and announced it was time for her to go. So she had her great-granddaughter-in-law bathe her and then dress her in her burial clothes, all 18 layers of them. Then she laid herself down and went to sleep. She never woke up again. She was 104. They had to break up the shifts so all members of the younger generations could have a chance to pay their respects at the vigil. At the funeral, everything was draped in red instead of white. There was no cause for mourning, everyone agreed, only for celebration.

"That's the way to go," Haopo always said.

The story made me wonder at the connection between Haopo's death and another piece of recent news from home: my father had decided to apply for an exit visa to visit the U.S. In my mind's eye, I saw Papa sitting down at the edge of Haopo's queen-sized bed to relay his decision. I recalled how dark and stuffy Haopo's bedroom could get — the eight-by-ten space Haopo had lived in since the Cultural Revolution. I heard Haopo telling Papa that she liked his plan of making my aunt's place his first stop upon arriving in the States. I saw Haopo give Papa's hand an extra squeeze when he stood up to leave: to say farewell and to have him carry it to his sister at their reunion.

I believed that Haopo had decided then and there that her time had come: she wanted to make sure that my father started this new turn in his life with a light heart. She did not want him to have any doubt or guilt over having to leave his elderly mother in the care of others. But, unlike her great-grandmother, Haopo could not simply announce her plan to lay herself down and never wake again. She knew that if she had, her filial son, the MD, would only have said — What bloody nonsense! — and would promptly have hooked her up with all kinds of tubes to keep her alive.

As I kept vigil, I heard once again my grandmother asking: "Are you going to be Haopo's good little girl?"

"Yes." I said, as I did when I was ten.

"Which is the key I've been telling you about?"

"This one, the one with the red cloth tag on it."

"Which of these trunks does this key open?"

"The third one from the bottom, in the second row."

"What do you do when they open it?"

"Look for the list pinned to the white satin shroud with the red rose cross embroidered on it."

"What would you do when they had me dressed?"

"Count the collars."

"How many?"

"Eighteen, not including the shroud."

"And you promise you'll do all that?"

I decided to keep my promise even though I was thousands of miles across the sea from where her body lay. I counted in my mind every single one of the 18 collars underneath the shroud I knew she would be wearing on her final journey. I trusted Ahfen to have done the actual counting before the funeral. And I was sure that, some time during the week, my aunt and the rest of Haopo's five granddaughters would be doing the same along the two coasts of the United States. So would Mmma, I thought, if there were indeed an afterlife, as both Haopo and Mmma believed.

I did more than that during my vigil. I pictured myself lining up each layer of her burial clothes, one next to another, along the edge of Haopo's queen-sized bed. I spent a long time mentally pressing the shroud, following the curves of the embroidered roses as they climbed up to form a cross at the center. I knew the shape of the rose-cross well from watching my mother and aunt picking and choosing through the pile of drawings Haopo had made, cut, and pasted from earlier drafts. From a copy of the final design kept in Haopo's embroidery box, I had stolen a bud here and a stem there when searching for patterns for a pillow or dress. I imagined myself twisting an iron around the stems of embroidered chrysanthemums, plum blossoms, orchids, and bamboo branches dovetailing one another along the border of the hood to the shroud. Then, I took my time dressing my grandmother, as I would have if her body had been in my attic room. I made sure that all the layers were put on properly, one after another: the four collars of the undershirts were arranged so that each hugged the next within 1/16th of an inch lower to form the spectrum of a rainbow. I carefully matched each pair of cloth loops and buttons with butterfly-, flower-, bat-, or fortune-character-shaped legs. I pulled at the legs to make sure the cloth buttons were securely snuggled inside the cloth loops, as I had previously on many mornings when the frog-buttons to Haopo's coats had refused to cooperate with her swollen knuckles.

When I had finished dressing her, I thanked Haopo for letting me help, for preparing me to know how to get her ready from so far away and in circumstances neither of us had wanted to anticipate.

I know many at the funeral would think it unfortunate that Papa was the only one actually there to send Haopo on her way. It was certainly not how Haopo had planned things when two women were hired after her 66th birthday, as was the custom, to work on the burial clothes in the work room next to the small dining room for over a year.

But I also know Haopo understood fortune differently. Fortune, I believe Haopo would say, is a living process sustained through efforts to love and let love. Haopo made plans to exercise our hearts as well as hers. She understood that plans — for funeral ceremonies or immigration to a freer place — had to be constantly tested and revised against the whims of human and natural catastrophes. Yet the experience of laboring over plans could never be taken away.

With the same intensity she poured into the designing of her burial clothes, Haopo had perfected the congee she had taken upon herself to make for my mother and me at the outbreak of the Cultural Revolution. Morning after morning, she'd rise at dawn and fumble her way through the empty house down to the kitchen, gradually developing a congee recipe for cooking every type of rice — brown, white, and long grain, whichever the ration coupons could buy at the state market. She thus reminded us that the Red Guards might take away all the symbols of her good fortune, but no one could take from her the right to labor for her loved ones. She inspired me to become the cook for our other meals, figuring out where to stand so that the stones revolutionary young heroes kept on throwing through the kitchen windows wouldn't get me, and how to come up with tasty and nutritious ways of stretching the meager rations of oil, sugar, meat. . . . Survival became more than a necessity. And I learned to care about food and to care for myself, my mother, and grandmother as I never had before.

In 1973, on the afternoon of Nixon's arrival in Shanghai and more than six years after the police took my father away, my father was shown his arrest warrant, read his prison sentence, and rushed home. Along with Haopo's newly "rehabilitated" son, the government duly returned Haopo's burial clothes with all the other things the Red Guards had confiscated during the Cultural Revolution. But the Gang of Four was still in power and the Four Old Elements — 18-layered-burial-clothes or shrouds decorated with Christian symbols — were strictly forbidden at funeral parlors. Haopo laughed as she dug her burial clothes out of the pillow case in which the Red Guards had stuffed them. Every morning, my 84-year-old grandmother celebrated her son's return by putting on a layer of her burial clothes underneath her normal clothes. "Might as well put them to use right away," she announced. And she alternated all 18 layers with the change of seasons for the next few years.

Shocking sight, Haopo moving around the house with pink, pale blue, gold, forest green, slipping through the neckline and sleeves of the brown, gray, or navy normal clothing she wore over them. But we got used to it. *My dear daughter* (who had migrated to the U.S.) *is here. . . . My beloved daughter-in-law* (who had recently died of cancer) *is here.* . . . Haopo seemed to be saying as her swollen knuckles caressed and coaxed the colors of her burial clothing back behind her normal clothes. She brought back images of an exhausted but excited aunt spreading the silk threads from her shopping bag on to the white satin: the palest lemon-green for the orchid against the richest mango-yellow for the chrysanthemum and maroon-tinted pink for the plum blossoms. We heard once again the voices of my mother, aunt, and grandmother echoing one another: "More blue in the bamboo, to bring contrast to the more muted greens of the leaves." We recalled the dimple on Mmma's left cheek as she quietly offered to look for that blue thread next Monday.

Around 1980 and with equal calm, Haopo had her burial clothes washed, pressed, and stored back in the trunk. Having already lost her sight to cataracts, she asked me to go through the satin pipings on the padded coats to put in a few stitches where it showed fraying: she knew my handiwork from the countless hours she had spent teaching me to sew and embroider. She had her burial clothes put away because she knew that, with the fall of the Gang of Four following Mao's death, old customs — Chinese or Western — would soon be tolerated again.

I realized while keeping my vigil thousands of miles from where (she and) I had planned to be that Haopo had not restored her burial clothes because she cared so much for her appearance at the funeral or in her afterlife. She had done so because she cared more for the loving exchanges which had taken place in the process of making, losing, regaining, and wearing the 18 layers. She restored them for all of us who had accepted her invitation to become partners in this making of life.

2

Ahfen

(1915–)

A Woman of Ill Fortune

Ahfen's Ill Fortune

I grew up knowing very few marriages worked out. Husbands died, left, refused to take jobs below them, put their devotion to ideals above family welfare, took care of their treasured caged birds while their wives cared for them and the children. . . . But women married and stayed married. Unless, of course, you were born with eight characters as bad as the ones Ahfen had.

Anyone downstairs could tell you about Ahfen's bad eight characters. But I liked Ahma's version the best:

How could anyone blame me for being stunned when one day, out of the blue, Ahfen showed up in Shanghai looking for work? Back home, we called her Miss Dainty Feet, the favorite daughter of our village elder. I used to watch her pass by the store, half hidden under that black foreign umbrella her father had brought from the city. And those embroidered slippers as she inched ahead!

How would I in my wildest dreams ever think that one day Miss Dainty Feet would show up in Shanghai and ask for me, a child daughter-in-law sold at eight into her village for a few silver dollars? Last I saw Miss Dainty Feet was when an eight puller bridal sedan was carrying her away. Lots of dowry. A good match, they said. He was from a good family in the next village, worked in that big school in the city as an accountant or something.

I asked myself: what the hell is Miss Dainty Feet doing here? Then I noticed her gray cotton top with white borders, in heavy mourning. It turned out that her husband had died less than a year after the wedding and her little boy, who was born after he died, was also dead. Lately, several matchmakers had shown up at her in-laws'. That scared her. She had already killed one husband and one son. She did not want to harm more people. So Ahfen ran away.

She had the address of a cousin who was working as a wet nurse in the Chinese City. But the cousin told her to look me up. The cousin was just trying to palm Ahfen off her hands. I would have, too, if I could have come up with another name. Didn't think Miss Dainty Feet would last a day with any family. But I couldn't very well turn her onto the street. So I told her she could stay for a few days. I figured once she saw us work around here, she'd run right back to her parents.

Then. . . . (Ahma always lowered her voice, and looked around to make sure that Ahfen wasn't close by before continuing) . . . she told me about her eight characters. Boy! Born a female rabbit in the middle of December when there was no grass. Worse still, wrong date, wrong hour. "This rabbit would eat up her husbands and sons," a fortune teller had predicted. So the father switched Ahfen's eight characters to fool the groom's family. Deed of evil, Ahfen said.

As soon as Ahfen told me about her eight characters, I knew she meant business. So I took her upstairs to your Haopo, who took her to your Mmma, who took to Ahfen right away.

Upstairs, we didn't believe in eight characters and fortune telling. So Papa grilled Ahfen, diagnosed TB for her husband, and took her to the clinic to have her X-rayed.

"Poor woman," Haopo would mutter to our guests on Ahfen's Bad Days, when Ahfen, probably so caught up in her own thoughts, would depart with the same tray of tea she had originally brought in to serve but had never bothered to set down. Haopo would go on to explain: Ahfen and her husband were barely together. He married her during the winter break, returned to the university in the city in February, was brought home on a stretcher by May, and died within a month. That, according to Papa, was why the poor woman escaped TB. For Haopo, that also explained the depth of Ahfen's longing for her husband: they had been together just long enough for her to develop feelings for him yet not long enough for him to leave her any bad memories. "Imagine that and her sense of guilt for his death and the death of her son! She believed they died because of her bad eight characters." Haopo then asked that we all be more understanding toward the poor woman on her Bad Days.

Because of Ahfen's ill-fortune past, they nicknamed her Sister-in-Law Xianglin. I knew the story of *Sister-in-Law Xianglin* long before I was assigned to read it in high school, after Haopo took us to a film adaptation of the novel by Lu Xun — "the founding father of modern Chinese literature." The comparison between Ahfen and Sister-in-law Xianglin was inescapable: early widowhood, the loss of a baby boy, the eating of vegetarian dishes and mumbling of Buddhist chants to cultivate good fortune for the next life. They said that on her good days, Ahfen remembered what everyone upstairs had been telling her: TB and typhoid took away her loved ones. On her bad days, the fortune teller got the upper hand. Like Sister-in-Law Xianglin in the movie, who wailed over her baby boy's body. . . . *I thought there was no wolf around in the winter,* Ahfen wandered around the house blaming herself, *I thought the fortune teller was just a quack.* She should have shaved her head and joined the nunnery near her village rather than obey her father. Now she would never be able to atone for the evil deeds she had helped him commit.

The upstairs agreed that, luckily for us, Ahfen's bad days came few and far between. Ninety-nine percent of the time, Ahfen remained the godsend Haopo had predicted as soon as Ahma brought her upstairs. Ahfen could not have chosen a better time to run away from her in-laws. Mmma, who was in her eighth month with me, hadn't had much luck finding a suitable new nanny. (Environment is extremely important to children's growth: soft music, soothing colors, pretty faces. . . .) Then God sent Ahfen: soft-spoken, fair-skinned, delicate features, young, fine mannered.

"What more can anyone hope for?" Haopo always said. "The child was blessed."

The child herself was of two minds about this idea of Ahfen as a blessing sent on her behalf. I loved being considered special. Yet, if Ahfen was indeed a sign of my good fortune, it could also mean that God had made Ahfen *the poor superstitious bloody fool* Papa said she was just to bless me. Didn't that then make me the cause of her ill fortune?

I reasoned that if Ahfen hadn't believed in fortune telling, she might have stayed home, got re-married, and borne little ones of her own. Then, my sisters and I could have been stuck with an ugly nanny like the one Ahma had recommended for my cousin. The very thought scared me so much that I'd say a Hail Mary, even though Papa had said that Hail Marys, too, were bloody nonsense.

"Please make Ahfen stay superstitious!" I was ashamed of myself as soon as I uttered the plea. I had wanted to be that child in Haopo's pear story, the one who chooses the smallest piece of fruit in the basket so that others, his brothers and elders, could have the good ones. I considered teaching Ahfen to say a Hail Mary. My prayers against hers, let God decide whose side to take. But I knew that could never happen: Ahfen would never do anything to offend her Goddess of Mercy, even though it seemed obvious that she was losing ground in choosing Buddha over God. People blessed by God just seemed always to have so much better fortune than people like Ahfen. I decided I was praying for Ahfen's own good. Ahma always said husbands were real pains in the neck! This way, Ahfen could have us — children, which even Ahma agreed could be a good thing to have — without having to put up with any husband. We would take Ahfen with us when we got married, as Haopo had her nanny. We would never turn her onto the streets when she became old or nutty, as Sister-in-Law Xianglin was in the movie. We treated our servants right, as family.

Ahfen's Child

"You girls have been so good to Ahfen! The visits, gifts, checks. . . ." relatives and family friends are always saying.

"As we should be," my sisters and I insist. "She's been like a mother to us."

A simple and safe story: everyone's heard some version of it somewhere and knows how to make sense of it. A tale of the meeting of two good hearts. Of instinctual — maternal and filial — love triumphing over that unspeakable, ugly divide between labor and capital. So much more pleasant to the ears and easier on the stomach in the free marketplace of a corporate America or a post-Mao China.

The script I'd clung to through the years traces our mother-daughter relation to that traumatic half-year after I turned two and the Stranger came home to usurp my place in my mother's bed. My father had left for surgical training at Johns Hopkins right after I was born. During his absence, he was no more than a face in the wedding picture on the fireplace mantel, someone called Your Papa, The Young Master, or Eddie. I vaguely remember being shown a postcard sent by Your Papa, with the picture of a lake and a pinch of salt sealed in a plastic bag on one corner. From family stories, I put together this picture of Haopo breaking the seal at the dinner table. Everyone, including the servants, took a taste of the salt while speculating about Your Papa's trip across the Nation Beautiful in the new car he was soon to bring home with nylons for the ladies, dolls for the girls, and his golden credentials.

Until the night of my father's actual return, I was quite eager to love Your Papa as my elders claimed I did. That is, until they informed me that what was to me the natural setup — me and my mother in our bed — was actually temporary. Imagine my indignation at the inconvenience caused by Your Papa's return. My first taste of a mother's betrayal and the beginning of a lifelong rivalry between me and the Stranger, as I insisted on calling my father to the great delight of the downstairs. They said that after the first month, my father got over his anger at my mother's lapse into old-fashioned childrearing methods and learned to ignore rather than discipline me during my midnight screaming sessions. Every time he waved a new toy in front of my two-year-old already greedy (!) eyes, I grudgingly called him Papa before seeking shelter behind Ahfen's pant legs.

Years later, lying in my moonlit bedroom on the third floor of our house on HengShan Road, with my heart pounding from the free-fall through the air I'd just taken in my dream, I would lull myself back to sleep by revisiting this scene: I was two and holding one of my nightly protests in the bedroom where, according to the Stranger, I should have slept from the beginning. Ahfen sneaked into the room to keep me company so that I would not choke on my tears. I turned on my stomach with one arm and leg dangling over the edge, hugging on to Ahfen's arm as she dozed off on the hardwood floor beside my bed.

I clung on to this story long after I began to question its factual base. In my script, Ahfen comes to my rescue with me crying, alone, in my bedroom in our house on HengShan Road. Yet I realized years ago that my family lived in a third floor three-bedroom apartment until I was four. I could not have had a room to myself during the time the story was supposed to have taken place: I had instead been merely made to sleep in my own bed in Haopo's room. Neither do I know for sure whether it was really Ahfen who had come to the child's rescue or, to be more precise, whether it had always been Ahfen who came night after night. I've heard other servants mentioned who also cared for me during those early years.

I have never really bothered to get the story straight. I think a part of me had long understood what the story is really about — a child's attempt to give a human face to that amorphous love she had learned to depend on but could not quite comprehend, nor justify. It records my early perception of Ahfen and our relationship: Ahfen stands for all the *loyal servants* my family took pride in attracting. She personifies that loving care supposedly deserved by only the most special of young mistresses — the descendants of an Exception. An arrogant but familiar tale. A hard fact for me to face.

Once in a long while, when explaining to strangers the source of my attachment to Ahfen, I still catch myself resorting to this story of a sobbing two-year-old hugging at the arm of an all-giving nanny. "Like daughter and mother," I've heard myself, my sisters, and Ahfen make this claim to others and to one another. I've held on to this story line even though I am acutely aware that the actual history of our relationship is much more convoluted. I do so because I do not trust words to do justice to that history.

I know that when we say we've been like mother and daughter to one another, we alone know what we mean. But we don't tell this to others. We don't trust them to understand. We don't tell it to one another either. We have for so long packaged this history within the mother-daughter wrapping that we see it as some sort of a talisman. We are afraid that the magic of our relation might break if we tamper with the story line. Besides, what's the point of telling one another what we know so well?

We knew what we were doing in the spring of 1996, when I returned to Shanghai after 15 years in the States and the two of us fought over whether she, at 81, should be allowed to cook me my favorite food on her single gas burner stove at the narrow landing of a rickety stairway right outside her eight-by-eight foot room.

"I don't want you to go to all this trouble for me," I insisted. "Let's just eat at the hotel, so we can have more time to catch up."

She won. She had me over to her place. Sitting side by side on the boards which served as her bed at night and our dining chairs for the occasion, she pointed to the mahogany chairs used to prop up the boards and asked: "Remember these?" "Haopo's wedding furniture," we answered in unison, slapping one another's laps to let each other know how much we both missed Haopo.

She showed me the shelves she had recently had installed on the wall above the bed. "The side I put my feet," she assured me. We agreed, working woman to working woman, that she got a good price on the shelves and that they were a smart use of space. Then we talked about my remodeled kitchen and how my husband and I planned to pay off the loan we took out for it.

Right afterwards, we had to start fighting all over again, this time about whether I should be allowed to spend the night with her in her unheated room. "You'll catch pneumonia," she yelled. I won: we crawled under the heavy blankets in our longjohns and lay awake for hours, with me hugging at her arm against my stomach.

Throughout my visit, we fought as if we had never been apart for the last 15 years. That, I think, was our way of telling one another that we'd both come a long way from that loyal nanny and deserving child in my story and from the women we were when we last hugged in 1981, on the morning of my departure for the States. Not the same Ahfen, nor the same Little Sister, as Ahfen calls me. But somehow, we would learn to know and love the new women as we had before. We knew the labor we put into plaiting the strands of our lives, the new with the old.

I said *I think.* I don't really know how Ahfen would tell any of this. I know only her way would not be the same as mine. Will I ever get to hear hers? I often wonder. How does a servant share her story with a mistress, a semi-literate with a university professor, a student of Buddhism to a student of Marxist philosophy, when the latter was also her child? What would be her motives? I have lots of theories on this sort of question. But I have yet to find the courage to test out any of them with Ahfen.

I love Ahfen too much to pretend that I can or have, as they put it in academic jargon, *let her speak.* I don't have her permission, either, to write down any of this. I had wanted to warn Ahfen during my visit: "I'm going to write about us some day when I find the time to put together a family history." But I never did. I never told her about my plan to leave my first husband either, not until after the fact. I was afraid she would not understand. She proved me wrong. But I am still scared. And I doubt I would, would know how to, translate any of this into Chinese for her. I can only wonder what she would have to say after hearing my version.

It seems that much of my attachment to Ahfen while growing up was spurred by my concern to be, and to stay, special. When I turned five and my parents decided to enroll me in first grade, I took it as a personal insult that Ahma but not Ahfen was assigned to accompany me between home, school, and my ballet lessons. My elders claimed that Ahfen was terrified of city traffic. On the few occasions she'd been sent on errands, she had always managed to get lost. But I felt I knew better than to believe the grownups. I had noticed that ever since the return of the Stranger, my parents had been scheming, as Ahma put it when teasing us, to steal Ahfen from us children. First it was discovered that Ahfen could starch and iron Papa's three changes per day of white shirts better than any of the other servants. Then it became clear that Papa joined Mmma in finding Ahfen's presence around their suite the least disruptive. The greed of grownups! And, their power! They simply wanted her all to themselves.

And then, there was my baby sister, who had somehow become known as *Ahfen's daughter.* Downstairs, they teased that my parents had *given* my younger sister to Ahfen from the day she was born: she was completely bottle fed, and slept with Ahfen in the servants' quarter. *She who has the milk is the mother,* my elders joked over the baby's *confusion.* I was too young to fully grasp the subtext to the teasing: the downstairs' concern to remind Ahfen of the exploitive nature of the deal and the upstairs' effort to assure Ahfen that her devotion had been duly noticed and would be amply rewarded. But I took my sister's special status to heart and blamed the whole thing on the Stranger. If he had stayed away, there would have been no baby. If he were not so greedy, Mmma would have had more time for the baby than to *give* it to Ahfen. Either way, I would have had more of Mmma and Ahfen to myself.

As it was, my elders couldn't even wait until I turned seven, the new government-approved age for starting school. They said I was sent to school two whole years early because I was so quick and smart, as my middle name had predicted. *Might as well get her used to it* was another reason my elders gave, only, of course, to our closest relatives and friends. *It,* I learned later, meant communist education. My parents had tried to keep my elder sister from *it* until third grade. Starting me with *it,* I believe, was their way of admitting to themselves and others that the communists were here to stay. But to express their resentment, they fought to start me at the age they thought appropriate. Wait until I turn seven? No, no! They couldn't be expected to follow such Russian rubbish. Fortunately, the year was 1951. Some schools were still semi-private. So they persuaded a founder-turned-principal who lived down the street to break the rule for me.

But I wasn't fooled. I agreed with Ahma, even though I knew Ahma said that just to tease me, to make me cry: my parents sent me to school just to get me away from Mmma and Ahfen. So I was all the more determined to remind them that she was mine, first and foremost. As soon as I got home, I doggedly followed Ahfen around to stake my rights over her. I jealously guarded Ahfen's lap against my sisters, whether it was around the dinner table down at the pantry or during storytelling time upstairs in Haopo's suite.

I had other shameful reasons for wanting to claim Ahfen as my downstairs mother. Subconsciously, I deemed it a badge of honor that the best of our servants should belong to me. Everyone upstairs — hosts and guests — voted Ahfen the most pleasant and refined in looks and manners, and thus, most suited to be directly serving the best of us. Ahfen was in a class of her own: she was from a good family in the country. She was not used to hard physical labor. She was not meant to be a servant. Her devotion was proof of my distinction.

For the same reason, I bitterly resisted being demoted to the charge of Wanma and Ahma. Hadn't Haopo and Mmma always apologized to our guests for Ahma's coarse manners? They explained: Ahma had a rough child daughter-in-law past. Honest and hard-working though, they always added, as if the family needed justifications for keeping Ahma. (I was later to find out at the club that we did indeed. "My Mom said your family is weird. It's not even as if you couldn't afford to hire someone more refined," a girl in my ballet class informed me one day. Ahma overheard it and coached me to tell the girl that *my Mmma pays our Ahma a whole five yuan more than your mom pays your Miss Dainty.* "Tell her your family knows how to tell real goods from fake ones," Ahma added.)

They called Wanma the smartest. She could read. They said that in spite of her over 200-pound weight and sight problems (one damaged eyeball and one nearsighted good eye), she could find her way around any part of the city on public transportation. But how many times had I overheard my elders wonder if it was wise for Wanma to be seen upstairs when so-and-so of our relatives and friends came to visit.

I decided I was too good for the coarse Ahma and ungainly Wanma. I could never bring myself to think of either as my downstairs mother, even though I was spending much more time around both. I loved the different but equally colorful ways Ahma and Wanma told stories. Ahfen, on the other hand, had little sense of drama. Her stories lacked suspense, just the beginning and the ending. When you probed really hard, she would only add some odd details which were sure to leave you wondering why they should be important to anyone. Besides, when it came to breaking my father's rules on snack foods, both Wanma and Ahma were so much more easily persuaded. A bowl of wontons at a roadside stand? An icicle from a street vendor? No problem (!) if I could come up with the money to treat them and myself. Of course, that often got us into trouble. Some little jealous brat would see us devouring our treats and go home and whine to his parents: Why can't I have this and that if the Doctor's own daughter is allowed to? This, ironically, further put Ahfen in a league above the likes of Ahma and Wanma in my parents' and thus, my eyes, heightening my interest to vie with my parents and my younger sister for Ahfen.

My determination and my sisters' to claim Ahfen as our Downstairs Mother caused a lot of teasing around the pantry: my first introduction to labor relations between the needy child and her loving nanny.

"Whose child are you today?" Wanma would start.

"Her child," one of us would announce defiantly from the back of Ahfen's chair, standing with our arms around Ahfen's neck and body hanging limp onto Ahfen, piggy-back style.

"A pea blossom, that's what you are." Wanma would moan half mockingly if I happened to be the target. "Pretty and white on the outside but dark at the core! Have you forgotten so soon the sweet-talk you gave me on the way home? Don't expect to pull this one on me again next time you fancy a stop at the wonton stand! No more stories from me either!"

"Yeah, she's a regular little ungrateful Chen-Shi-Mei all right," Ahma would chime in. And if she happened to have already had a few cups of rice wine down her, she'd break into a sketch from the famous opera, impersonating Chen-Shi-Mei's wife, who had slaved over the loom to support him through his ten-year study period and then been abandoned by him soon after he passed the scholar's exams, at the prospect of marrying the daughter of a high official.

"Don't expect her to repay you for any of this extra work you are doing for her." Ahma would then turn to Ahfen. "You foolish woman, with your soft ears. Remember, her parents are not paying you enough to be both nanny and mother."

"Yeah, how long do you think she'll stay your child?" Cook would join in. "See what she calls you when her wings grow hard and you're too old to run around and answer her do-this and do-that for me!"

I dreaded and looked forward to this type of evening ritual. No matter how many times I had gone through it, it always got me to a point when I was almost sure that Ahfen was going to join in and say: "You are right." Then she'd turn to me and add: "And you spoilt brat, get off my back and find yourself another sucker."

But she never did. Instead, she always took it all in with what Papa called her Goddess of Mercy vapid beam. Occasionally, she'd give my hands or arms a soft pet as they began to twitch and tighten around her neck. This silent love-talk was my sweet reward for having to go through the teasing. No one, upstairs or downstairs, could ever come between Ahfen and me.

Incidentally, this ritual teasing also gave me a nascent understanding of the convoluted nature of Ahfen's relation with her upstairs daughters. Her loving care was something she could exchange for money. And yet, it was something she had often given to us for free. I understood the meaning of money to Ahfen. I had watched her empty her savings — half of a gold bracelet, gold rings of all sizes, single pieces of gold earrings, odd bits and pieces of gold — from the bright red Lucky Strike cigarette can Haopo had given to her. I had seen the expression on her face and in the shape of her shoulders as she slowly rubbed each piece and weighed it in her palm before putting it back into the can and then tucking the can back to its hiding place on the underside of her bed frame. So I tabulated the expense of Ahfen's free love for us. It was something I should someday pay back in real money. It was something which no amount of my money could ever buy, nor repay.

What was there for Ahfen? The teasing from downstairs prompted me to wonder. In 1957, I entered junior high and was told (and believed) that I was too grown up to be hanging around the servants as if I had nothing better to do. Fortunately for me, the question posed by their teasing — the question of what was there for Ahfen — continued to nag me throughout my adolescence.

At the time, the question translated to simple arithmetic. I had two mothers: one real and one almost real. Ahfen had no children: one dead baby boy and three girls not really her own. It cost her more to love us as her own than for us to be almost her own (or to love her as our own). Thoughts like those made me even more curious about the significance of those cotton baby shoes Ahfen kept in her dresser.

Before I turned four and started school, Ahfen used to entertain me with her cotton baby shoes whenever I got cranky. "Feel this satin, soft eh?" Ahfen would ramble on as I dug into the drawer and lined up the shoes on the edge of her bed. "Leftover fabric from that padded coat you wore on your first full month feast. I knew you were going to be pretty, although they called you the little God of Longevity. Ugly forehead, they said, jutting all the way out, shiny like a shelled hard boiled egg. Like a boy. . . ." I learned never to ask Ahfen if she had made the shoes for me or my sisters: it would only make her put the shoes away and be in a bad mood for the rest of the day. So I'd sensed from the beginning that these shoes had something to do with her feelings towards us.

Later, it dawned on me that the shoes could not have been intended for any of us, since Ahfen kept on making more long after my baby sister's feet had outgrown their size. For whom, then? For a while, I thought she'd made the shoes for her dead baby, to be burnt on his birthdays with the paper money she folded out of tinfoil paper after saying so many chants. But then, she never did burn any of the shoes. So I changed my mind and thought maybe they were after all intended for us: a record of our life through the dresses we had worn, like the markings other mothers make on door frames to keep track of the changing heights of their children.

During my first year at junior high, I began to wonder if Ahfen had made the cotton baby shoes for herself, as a record of her love for a boy taken away from her too soon and three girls she was afraid she was soon to lose. The idea came after I caught her staring at the shoes on one of her bad days, which, as I got older, seemed to grow more intense and come more frequently. By the late '50s, on her bad days, Ahfen had gotten into the habit of locking herself up in the room she shared with Ahma instead of ghost-walking through her routines. I'd been secretly glad of this change, although I would never have admitted this to anyone or myself. Not long ago, my older sister had shown me a book illustration of a female ghost who had hung herself after having been grossly wronged. Ever since my sister pointed out the resemblance between this image of a wronged ghost and Ahfen's gap-mouthed, vacant-eyed face and stiff body during her bad days, Ahfen's ghost-walking had given me the creeps.

Who had wronged her? I wondered. Fate? Definitely. My parents? Everyone had always said they had been so understanding. My ungrateful self? I comforted myself: Hadn't I faked enthusiasm over those wild nuts and baked yam chips she was always smuggling into my room as soon as a fresh crop arrived from her village, even though they had long since lost their appeal? Because I felt guilty for sensing that I had outgrown Ahfen, I was all the more drawn to her on her bad days. So I developed this new habit of visiting her through the keyhole to her door, to keep an eye on her. And that was how I bumped into Ahfen staring at the cotton shoes behind her locked room. I also began to notice that it was usually a little before or after her bad days that a new pair of cotton shoes would appear in her drawer. So I developed this theory. It was not just the memories of her dead husband and baby that haunted Ahfen on her bad days. It was the choke of that lump in her chest bursting with all that love that had no place to go. A mother without a child: only a dead baby of her own and someone else's children, who could be taken away from her any minute.

I developed this notion of a lump in Ahfen's chest from one of the books assigned to me in my first year at junior high, during a movement called Remember Pre-Liberation Bitterness to Appreciate Current Sweetness. It was a novel set in the 1940s on the northern banks of the Yangtze River and during a flood followed by a famine. In order to pull the family through, the central character, a country woman, had to leave her two-day-old baby girl and work as a wet-nurse for the son of a landlord in the next village. Her family survived, but the baby girl died.

Except for a short, short passage, I don't remember much else about the novel. This is how I recall the passage: the woman was nursing the landlord's baby at night and had dozed off while hugging and rocking the cuddly thing. When she woke up, her lips were brushing against the baby's soft cheeks as it lay asleep against her chest, with his hands cupping her breast. Gone was the burn of her swollen breasts. Instead, she was ravaged by anger and guilt for having grown so attached to this killer of her own baby.

The passage made me think of that image of myself hugging at Ahfen's arm and link it with this image of Ahfen staring at the cotton baby shoes lined up on top of her dresser. And I broke into uncontrollable sobs, although I had no clue as to why. I remember thinking that there was little resemblance between Ahfen and this woman beyond the fact that both had lost a baby and gone into domestic service. In fact, Ahfen herself would have been quite appalled to find out that I was comparing her to some poverty-stricken, North of the River woman! I told this to myself, all the while worried that my sisters in the next room would hear my sobbing and catch me once again weeping over some stupid Revolutionary book. And I was irritated at myself for having so wasted my time. I barely had time to skim the book and write my two paragraph self-criticism before joining my parents for a movie at the British Consulate.

What could Ahfen have meant when she called us her little ones, I asked myself after reading the novel. Little one, the one she wished was still alive? The one she wished we were but had not been? These questions made me burn with shame and guilt: the expanse of her love for me and my sisters mirrored the paucity of mine for her. So I convinced myself that I was too busy growing up to bother with these questions. I got my period during my second year at junior high. My body filled out and my face got longer. No longer cute. Just plain, awkward. Entering junior high also meant that I now suddenly had a "consciousness" to take care of, something I had to critique and reform along with other Intellectuals during every political movement, Anti-Rightist, the Great Leap Forward. . . . Sometime during my sophomore year, I stopped visiting Ahfen at her room in the servants' quarters. And I lost track of her cotton shoes.

In the summer of 1966, the year of the Cultural Revolution, the Red Guards came and searched our house. On the 60-some-page list of things the Red Guards confiscated, a list the Red Guards left for us along with the empty house, one entry puzzled my elders: 45 pairs of cloth baby shoes (new).

"Creepy, just like the Doctor in Dickens' *Tale of Two Cities.* Always knew the bloody woman was a little nutty," Papa said later when someone told him about the shoes.

"Or rather, the knitting of Madame Dufarge?" I thought to myself.

But I am jumping ahead. The day the Red Guards left us, I watched myself going over the entry again and again, thinking that I could not remember the last time I'd seen any of Ahfen's baby shoes.

Did she ever stop making them? When? Why? I asked myself.

I would never know.

For the first time since that hot summer afternoon a few weeks earlier, when I'd heard the Red Guards' drum and slogan chants approaching our driveway, I felt sad. I knew how that sadness looked. I had seen it in Mmma's eyes when she talked about her family's house in the Old Chinese City, the one burned down by the Japanese. It struck me as odd that out of the 60-some pages of things confiscated by the Red Guards, it was Ahfen's baby shoes which brought this sadness home. It started as an itch around my throat and squeezed its way through my spine and limbs, gradually rolling away the fear that had taken hold of me since that summer afternoon. I suddenly became conscious of the clamp of my jaw and my knotted muscles, even as I noticed them being slowly loosened by the sorrow easing through me. I fell asleep. When I woke up, I put on the black cotton revolutionary-style shoes Ahfen had just bought me and followed Haopo's footsteps down the stairs, through the pantry, into the kitchen.

Ahfen's Life Plan

Ahfen and I seldom talk about the three years before the Cultural Revolution, between the time I turned 17 and graduated from high school and that day in the summer of 1966 when the Red Guards marched into our house.

"I was so not understanding. . . ." I tried to bring it up on several occasions. My way of apologizing for having been so wrapped up in myself during those three years.

"You had a lot on your mind," Ahfen would say as she patted the back of my hand resting on her lap.

"You too," I'd reply, hesitant to go into further details, to sadden her with unpleasant memories.

She'd sigh and give my hand a little squeeze.

She knew what I meant, I took her to be saying.

It pains me to imagine what Ahfen was going through during those three years. Nothing in her whole life plan, as we call it in Chinese, seemed to be working out. Her Upstairs Children wanted to go abroad. Her Small Sister, Ahma, left to get married. And her adopted daughter, Yinyin, whom she had raised and then married to her adopted son, blamed her for having ruined her life.

Every few weeks, when my parents and I would appear at the breakfast table at 8:30 sharp in the second floor small dining room, we would find our toast burnt and the silver electric coffee pot lifeless.

"Ahfen's having her dizzy spells again," Chenma would sheepishly confirm.

"This," Papa concluded with a tap on his head, "and menopause."

"See if she needs anything," said Mmma, who was also going through menopause and dizzy spells.

I would dutifully go and whisper through the closed door to Ahfen's room: "Do you need anything?" I waited a few more seconds before taking the silence for a *No*. Then I returned to my overcooked and by now cold egg.

The next morning, sometimes two mornings later, I would give Ahfen's hand a little squeeze as she put my soft-boiled egg in front of me. My way of letting her know — before I returned to my studies, Chinese brush painting, and housekeeping duties — I had missed her. I had a lot on my mind.

This is the story I give when discussing my Society Youth status. After graduating with excellent grades from the best science-focused high school in Shanghai, I had applied to the best university for electrical engineering when taking the national entrance exams. My teachers at the high school had other plans. To maintain the pres- tige of the school — that is, the number of graduates accepted into major universities — they had recommended me to the government examination boards as a future English major. So I was officially en- couraged to reapply to a two-year teaching program in a foreign lan- guage department. (My politically dubious family background had ruled out my other options for serving the motherland: becoming a diplomat or an interpreter.)

"What a joke," my parents complained. "Her English is already better than most of the teachers at the university. Besides, who wants to be a low status school teacher?"

So I stayed home. To the government, I became a Society Youth, a label used to identify the 99 percent of high school graduates from the city who had failed the entrance exams and would be waiting for the next ten years to become one of the lucky five percent to be assigned a city job. Within the family and among friends, my parents announced that I was getting ready to study abroad. That was, after my parents worked out an acceptable excuse for me to apply for and obtain an exit permit.

To prove to myself and others that I hadn't flunked the exams out of stupidity or laziness, I read every text in English I could lay my hands on and taught myself college-level math and physics from textbooks borrowed from friends. I measured my progress with my scores on the "It Pays to Enrich Your Word Power" tests in *Reader's Digest*, which arrived monthly through the British Consulate. I doubled my score on any word that Mmma had missed and I mastered.

To others, I repeated the same story of how I ended up being a Society Youth. To myself, I asked if maybe I was recommended to be an English teacher because I had not done as well on the science portion of the exams. I asked if I was being foolish, as many had cau- tioned, in turning down my opportunity for a certificate. (In my 50- year-old nightmare, I am in my mid-30s and back in China. I don't have a job because I don't have a B.A. But I have a Ph.D. in English from the U.S., I keep on saying into the phone. Sometimes, I am passed from one to another but not to the person in charge to whom I must speak to get my job assignment. At other times, I hear a voice but cannot make out what is being said.)

To boost my spirit, my parents increased my allowance to the equivalent of the wage of a factory worker and twice Ahfen's *exorbitantly generous* pay. They entrusted me with the writing of all my parents' invitations and thank-you notes. I also oversaw their party preparations and arranged to have the right size flower baskets delivered to their various hosts. And I served as dinner or bridge partners to their young and old bachelor diplomat and banker guests. I took lessons in Chinese brush painting — flora and birds — and perfected my knack for flower arrangements. I updated myself with the *London Illustrated* and all sorts of ladies' journals passed down from my parents' Western friends. My parents wanted to make sure that I would know how to act wherever I went. After all, as the mother of a childhood friend of mine reassured my husband a few years ago: "Your wife is from the best of Shanghai families." ("My father was a farm boy from Pennsylvania," my husband replied with equal enthusiasm.)

The year was 1963. My sisters were both away at school. Theoretically, I had Ahfen all to myself. But things had changed. In the daytime, I gave her orders with, of course, my arm wrapped fondly around her shoulders and my cheek brushing against the top of her graying hair. "I hope she snaps out of her moods soon," my elders would say of Ahfen. Then they'd ask me to go talk to her, especially when they wanted something done as only Ahfen knew how to. My visits to the pantry were brief: I had other orders to give to others downstairs.

No more reasons for her to visit my room either. "I'm home now, I can dust it later myself," I told her politely. I was as messy then as I am now. But my room remained clean. How? I would not let myself ask then. I remember this time when I found her sitting on the floor in front of a bookcase with her mop on her lap, lining up, as we used to when I was younger, the 12 wooden Russian dolls nestled inside one another bought from the opening celebration of the Sino-Russian Friendship Hall. I don't think I learned to tidy my room. I just taught her to do it when she wouldn't be disturbing me.

Like Ahfen tells me, I had a lot on my mind.

I knew but did not want to know that Ahfen too had a lot on her mind.

"How are you girls going to repay her when you grow up?" My elders were always asking when we were very young.

"She goes where I go," I solemnly proclaimed.

By the time I turned 17, I had long since grown reconciled to the fact that working for me or one of my sisters was only one part of Ahfen's life plan. There was, as they say, always the question of the final resting place. All fallen leaves must go back to the roots. Ahfen's roots were that strip of land next to where her husband and baby boy lay, which now belonged to her husband's brother (from whom she had fled) and, later, to one of his two sons.

So Ahfen had been advised to approach the brother-in-law and arrange to adopt her younger nephew. To make sure that her adopted son would honor her right to return to the side of her husband and baby boy, Ahfen had also been urged to adopt Yinyin, an orphan girl from a poor village in the hill district. Yinyin was to be raised in Shanghai and then married to her adopted son. The idea was that the girl's indebtedness to Ahfen could also serve as a failsafe measure against illnesses towards the end, when Ahfen might need physical assistance. In the meantime, Ahfen should do everything she could to stay fit and save her earnings. An elderly person with money is always a more welcome burden to her children, alive or dead. The *meantime* part of Ahfen's life plan was where Ahma came in, although I was reluctant to accept Ahma's role in Ahfen's well-being.

I had always known that except for Cook, everyone downstairs came to us to run away from home. There was Wanma, who lost an eye to a pencil she and her brother were fighting over. A Nobody-Wants Old Maid, she stayed with us ten months out of the year to escape her mother, who at 90 still reigned over the household with a lashing tongue. Dongma's problem was her loghead husband, whose beatings regularly chased her to Shanghai for years at a stretch. That was, until letters of pleading from her seven sons would coax her back home for a short period to darn their clothing and feed them food fit for humans. Then there was Chenma, who had five daughters and thus infinite need to generate dowry money every few years. Before we learned to chronicle our life in terms of the Anti-Three and Anti-Five Movement, the Anti-Rightist Movement, or the Great Leap Forward, my sisters and I used to settle our arguments on what happened when by counting the faces present or absent at the pantry table.

This constant flux also taught us the essence of the ill forture of the Permanent Two, as we called Ahfen and Ahma. Family (or the lack of) was the cement between the Permanent Two, who had sworn to sisterhood years ago. Of the two, Ahfen at least had a married family name to carry and a paternal family to visit. If she had wanted to, she could have rightfully been Zhouma, meaning, the Ahma married into the Zhou family. Ahma, on the other hand, was called Ahma, because, as she liked to insist, she had no family name.

"Look at this," Ahma raved whenever her brother wrote, usually to ask for money.

"And look at this and this," she'd continue, pointing to the bald patches on her scalp and the scars on her arms and legs. "He calls me Sis now. Where was he when they sold me to the Old Bitch? (May she soon go to the 18th bottom of hell.) Where was he when the Old Bitch dragged me around by my hair and applauded when the Son of a Bitch bit me? Who was there when I popped, in the little shed behind the store? No one. Now that I have money, he tells me we are family. Family, a bunch of leeches ready to suck me dead."

According to downstairs gossip, the family to which Ahma was sold as a child daughter-in-law was actually a Good Family, owners of a grain store. The It which Ahma popped at 14 was by the Old Man rather than That Son of a Bitch, since the son was attending school in the city at the time. It was brought up by the Old Bitch as a man of the family. So It, too, was sent to school. Ahma was let go after she popped and just before That Son of a Bitch returned with a modern girl from the city.

"Your brother is a bottomless hole. The more you pour into it, the deeper it gets," Ahfen always warned as soon as a letter showed up.

"I know, I know. When we get old, you'll return with your gold bars and I, a pauper. Well, we'll just be back where we started, right?" Ahma would mumble, chuckling at her own humor as she made her way up to Haopo's rooms to have the letter read. "How many times do I have to tell you? It's all in my eight characters. I get sick whenever I have idle money sitting in my pocket. Someone has to bleed me, if not my brother, then the doctor."

That evening, after she had mailed out the money, Ahma would gloat over her rice wine: "I'd just love to see the Old Bitch's eyes pop when she hears I am sending money home again. Heaven's revenge: she, labeled a wife of the Anti-Revolutionary Landlord, with all her property confiscated, while me, the low and worthless to the bone child daughter-in-law, has money to burn. Ha, ha, ha."

"Forget about the Old Bitch. She's blind, deaf, and with one foot in her coffin," Ahfen would counter.

"I know, I know," Ahma agreed quickly to spare herself the rest of Ahfen's lecture. Taking another sip from her cup, she'd clear her throat and sing in Ahfen's softer voice: "Save up for when we get old." Taking another sip, Ahma would switch to the voice of an old man in Shaoxing opera style and sing: "Get drunk when there is wine!" Then she would wink and take her bow to the others tittering around the pantry table.

"You fool," Ahfen would shake her head while trying to keep a straight face. "You know what I'll say when your worthless brother kicks you out."

All of us at the table knew what Ahfen would say. But we also knew what Ahfen would do after she had had her say. She would take Ahma in, as Ahma had Ahfen when Ahfen first arrived in Shanghai. That's what Small Sisters were for.

For a long time, I didn't think it was fair that Ahfen should someday have to provide for Ahma, especially since Ahma always seemed to be having so much more fun than Ahfen. Then my sister read *The Journey to the West* and began calling the Permanent Two the Monk and the Monkey. I caught the physical resemblance after watching a Peking Opera version of the classic novel. Like the Monkey in the opera, who was always twitching his face and scratching himself, Ahma had a habit of fidgeting around whenever she was spoken to. Like the Monk, a white-faced scholar in a world of animals and monsters, Ahfen's delicate features and fair skin always made her seem out of place at the pantry table. Furthermore, like the Monkey, Ahma had a quick temper and a weakness for wine. Even Papa understood that a shot of brandy worked better for Ahma's cramps than his pills, which Ahma would only flush down the toilet as soon as his back was turned. Everyone upstairs and downstairs knew not to ruffle Ahma. Cook didn't know when he first came. He took offense when the Permanent Two insisted on cooking their own food. So he put his foot down: no more carrying produce from the market for the two, and no messing around in his kitchen, after he left, to make their stinky country folk food. The three got into an argument. And the next thing you knew, Ahma was chasing Cook around the house with his cleaver in her hand. Haopo had to be brought down to settle things. Ahma was made to admit that she had had a bit too much to drink, so that Cook could save a little face. But Cook also learned to quietly leave pickled greens and tofu by the pantry sink and make no further inquiry as to how and where the produce was later turned into those dishes the two munched on across the pantry table from him.

As I got older and read *The Journey to the West* in its original, I noticed other parallels. In the novel, the Monkey was assigned by the Father of Heaven to assist the Monk on his journey to bring back the holy writ. Because the monsters believed that eating the Monk's tender flesh could give them eternal life and youth, they were always disguising themselves in the form of devout pilgrims and chaste maidens to lure the Monk to their caves. It was the Monkey's job to protect the Monk by clearing the paths of those monsters. Yet in spite of the Monk's sacred knowledge, he was forever fooled by the monsters and thus wrongly punishing the Monkey for chasing after the monsters in their disguised forms. But the Monkey never bore the Monk any grudges. He always returned to save the Monk just when the monsters were about to toss the Monk into their smoldering cauldrons.

Like the Monk, Ahfen needed Ahma's Monkey street wisdom to get her through her dealings with the world outside. Ahfen's holy mission: save up more for old age by lending her savings out on interest. This made Ahfen an easy prey for monsters such as the Egg Woman. Story had it that the Egg Woman was popular downstairs because, besides selling her day-fresh eggs, she also let the servants have things her husband vended on the streets at a special discount. "Trash," Haopo was always warning them. But Egg Woman knew how to sweet talk anyone. Years ago, the Egg Woman had talked Ahfen into lending her a large sum of money at a higher interest rate than that offered by the government bank for saving accounts. But she went back on her promise as soon as Ahfen loaned her the money. Since it had been illegal since 1949 for private citizens to lend money for interest, the terms did not appear on the contract Ahfen had asked someone to draw. (Haopo had flatly refused to have any part in the deal.) So Ahfen had no hold on the Egg Woman and ended up losing on the money she would have earned if the sum had remained in her savings account at the government bank.

"Do a good deed to accumulate good fortune for the next life," the money-hungry monsters would pester Ahfen the Monk.

"Remember the Egg Woman!" Ahma the Monkey would caution at the risk of angering her Monk master. "Close your soft ears, they are only trying to sweet talk you out of your blood and sweat money."

Once a month, Haopo treated the Permanent Two to a Shaoxing opera. And once during every Spring Festival, the Permanent Two got to spend a day at the Great World, a five-story entertainment center in downtown Shanghai with funny-mirrors, local operas in all dialects, acrobatic performances, magicians, circus, souvenir and food vendors and, of course, tourists from all over the country as well as the most skilled of pickpockets and swindlers. These outings always left Ahma in the highest of spirits for nights to come, describing the plots and impersonating the singers in the opera they had watched. Ahfen, on the other hand, would be sulking in her corner, nursing a headache or moaning over a scarf or something she had lost. Ahma got the biggest kick out of the fact that the pickpockets continued to target Ahfen even after Ahfen had learned to keep most of her money with Ahma. Ahma always said: "It's my worthless-to-the-bone look. I could be wearing the Young Mistress's mink coat and they would have no interest in my pockets." So we all shuddered to think what could have happened to Ahfen if Ahma the Monkey was not there to protect her.

Like the Monkey, Ahma also let Ahfen lord over her. Who else downstairs could make Ahma cringe and wince but Ahfen with her soft-spoken words?

"Forget about them, they can't harm you anymore," Ahfen would chant when Ahma schemed about sending her brother things and money for the sole purpose of burning the Old Bitch and That Son of a Bitch with envy and regret.

Nevertheless, the parallel between the Permanent Two and the Monk/Monkey coupling breaks at a crucial point, which I would not realize until much later. In the classic novel, whenever the Monkey acts unruly, the Monk chants to inflict a splitting headache upon the

Monkey: a magic power given to the Monk by the Father of Heaven to ensure the Monkey's service during the journey west. Ahfen, on the other hand, chanted to calm Ahma by reminding her to focus on the present and the future: to remind Ahma that she was now Ahfen's Small Sister and no longer the *Old Bitch*'s Child Daughter-in-Law. In return, Ahma put up with Ahfen on her bad days when Ahfen locked herself in and Ahma out of the room the two shared. On nights Ahfen responded to Ahma's knocking, she brought Ahfen food and coaxed it down. On nights Ahfen didn't, Ahma just slept wherever she could without a word of complaint.

I don't know what the Permanent Two talked about or did at night in the room they shared from age 30 to almost mid-40s. I can only guess from what I'd seen of them around the pantry table. I imagine Ahfen was the voice of love that Ahma never had from anyone else. And Ahma was the voice of doubt, reason, and rebellion that Ahfen never knew how to let out. Whatever feelings of ambivalence toward the upstairs Ahfen might have sensed and tried to suppress on her bad days, Ahma voiced them aloud for Ahfen before and afterwards. Ahma's teasing and chiding reassured Ahfen that she was not alone, nor crazy, to have felt any of her ambivalence. Ahma's teasing insisted: there were others, real people and opera characters, who had shared Ahfen's sentiments and had not been too shy to put them into words. As a reader, I admired the Monkey for his feisty suspicions toward the gods of the Western Heaven, and I considered him an excellent role model for my combats with the grownups. Yet, being a part of the upstairs and often the butt of Ahma's teasing, I was not thrilled by Ahma's Monkey-like opinions and behavior toward us. I believed in our benevolence and thus, in our right to receive proper reverence.

Nevertheless, by the time I entered junior high, I no longer resented Ahma's part in Ahfen's life. In fact, I began to take secret comfort in knowing that Ahfen would always have Ahma to fall back on: it appeased my conscience to know that Ahfen's love was being appropriately reciprocated by someone else. So I learned to accept and then take for granted that Ahma goes where Ahfen goes where one of us goes. After all, as my elders always claimed, in many ways, Ahma could be just as indispensable.

Then, in the spring of 1965, Ahma surprised all of us by announcing her decision to marry an old widower, a retired silk weaver with a modest pension.

"How could she," I asked the question I presumed Ahfen would be fuming over: "leaving us at the (such!) old age of 49?"

"What could I lose," Ahma asked when explaining her decision. The upstairs had agreed that Ahma could continue working for us, except now she got to go home at night and have half of Sunday off every other week. Instead of being bled by her no-good brother, she'd just pour her blood sweat money into the old widower's wine jug, braised soy beans and fried small yellow fish. This way, at least she'd get to share the wine and food and have someone to warm her feet at night. As we were soon to find out, she also got to take home the many stray cats she was always finding outside our house but could only, up till then, feed and woo from across the garden fence. Besides, if he who was ten years older were to go before her, she'd have a room under her name. If it were to be the other way round, she'd have someone to send her on her way.

I don't know what the Permanent Two said to each other before or after Ahma made her decision. My guess is, as the saying goes, the Two let their hearts enlighten each other without ever uttering a word. Ahfen took money saved up for when the Two got old to supplement the gift from upstairs, so Ahma, at 49, had the wedding denied her when her parents sold her at age 8. For her part, Ahma regularly arrived in the mornings carrying a bowl wrapped inside a handkerchief filled with braised soy bean or steamed stinky tofu. This, I believe, was their way of telling one another that, if things did not work out with the widower, Ahfen would take Ahma in after, of course, Ahfen had had her say. And if the marriage worked, Ahma would never leave Ahfen behind, only the room they had shared for the last decade and half.

All knew that no one could fill the silence around the pantry table, nor the empty bed in their room. But only Ahfen knew how she passed those hours without her Small Sister. I didn't bother to find out. I was too busy growing up.

"Her fate turns out to be better than it appeared." That was all Ahfen would say when Ahma's marriage came up in conversation.

Some suggested that maybe Ahfen should consider marriage herself. What about Chauffeur Wang, who was always asking after her? Financially secure, not too old, warm-hearted. . . .

Others argued Ahfen would be foolish to take the risk. Why waste all that money adopting children if she wasn't going to make them pay back?

Ahfen seemed to agree with the latter. (She gave other reasons. *Don't need someone to boss over me*, Ahfen always added after her *not me*. But I wouldn't really hear those words until years later.)

I sided with the first group, which included everyone upstairs. I wished Ahfen could be less superstitious. With things being so strained between her and her adopted daughter, Yinyin, it was time for Ahfen to revise her life plan.

I was 10 when I first met Yinyin, who was 15 but looked 11. They said Yinyin's mother had left her with her grandparents when Yinyin was two, after her father died in an accident at the textile mill where both her parents had worked. Yinyin had never been outside her village in the hills until one of Ahfen's sisters-in-law, a native from Yinyin's village, took Yinyin down to meet Ahfen. Yinyin came with nothing but the cotton shirt and pants her grandparents had scraped to put together for the occasion.

"A sharp kid, knew how to intuit her surroundings and elders' mood."

"Pleasant face. Tough, could shoulder a hundred pounds up those mountain steps on that stunted body."

"Poor child, never enough food around the house."

Ahfen took to the girl and made a three-way deal. She paid Yinyin's grandparents for having raised Yinyin from infancy in return for the right to adopt Yinyin. She sent a matchmaker to the brother of her dead husband, who accepted Yinyin as the future bride of his younger son (whom Ahfen had adopted and been semi-supporting since ten) with, of course, Ahfen footing a respectable dowry. They said that the third part of the deal was sealed as soon as Mmma laid eyes on Yinyin. Room and board? No problem. How about a little allowance of ten yuan for working as Ahma's helper?

Mmma and Haopo predicted: "This kid will make good at anything she sets her heart to." They insisted that Yinyin address them as Haopo and the Mmma of the Lu Family, as did the children of family friends. The upstairs did not approve of arranged marriages. "Foolish idea," my elders said behind Ahfen's back. "Who knows what will happen to that boy and this girl in three or four years!" But we liked the idea of Ahfen adopting Yinyin: a healthy outlet for Ahfen and a truly good deed for the girl.

We also had a lot of ideas about what should be done for Ahfen's adopted daughter. "Eat more," my elders ordered. When Yinyin got her first period, it was passed around as proof of the proper nutrition she was getting from us. "Enroll Yinyin at the night school," they urged. It would only be fair, Haopo argued upon hearing that Yinyin had been forced to leave school at third grade. Wasn't Ahfen helping with her adopted son's high school expenses? "Be nice to her," they told us girls. So we shared our things to ease our guilt for being so *lucky*. For me, the discrepancy between my allowance and the wage of a servant, not to mention all the other things, was suddenly driven home by the realization that Yinyin was the same age as my sister, could have been her and vice versa.

During the first year, Yinyin and I played together in my room a lot: she was about my height and a third grader, so everyone assumed we were about the same mental age even though she was 15 and her heart, they agreed, was as mature and wise as any grownup's could ever be! We'd start with me straddling her shoulders, thighs wrapped tightly around her neck and hands clinching on to her scalp. Yinyin would circle around the room with her hands gripping my ankles (dangling down her chest) while I screamed with joy as she quickened her pace. (My favorite pastime with Papa until the ceiling got in the way of my head when he stood up and his chain-smoker's breath got shorter and shorter.) Afterwards, we'd dress Yinyin up in my and my sister's clothes.

Then a little misunderstanding happened. Haopo told me one day that I was too grown up to continue my (bad) habit of leaving my 10-yuan bills all over the place. Yinyin, Haopo explained to me, thought maybe I was doing that to test her honesty.

I felt hurt (even though it hurts more to remember my crass reaction): "Couldn't she tell that was just me? I do that all the time!" How could she doubt my intention? I thought we were friends.

Haopo advised me to consider Yinyin's side: "That's what friends do!"

But I didn't know how. I could not begin to tackle the question my grandmother was prompting me to form: What would it have been like to have worked in the fields since age 10 for less than 20 cents a day and then to have to fathom why another 10-year-old could simply forget about two 10-yuan bills inside a red New Year's gift envelope crumpled inside a coat pocket? So instead, I stopped inviting Yinyin to my room.

Other than a few isolated vignettes, I had little recollection of Yinyin during the next four years. One image had the four of us squeezed in the back of my father's little forest-green Rover, *the brand the Queen of England rides in.* It was probably during one of those Sunday outings Papa liked to make. My elder sister and I exchanged looks when my younger sister, who, being the youngest, was made to sit with Yinyin in the middle, complained about the weight of my thigh leaning against hers. We, the look between my elder sister and I implied, were mature enough to know not to do or say anything that might make Yinyin feel out of place.

Then there was this picture of Ahfen moving her forefinger slowly across the block-size characters printed in her adult primer and mumbling with quiet pride: "Workers, farmers, trade-personnel, students, and soldiers, reunite!" Next to her sat Ahma, sipping her rice wine and arguing with Cook from across the table. And next to Ahma was Yinyin doing her math homework with the Little Doctor fountain pen Haopo and Mmma had given her on her birthday.

This scene had to have taken place during the Great Leap Forward movement of the 1960s, when Mao announced the new five-year plan to rid China of illiteracy and the four pests (of rat, fly, mosquito, and sparrow) and, of course, make China catch up with the British American Imperialists in productivity. Upstairs, we believed in education. So everyone downstairs was encouraged to attend the free evening classes offered by the lane organization as long as, needless to say, it did not inconvenience the upstairs. Ahfen, as I recall, was the only one who went through the whole thing and passed the 100 characters test at the end.

A romantic sight, I observed from the top of the back stairway after I relayed an order. Seeing Ahfen and Yinyin doing their homework at the pantry table made me think of Mmma's summer school, of the mahogany table she had had set in the downstairs hallway where the marble floor and the breeze from the open doors and windows in all directions would keep us cool on the muggiest of Shanghai mornings. I thought of Mmma hovering over her French dictionary and the entire works of de Maupassant as she kept us company while we did our homework for our private English lessons.

Unfortunately, this image of mother and adopted daughter getting ready for evening school was superimposed on another I'd rather forget. A raging Ahfen shaking Yinyin by the shoulders against the back of her chair and frantically tossing Yinyin's exercise books into the furnace in the corner of the pantry. "Who do you think you are, a young mistress who can just eat already prepared meals without having to do any work?" Ahfen would cry.

Ahfen's old-fashioned behavior shamed me: treating Yinyin as if she were a Child Daughter-in-Law bought with a few silver dollars.

"Her manners might be harsh but her heart is pure," Ahma always consoled Yinyin afterwards, reminding Yinyin of the many expressions of love — clothing, a wristwatch, and new school supplies — an Ahfen in remorse was always showering on her.

I thought Ahfen was mad at Yinyin because she had neglected the house chores assigned her by Ahfen and Ahma. How silly! I agreed with Ahma, Haopo, and Mmma that there was absolutely no need to get so worked up just for that. No one upstairs was complaining.

The word *just* makes me think that my elders had in mind other reasons I was too young to contemplate. I could not hear the fear and frustration of a mother watching her child slip away as a result of the very (best) thing she was fighting to give the child, not until years later, in the U.S., when I learned to measure my own daughter's progress at school with the frequency by which she corrected my accented English.

I think Ahfen had to have wondered: Where was all this schooling taking her adopted daughter? The upstairs claimed that if you have knowledge, you'll never be afraid of not having food to eat. The characters in Ahfen's night school primer taught: "Study hard so that we might be the new masters of China." Visitors from the village warned: "You let them put ideas into that girl's head and soon she'll want to stay in Shanghai and ruin your plans." "So what," the upstairs replied, "so long as her heart stays with you. Look at her friend the maid next door (who was soon to marry Cook's son). Find her a husband in the city and she can be there for you, a mere phone call away."

I remember the look of pride on Ahfen's face in a photo taken at the wedding of Cook's son to the maid next door: Ahfen's slight frame cradled inside Yinyin's firm arms. "Could easily pass as a Shanghai girl, a high school student," we applauded before mother and adopted daughter took off for the wedding banquet. The highest compliment we could imagine. We passed it after carefully inspecting Yinyin's wrist-watched arm, her white linen shirt with a fountain pen pinned to the chest pocket, her starched skirt made out of export turned local retailing fabric (with bright colored hand-bag, high-heeled slippers, and sunglasses scattered across an off-white background), and her white bobby-socked, black leather-shoed feet.

How was Ahfen to think of her adopted daughter, herself, and her life plan upon hearing such compliments? The original idea was to groom Yinyin to marry her adopted son back home, to guarantee Ahfen a final place of return. Did Ahfen let *them* put ideas into Yinyin's head because Ahfen was reconciled to the fact that she alone could not withstand the flow of time which always seemed to travel with others — the upstairs and the government? Or did she let it happen because she wanted for her adopted daughter what *they* had and could give, what she herself had never had the opportunity to obtain? A little of both is my guess. So how do you fight against something you both desire and fear out of love?

In the winter of 1960, the Country Mouse, as my younger sister called Ahfen's adopted son and Yinyin's prospective husband, came to visit. Mmma sponsored the trip so the two could get to know one another before the wedding, which had been set for the coming spring. Haopo bought movie tickets to give the two a little privacy. My sister and I watched them leaving the house from the third floor bedroom windows, he tagging 15 feet behind her. And we laid bets on the number of times he would speak during the entire evening.

They said that Yinyin went to Haopo after the City Mouse, a factory worker she'd met in evening school, proposed. He was in his mid-30s and an orphan like herself. Haopo asked what Yinyin thought. Yinyin knew whom she would like to marry. But she also understood her debt to Ahfen. She would not do anything without Ahfen's blessing.

Haopo and Mmma tried to mediate. "The child understands her obligations," they reassured Ahfen. "Yinyin would go back, if you tell her to. But what about how she would then feel toward you? The child takes things to heart," they warned. "You'll gain a daughter-in-law but lose a daughter." They advised Yinyin to talk to the guy, to think of some ways to appease Ahfen's worries about her life plan. How about having him offer to become Ahfen's adopted son? "No problem," the City Mouse said. Ahfen would just be the mother he had never had. She could even move in with them after his work-unit got around to assigning the couple an eight-by-eight room in the dormitory. She could work for the family during the day, as Ahma did.

But everyone knew that no amount of understanding amongst the three could stop the wrath this change of plan would bring from the villagers. Forget about that strip of land by the side of her husband and baby boy. Get ready for the reputation of stealing and corrupting innocent girls from the village. Like mother like daughter, they'd say of Yinyin. And Yinyin remembered only too well what they had called her biological mother.

"I should have let her stay in Shanghai," Ahfen told me in 1996.

She was showing me a color photo of herself, Yinyin, her adopted son, and three grandsons in front of Yinyin's newly completed four-story house in the village. Good fortune, people in the village say of Ahfen and Yinyin: a household full of sons and grandsons. Four TVs, one on each floor. But through the years, Ahfen's visits got shorter and shorter. It pained Ahfen to watch Yinyin: always pinching the penny, so harsh on the hired farmers, so picky toward the daughters-in-law. Expand the household was what Yinyin was sent back to do, and that seemed to have become the only thing keeping her going. Yinyin was making everyone pay for what she had had to pay.

All my fault! I understood Ahfen's long sigh to be saying. So I gave Ahfen's hand a gentle squeeze to let her know that I agreed but did not condemn. But condemn I did during the 1960s, burning with shame at Ahfen's old-fashioned decision.

"Foolish," my elders concluded. "Things between Ahfen and Yinyin could never be the same again. Five years of loving and thousands of yuan down the drain, just for a burial place at the end."

I agreed. Why couldn't Ahfen just go with the flow of time? I asked every time I missed Ahfen's greetings at the breakfast table. I had yet to experience the fear of collective consternation awaiting those who burn their bridges. I was not ready to consider that Ahfen, however, would have known well the full scope of such consternation from when she first ran away from her in-laws. Well enough to dread it. I was merely able to realize that Ahfen had a lot on her mind. But I had more, I reassured myself.

In Exile

"It is time for me to go home," Ahfen announced in the fall of 1966, at the beginning of the Cultural Revolution.

Everyone downstairs was told to quit serving my Rotten Nine Category family. But all agreed there was no need for Ahfen to look for new employment. She could never manage the load expected of the do-it-all helpers revolutionary cadre families hired. She should go back to her adopted children and live off the interest from her savings in the bank. Yinyin would welcome her help: Yinyin had been adding boys, silkworms, and livestock to the household she had been adopted to expand.

To everyone's surprise, Ahfen was back in Shanghai before the end of the month. Yes, the adopted children were wonderful. So was the air and the produce. No, she couldn't get used to living that way anymore.

So Ahma and her husband helped Ahfen settle back into her room in the servants' quarters of our house on HengShan Road. It was clear by then that, like all the other Rotten Nine Category families, we would soon be swept outside the door of our house like the dust on the floor. When the time came, Ahfen should use her working-person status to demand that the Revolutionary Housing Bureau assign her a permanent place of residency. In the meantime, to protect Ahfen's belongings from the Wildcats — what we called the thugs in Red Guard armbands coming nightly to loot the house for whatever was left — Ahma nailed up the door connecting the servants' quarters to the rest of the house. Then they put up a sign marking Ahfen's quarters as belonging to a separate, working-class household.

Soon afterwards, Ahfen found work with a cadre family. She learned to shop in the food market, cook three meals, wash and clean besides taking care of a ten-year-old boy and a four-year-old girl. Nothing fancy, Ahfen assured us. The family had a suite the size of my old bedroom and did not even own an electric iron. Like everyone else, I did not expect Ahfen to last more than a week: the crowd at the food market was easily worse than the one at the Great World amusement park.

Ahfen stayed with the family for six and a half years. Then she figured out a way to double her income by contracting herself out, by the hour, to four families.

When Ahfen got her first paycheck from her cadre employers, she and Ahma sneaked back to our part of the house one night to bring us food, clothing, and news from the outside.

They also offered money.

"It's yours anyway," Ahma muttered as Ahfen slipped a roll of 10-yuan bills into Haopo's hand.

We knew they were referring to the six-years' severance pay Mmma had insisted to the Red Guards that we owed the two. When Mmma asked that the two be paid out of the account confiscated by the Red Guards, I couldn't tell whether the leader was more stunned or angered. "This money belongs to the people now, you crazy old woman," he yelled. "I know," Mmma reasoned, "but the people wouldn't want to deny the working persons what they had labored for, would they?" I watched, digging my nails into the soft of my hands as if the pressure on my flesh might somehow be transmitted across the room to curb the look of contempt and triumph on Mmma's face. (In my dreams, I am still explaining to Mmma about the psychology of these animals: "Don't go out of your way to provoke them!")

On the night when Ahfen and Ahma sneaked back to leave us some money, Haopo reassured the two once again that the money was theirs: "You earned it."

In the end, we took 20 yuan, which was about a whole month's salary for Ahfen or Ahma and a loan we knew we might never be able to return. We could use the help. A group of Wildcats had visited the night before and took what grocery money we had left from our monthly subsistence fee of 12-yuan-per-person. We were glad the money was there for the Wildcats, knowing that if they had had to leave emptyhanded, they might have taken out their disappointment on us.

"Thank you," Mmma whispered as Haopo accepted the two ten-yuan bills.

Mmma had always said that knowing how to thank those who waited on you (*with a gentle smile and eye contact!*) was a sign of good breeding. But that night, all of us in the room heard the difference in her use of the only two words she had uttered all evening.

A friendship cemented in adversity, as the saying goes.

When the initial turmoil of the Cultural Revolution was over and the nocturnal visits from the Wildcats gradually stopped, the Shanghai gas company decided that our house would be an ideal location for a main office. So it had us moved to a one-and-one-half-room residency in a lane of rowhouses. Ahfen stayed behind as planned and was duly assigned an eight-by-eight back room above the kitchen of a one-down-one-up rowhouse with stone-framed doors in a place called the Garden

Lane. Every evening after work and before returning to the Garden Lane, Ahfen would stop to spend a half hour with us.

She would begin by sitting a little bit with Mmma, who stared into the night by the window, clenching a cup of hot water. "Deeds of evil," Ahfen would mutter. We knew what Ahfen meant: neither Papa nor Mmma deserved what had happened to them. "Heaven will protect and bless the family," Ahfen would add softly.

Then she would get up to see if there was any washed clothing soaking in the tub. "My new hobby," Mmma explained when others caught her pounding away at the wooden washboard. "Leave the heavy things to the children," they advised as they eyed the weight of the denim sheets against Mmma's bird-frame of a body. But Ahfen had watched Mmma soap, scrub and rinse her grief and anger away. So she knew not to offer her own firmer wrists and grip to the Young Mistress, other than giving the heavy pieces a final wring so that, when Mmma hung the sheets outside the windows the next morning, they would not drip water onto the downstairs neighbors' clothing and make them mad.

Next, Ahfen went to sit with the Old Mistress. "Any mail?" Ahfen asked on Thursdays (or, was it Tuesdays?), the day of delivery for mail from Hong Kong. Haopo relayed the good tidings of vacation trips, promotions, graduations, and weddings, as she showed Ahfen the postcard-sized color photos that had come with my aunt's letters. Yes, the dress was in red. No, that looked more like a table lamp. Ahfen lent her clear sight, which followed Haopo's swollen forefinger as they traced the cataract-blurred objects in the prints. Sometimes Ahfen had news of Yinyin and family. Then the two held hands and sighed. "If only I could exchange the remainder of my years for Eddie's freedom," Haopo moaned. "Why don't I give you a sponge bath," Ahfen offered, rubbing the corner of her eyes. Her way of reminding Haopo that the Young Master would want his mother to live and live well. "He's a good man — there will be a good end," Ahfen muttered as she went to get water. Afterward, they talked about how to get Haopo some cotton ration coupons so that they could add a new layer of silk wool to Haopo's winter blanket.

Ahfen's face and body filled out. Gone were the dizzy spells. No more bad days. People called it a clear case of someone forced to go up the Liang mountain, meaning, learning to thrive in situations not of their own choosing.

So much healthier looking, they said.

So much happier, was how I would put it now.

Back then, I didn't know how to talk without guilt about the new openings I was noticing in people's lives in spite (because?) of the Cultural Revolution. I realized that good ends could result from bad happenings. But I had trouble admitting that.

To express my delight with the new Ahfen, I sometimes addressed her as Elder Sister Lou, revolutionary style, even though Ahfen and Ahma had insisted that in the privacy of home we stick to our old way of addressing each other. They would only refer to Mmma as Elder Sister Li in public. At home, Mmma remained their Young Mistress. I understood this to be their way of saying that no amount of political-consciousness building could change their gratitude for the good life they had had with the family. We, on the other hand, sometimes called them Elder Sister Lou and Elder Sister Chow to acknowledge the new turn in their lives and in our relationship.

However, I didn't think the Elder Sister Lou I knew was the same as the one Haopo and Mmma had in mind, for they had never been with Ahfen at the food market nor visited her place at the Garden Lane. At the food market, I was known as the daughter of Elder Sister Lou's former employers. At 6:00 in the morning, on my way home from the night shift at the factory where I was being re-educated during a six-month period at the beginning of the Cultural Revolution, I'd slip quietly in between two of Elder Sister Lou's friends at the beginning of a line of over 500 people formed since midnight for any fresh produce, which was in perpetual short supply in spite of heavy rationing. I learned the popularity of this new Ahfen every time I was caught trying to sneak into the line, when friend after friend of Elder Sister Lou would come forward to vouch for my rightful place in it.

I liked our walk home afterwards the best: Ahma in the middle about half a step ahead with Ahfen and me on the flanks, squeezing our way through the little gap Ahma had cleared through the crowd. We bathed in the envy of strangers as they noticed the shimmering silver gray of the belt-fish resting on top of the greens in our baskets. We laughed as Ahma impersonated the mean North of the River woman who headed the meat counter, with whom Ahma was always battling to get a piece of pork which weighed no less than what was allowed by the ration coupons she had. And we'd describe to one another how we planned to cook the tofu we had bought with our monthly ration cards, sharing tips on how to make it tasty with the least of the also rationed oil and sugar.

Once in a long while, we would stop for a treat by the breakfast stand on the street corner where Ahma and Ahfen daily picked up soy drinks for their employers. A piping hot pancake with sugar fillings and sesame seeds on the shell, my favorite, or a steamed vegetarian bun. Ahma teased me about the old days when I'd begged and bribed her to buy me such food on the way back from school and got us all into trouble. We laughed. Then we sighed, to let the others know how much we missed Papa's tirades on the lack of sanitation in these places. Then we fought to pay for the treats. Mostly, they paid. I was making 70 cents a day and they, 85.

I don't remember exactly when Ahfen began to refer to her eight-by-eight room as *home* or *my place*. I know for years she simply called it the Garden Lane. I think she did that for the same reason one of our HengShan Road neighbors called their favorite son Ugly-Ugly: to deflect the red eyes of envy.

I could tell that Ahfen liked it when I stopped by the Garden Lane to taste the tea eggs she had made on the single burner stationed at the one-by-one foot landing outside her door. So, to please her, I did from time to time. Because I went with my nostalgia for our old house, I sensed but had difficulty comprehending that mixture of novelty, pleasure, pride, and anguish her place seemed to evoke in Ahfen. "Half the size of her old room with us and without indoor plumbing," I reported to Mmma and Haopo after my first visit. I heard the rickety stairway, smelled the chamber pot behind the badly chipped wooden door, and felt the draft through the crack in the single window which she had to climb onto the bed frame to close. And I joined my elders in urging Ahfen to come and eat with us on her half day off every other Sunday and to take advantage of the bathtub we shared with a family of eight that lived below us. But she seldom did.

Nevertheless, I tucked away several images of Ahfen at her place: her shy pride when others came for tips on cooking and child rearing, her grace as she introduced me to a neighbor passing by the open door of her room, her excitement as she showed me the new wood stand she had had built, which could be stored underneath the desk-sized table, to hold her wash basins and cooking pots.

"Never lost a single coupon," I can still hear Ahfen's voice as she put away the coupons for something Mmma was asking her to get from the market. She stashed them in a little wallet she wore on the inside of her shirt and next to her own coupons and that of other families she worked for, four at one point. I knew why she had never lost a single coupon. I'd witnessed the confidence in her gait: no monsters would be foolish enough to take her for the guileless Monk in *Journey to the West*. I noticed something else in that gait, what I now call the shy pride of someone taken by surprise at her own capacity and the gratification it brought. Back then, I only sensed the significance of this something I didn't quite have the words for.

Luckily, I hoarded this image of Ahfen's gait along with the images of Ahfen at *her place* and, without knowing what I had, smuggled these images across the border upon leaving China in 1981. Over in the U.S., well-intentioned friends and relatives were eager to volunteer warnings against my career choice: professors are the worst paid the world over. No job for Ph.Ds in English Literature here, not even for native speakers! So I had many occasions to remind my 30-something, single mother, non-native speaking, penniless self: no one, myself included, thought Ahfen would make it in the world outside our house on HengShan Road. Then I practiced Ahfen's gait from the food market days down the corridors of the building where the English Department was housed, learning to take cautious delight in watching myself outgrow myself.

It was during the same period in my life when, separated by a 19-hour jet ride, I found a new intimacy with the Ahfen of my early childhood. I had met Liz through a newspaper ad within a week of my arrival in the States: free room and board in exchange for 20 hours a week of babysitting. We hit it off right away: two married, but separated, 30-something, returning graduate students from upper-class backgrounds. She hired me on the spot and I moved in the next day. I was in such a hurry that I never paused to consider the hurt it might have caused Slu and Phil, who had devoted almost a whole year's time persuading university administrators at all levels to admit me into the MA program in spite of the fact that I had no undergraduate degree. Upon my arrival, they had opened their home to me for as long as I needed. I told myself and them I did not want to overburden their hospitality. I hope they understood better than I did what I was hiding behind my politeness: my insecurity about my much doubted ability to make it on my own, and my fear of being indebted to anyone. I am, after all, every bit my father's and my mother's daughter.

During my days at Liz's, I thought a lot about Ahfen and her baby cotton shoes. "I want my mommy," Emily, who was two and took to me from the beginning, never failed to wail when I was putting her to bed.

After I had reassured her for the umpteenth time that her mommy would be there to greet her when she woke up the next morning, Emily would ask, "Where is *your* little girl?" "In China, where I came from," I'd answer. "Where is China? Why did you leave your little girl there? When is she coming to live with us?"

Adam, Liz's nine-year-old son, remained politely aloof. He would not forget that somewhere in China there was a child of about his age left behind by a mother who, like his own father, had taken off to chase a new life. I couldn't decide which was worse, Emily's affectionate probing or Adam's sullen reminders of my motherly betrayal. As I warmed to the heat of Emily's silky skin, I froze at its power to replace in my memory the feel of my own little girl's body against mine. (To this day, I have to resort to my dreams to relive the sensation of my daughter's tiny hands around my neck.)

I realized during moments like that that I only escaped having bad days because I had other things to look forward to, not because I had stronger *nerves* or was less *superstitious*. Jacobean drama, metaphysical poetry, women's liberation, the flower generation, affirmative action. I tried out my new vocabulary with Liz after the children were tucked in, me sipping green tea across the counter from where Liz rinsed the dishes and occasionally took a swig from her Diet Pepsi. In return for reading and critiquing her papers, she copyedited and typed mine. With that, she gave me a lesson in composition few literature professors knew to offer: stop worrying about errors in spelling and grammar; focus instead on refining the ideas she taught me to believe I was able to produce. To remind me of what a fun and loving mother I was and could be, she lent me her Jewish children for my first Easter in the U.S. to take on an egg hunt modeled after the ones Mmma used to give in our garden at HengShan Road.

Lying on my stomach at night, I groped for the arm of my Downstairs Mother even as I waited anxiously for the feel of my daughter's eight-year-old skin on my fingertips. And I told myself: Fate might take my little girl away (temporarily, I prayed), as it had robbed Ahfen of her baby boy. Like Ahfen, I could refuse to let fate take away my desire and ability to love the child I was paid to hold as well as the child I had left behind.

Unfortunately, my new intimacy with the Ahfen of my childhood also increased my worry about the distance which news of my pending divorce might create between us.

On the few occasions I have talked about my divorce, I have always said: things worked out much better than expected. I trained others with my face, tone, and body to be content with the minimum plot. Three months after I arrived on the East Coast, my first husband got his visa to attend a school on the West Coast. That freed me to tell him of my decision to leave him. Out of a genuine love for our daughter and, I believe, thanks to the well-intentioned advice from friends and relatives — *Give the child to her and she'll come running back to you after a week. She would not know how to raise a child on so little money and all by herself* — my first husband cooperated when I tried to take advantage of the new and much more lenient rules for granting passports and entry visas to the dependents of international students. So my daughter joined me a mere ten months after I left.

At the time, Papa was the only one back home to whom I had written to break the news of my request for a divorce. I didn't think my *it's not working out for me* would make much sense to most people. In fact, I stopped writing altogether to everyone else so that I might be spared the humiliation of the silent rejections I feared to get. However, nothing could stop me from filling the very silence I myself had created with imaginary conversations.

"You lied," I heard Ahfen say upon hearing the news. (From whom, I wondered?)

When telling her of my decision to study abroad, I'd explained, as I did to everyone else, that I was doing it for my daughter, for her future. A familiar story. My aunt and her husband did it, so had many other friends and relatives. Like my sisters, I'd be the trailblazer. The husbands and children would follow after the expected long separation, so that the younger ones could someday make it good in the land of freedom and bounty.

"I'll pray for the Buddha's protection so you and your family will soon be reunited," Ahfen had said when handing me her one-ounce solid gold bracelet. At the time, persons traveling with a student visa were not allowed to depart with more than $40 and two suitcases of belongings. Rumor had it that you might be allowed one piece of gold jewelry if you bumped into a lenient customs officer. I knew the value of Ahfen's bracelet. I'd seen her fondle the gold pieces she stored inside her Lucky Strike cigarette cans. I could count the years it had taken her to save the money to buy the bracelet. And I remembered its weight on my wrist as I stood anxiously in line for my turn at customs, calculating once again the dollars it could bring me and the days they might sustain me if I was allowed to bring it across.

Ahfen pledged her support for my migration in other ways. She left me with that image of her holding my daughter's hands and waving. Ahfen stops to wipe a tear from my little girl's cheeks and whispers something. The promise of her special shrimp wontons for lunch? That brought a half smile to my daughter's face, I tried to convince myself. I gripped my purse to null the throbbing left on my fingertips by the spasm of my daughter's tiny back when we last hugged. I knew Ahfen left me this image of her holding my daughter's hand to assure me that she would be there for my daughter and me, to make sure that my little girl would know me and my love for her no matter how long it might take for us to meet again.

As I fretted at night over whether I had made the right choice in ending my marriage, I heard Ahfen complain: "Remember, that was not the deal you made with me." She had given what she had and could so that I would make, not break, a family in the Nation Beautiful. My betrayal was worse and therefore less forgivable than Yinyin's, who had merely contemplated changing the terms of her pact with Ahfen.

"Who do you think you are, a foreign devil with nothing else to worry about but her sex life?" I could feel Ahfen shaking me by the shoulder until my teeth clattered as I sat and listened to other graduate students tell the thrills and throes of their latest date/lay.

I heard Ahfen continue relentlessly: "Well, you are not one of them."

She reminded me that I loved being alone and couldn't remember exactly when I last had one of those dreams. (I had just recently realized that "wet dreams" do not refer to sweating and peeing.) I knew I would have stayed with my marriage without the *Joy of Sex* if I thought I was being loved for who I was and aspired to be.

"See what your foreign friends would think if they knew of these thoughts," Ahfen went on with another hard push at my shoulders.

I knew what they thought of me now.

More like a recent graduate of Radcliffe than an international student fresh from the People's Republic of China, a journalist from the city newspaper had described me after an interview.

"A huge compliment," everyone assured me.

"But you know they are wrong," Ahfen shook me some more. "You are 36 and Chinese. Look at your sisters. Why couldn't you be more like them?"

Then, about two months after I got my daughter back, a letter came. It was addressed to my daughter and me and written in Ahfen's name. She was fine, it said, enjoying good health, so not to worry. She missed my daughter and me. Focus on my studies and take good care of the little one, no need to pay attention to idle talk. Mmma's spirit would protect us, as it did my sisters and their families. In a PS, Ahfen enclosed her Garden Lane address and a reminder to not have the foot of my daughter's bed facing the window. The draft would get into the stomach and cause cramps.

The letter was short and very formal in style. Ahfen's neighbor the school teacher had written it. But I heard the unspoken behind the generic greetings. I took note of the absence of any reference to my first husband. That suggested Ahfen had heard of our separation and accepted if not approved of my (rash) action. I took the Garden Lane address as a reminder that I should have relayed my news directly to Ahfen and should stop assuming that she always shared Papa's reactions to things or agreed with the idle talk of others.

The letter brought back those images of Ahfen at her place in the Garden Lane, images I had been hoarding for years without knowing why. I realized that Ahfen would understand the nervous pleasure I got from my efficiency apartment, with the slanted floor tilting us toward the bathroom — a convenience at night, I explained to my daughter when she complained. The evening after the letter arrived, I made Ahfen's braised tofu while going through with my daughter the list of new words I was teaching her to spell. And I let myself believe in the love I saw in the gleam of my daughter's eyes as she savored the dish.

That night, I mulled over Ahfen's reminder that Mmma's spirit would protect me. I took Ahfen to be saying that, like her, both my mother and grandmother understood the tyranny of idle talk. All three women knew what it was like to feel things were not working out and yet not to have the words to explain to others and yourself how and why. Ahfen's letter also brought home the fact that she had exiled herself twice, first in her 30s, when she came to work for my family and then, again, in her 50s, when she came back to Shanghai after returning to the home of her adopted children at the outbreak of the Cultural Revolution. When she said during her second exile that she *couldn't get used to living that way anymore*, I'd thought she was referring to the lack of indoor plumbing and the dirt floor. But she probably meant the way of living expected of the mother of her adopted children. After 20 years on her own, Ahfen could no longer, nor cared to, live like the biological mother of her adopted son, the wife of her dead husband's brother from whom Ahfen had run away at age 30. And she had not thought herself too old, in her 50s, to start all over again.

I reconsider the parallel between Ahfen and the Monk in the *Journey to the West.* A Nobody Woman, there was no holy script from God waiting for Ahfen to fetch and bring back to the home temple, as there was for the Monk in the classic novel. Her return could never have been the same as the one scripted for the master Monk (by a man for men?). The wisdom Ahfen gleaned from her journey only called attention to the cracks in the home temple. The monsters outside served different functions for the female servant. The need to remake oneself — a possibility to be avoided at all costs by the Monk with the support of the Heaven Father — turned out to be both inevitable and exhilarating for Ahfen. So Ahfen returned to find herself a changed person, the home temple stale and stifling. Ahfen realized that things could no longer work out for her at the very "home" to which she had longed to return. Besides, Ahfen knew the personal cost of settling for a life you have long outgrown: She had watched Yinyin fill her emptiness with new additions to her household. Ahfen would not make the same mistake she had made with her adopted daughter.

"I couldn't get used to living *that way* anymore," Ahfen had said in 1966 when she exiled herself from the home she had adopted with her savings. Yet, it would take me another eight years and a letter she sent from across the Pacific to realize that, when Ahfen began her second journey to Shanghai in 1966, she knew she was starting from the point of no return. She knew more about the ins and outs of exile than I had thought. She had many tales to tell, if I knew how to listen.

In 1996, 14 years after getting that letter, I got my first chance to confirm some of the speculations it had led me to concerning Ahfen's second exile. I was spending the night at her place after the meal she cooked me on the landing outside her small room at the Garden Lane. After catching up with my life overseas, she let me into a detail from her past which she had not bothered to mention when Ahma took her upstairs to Haopo and Mmma 50 years ago.

It turned out that the Cultural Revolution of 1966 was not the first time Ahfen had left home because she could not get used to a way of life she had longed to resume. Even though Ahfen had indeed never worked a single day in the field before coming to us, she had worked outside the house between 1942, the year of her husband's death, and 1945, the end of the Japanese occupation.

"As what?" I exclaimed in shock, thinking of all those stories of Ahfen's sheltered past I grew up hearing.

"A smuggler."

To cut off supplies to both the Nationalists and Communists, the Japanese had put Ahfen's native county, known as the country of rice and fish, under heavy surveillance. So smuggling became big time for the locals. A ringleader worked out a deal with her in-laws to borrow Ahfen as a front. Ahfen would swaddle packages of rice around her waist while pretending to be a pregnant mother (with a boy clinging onto her knee) being paddled to and from visiting her paternal family. At other times, she'd just bundle the rice in the shape of a nursing baby and press it to her breast as the boat passed the checkpoints.

"Not once," Ahfen assured me with pride, "was our boat even searched by the Japanese soldiers."

Who could have been more convincing, I realized as soon as Ahfen sketched the scene. Fair-skinned, demure, timid-looking Ahfen sitting speechless under the awning! In return for her performance, both Ahfen and her in-laws got a tiny cut of the profits. Unfair as it might sound to me now, Ahfen reminded me, as we huddled, shivering, in our longjohns under three layers of blankets on her wood bed frame propped up on Haopo's mahogany chairs, the cut meant big money to country folks like her in-laws. As for herself, Ahfen had never been given money to keep as her own. Besides, what option did she have, a young widow with a baby, both dependents of her dead husband's brother?

Ahfen hated every minute of her life as a smuggler. She had heard of innocent adults and children having their bellies slit open by the Japanese soldiers at the slightest suspicion. Terrified by this potential fate for herself and her boy son, Ahfen would have massive cramps and sometimes soil her pants during the trips.

"I still have nightmares," Ahfen whispered to me in the dark.

Lying on my stomach, I gave Ahfen's arm a gentle squeeze — my way of saying that I realized this was not a past Ahfen had trusted my Haopo and Mmma to understand 50 years ago. She rightly intuited the upstairs' attraction to her sheltered look and her not-meant-to-work-outside-the-house past. My elders would never have trusted a smuggler with the family's blessed offspring. I think Ahfen had only decided to trust me and my sisters with this detail from her past because she felt that we might finally be ready to know her, immigrant to immigrant. We, too, had had to assess what of our past would make sense (and what would not) to people who had not gone through what we had, people who had no clue to what it could have been like. We, too, had known the difficulty of admitting to people you later grow to trust, even love, things in your past which you had not felt safe to share when you first met.

That same night, Ahfen told me that, lately, she had realized that she might have left home in 1946 even if her baby had lived and her brother-in-law had not schemed to marry her off. In spite of her relief in learning by the end of 1945 that the Japanese occupation was over, when she did return to normal life, she felt like she was overcrowding the kitchen when she helped out, as she used to, with the mother and wife of her husband's brother. I took Ahfen to be telling me that she had sensed a change in herself, her real reason for taking off to Shanghai in 1946. But this understanding had only occurred to her *lately*, after having watched the Cultural Revolution force me to outgrow myself and then, seeing my inability to settle back into the pre-Cultural

Revolution life I had hoped to regain when marrying my first husband. Trying to understand my dilemma, she realized why she had exiled herself twice. And she wanted me to know she had no regrets.

This, I believe, was not only Ahfen's way of telling me that she understood why my first marriage might not have worked out for me but also, to prepare me for the surprises I might experience on my return after 15 years in the States. The joy of returning home to things we had missed most in exile — voluntary or involuntary — is often accompanied by this urge to take off again. She hoped that my return would charge my 50-year-old body, as hers had been changed back in 1946 and 1966, so I would take off again, eager to face all the complications in this new life I was building with my daughter and my foreigner husband, which Ahfen and I had just spent hours talking about before going to bed.

Lying there in the dark, hugging her arm, I was once again impressed by how much more she had yet to offer me, if and when she deemed me ready to hear more. For instance, I had long since realized my shameful role in desexualizing Ahfen through the years. I had often wondered: What did Ahfen and Ahma talk about, into the nights inside that room they shared during the prime of their lives? Sometimes I imagined them venting their frustration at the way the two men of the house, Papa and Cook, talked about women in front of them, speaking without any indication that they (Papa and Cook) understood that they were indeed also talking about them (Ahfen and Ahma). Other times I imagined them cracking jokes at the way Papa strutted naked and unself-consciously in and out of his bathroom in full view of his two most trusted servants. For some time now, I had been angry at my father for acting as if simple country women, as he called Ahfen and Ahma, were simple as children: not fully developed in intellect, emotions, and sexuality. But what words would Ahfen and Ahma have used to talk about my father's arrogant ignorance? How did they discuss Haopo's open complaints about her loneliness after Dada's stroke?

The question I could have asked then concerning any other women as smart, sensitive, and resourceful as those two would be: What did they do to satisfy their sexual needs and well-being? But I also knew that, long after I had learned to pose that question in relation to my grandmother and mother, I had not thought it relevant for Ahfen. This much I knew: just because my imagination froze at the mere hint of the question, it did not mean that women like Ahfen and Ahma had not thought, said, and done things which could help me live my own sexuality. This much I also knew: I could not trust any image my mind might conjure up when I tried to get inside Ahfen's skin. I knew where my images came from — books and movies about the sexuality of servant women written by masters and mistresses. Furthermore, I had no right to probe until she deemed me ready to hear what she had to tell. Until then, I wait.

Lying huddled in my longjohns, I gave Ahfen's arm one more squeeze before drifting into sleep — my way of telling her that when I said *I know*, I did not mean or expect her to hear me say that I *knew* in the way she knew. Rather, we both understood that I was beginning to know in such a way that it was finally possible for her to tell me more. I hoped there would be another night like this one in the years to come. Next time, I might be more ready to continue where we left off.

Ahfen's Place

"Such good fortune for Ahfen to have the three of you," people say. We, especially my younger sister, are always sending her money, bringing her stuff, going to visit her, and taking her places when we are in Shanghai.

"As we should," we insist. We tell of how good she was to us when we were children, *like a mother*. She offered us her life savings when we left China, when the rest of the world speculated on how long we'd last on the other side.

I don't know why my sisters talk like that. I know I do because I don't know how to tell the other story. A story of the good of knowing a woman who, at 80, is still revising her life plan. And the story of the good of being able to say *I know*, and to know that she trusts I know in ways many others might not.

Good fortune, people say when looking at the photo of the four-story house her adopted daughter Yinyin had just built in the village. In another photo, Ahfen's Big Grandson stands beside a Mercedes which had come, along with the Western mansion in the county capital, as part of his government job. Number Two Grandson worked as a chef in Italy and returned with enough savings to start a business and build a mansion to house his university graduate wife and their two boys. In each house, as the grandsons like to remind Ahfen, there is a room waiting for her. Truly a proud rabbit with three abodes, as we say in China.

"When are you coming home for good?" Yinyin asks with every letter. She wants to set a good example for the city girls her sons have married: so wasteful and lazy.

"Come live with us," the granddaughters-in-law compete with Yinyin and one another. They are eager to demonstrate that they know how to be filial, if their mother-in-law would only be as open-minded as Granny, more accepting of their new and better ideas. Ahfen visits them all but seldom stays for more than a week with each. She tells them, as the saying goes: Gold house, silver house, cannot compete with your own dog house.

"They don't understand," she told me upon my second return in the fall of 1996. "There is so much waiting for me at home."

I took her to mean that I might understand, because I too am deeply attached to my home in the Midwest, even though it seems a mere doghouse compared to the homes of my U.S. relatives. And my sisters and I seemed to have some sense of that *so much* waiting for her at home. We had commented on the mound of tin-foil-folding her friends entrusted her to burn for them at the temple when she visited it with me or my sisters. We had speculated on the hours she spent folding foil with her friends.

We had counted the number of friends she had made since we left. There was that retired schoolteacher who had lost the use of her legs to a stroke. She awaited Ahfen at the beginning and middle of the lunar month, to chant scriptures and meditate with her. Ahfen brought news from the outside. So did the teacher friend's husband and children, and the morning and afternoon newspaper, but not in the same way, the teacher friend insisted.

And then there was the grandmother who lived two houses down from Ahfen's place. She sat for a while with Ahfen every evening to get away from the daughter, son-in-law, and their two kids with whom she shared a 10-by-12 room. Also a native of Shaoxing, she and Ahfen listened to the opera on the Sony transistor my sister had bought Ahfen. And then there were all the other sons, daughters, nephews, and nieces of friends and relatives of whom I could not keep track. They brought her dishes that took a long time to make and had to be cooked in large quantities, seasonal fruits from other parts of the country they had just visited, and products one could only get through the back door.

So and so gave it to me. . . . She has good heart. Ahfen told me during my second return, while offering me and my foreigner husband the goodies.

"How come?" I wanted to know.

For something trivial Ahfen had said or done a long time ago, she assured me. Like that time when Ahfen felt she had to lend 100 yuan to the younger sister of her adopted son. Little Goose wanted to buy a sewing machine and take some lessons in the county capital to get started as the village seamstress.

"Smart and hard-working kid. Made better grades than my adopted son." Ahfen had to remind her brother-in-law to help raise the rest of the funds.

Little Goose now has a son who is an officer on an ocean liner. Little Goose tells the son: "Go and check on Granny when the ship docks in Shanghai, see what she needs and needs done." Knowing how much his mother respects Granny, whom she calls her life savior, the son brought his girlfriend to Ahfen for approval before he took her home. This same girl, whom he has since married, is the one who types the addresses in English for Ahfen. She also serves as a translator for the thank-you notes my daughter and husband send.

Sitting there at Ahfen's place, I realized that everything I touched had a person and a story behind it. It was almost as if, through her own distresses, she had come to know her porcelain statue of the Goddess of Mercy so intimately that it had become second nature for Ahfen to treat others in her situation with the same grace she had prayed for from the Goddess. I looked at that vapid smile which Papa had taught me to observe on Mmma's Madonna as well as on Ahfen's Goddess of Mercy. And I was surprised to notice how receptive and perceptive that smile can also appear to be from certain angles. I wondered if the expression looked different now because I too had lived through times when consternation, contempt, and pity were all I could get from those in a position to judge my words and deeds.

It made sense, I thought, that the Goddess of Mercy was always portrayed as holding a tiny branch of willow in one hand and in the other, a hand-sized vase with water trickling out of it. To remind us that the good deed needed to help those suffering in the sea of bitterness to stay afloat was often trivial in the eyes of those in a position to give. *It's not the market value of the things you have to offer but your knack for listening and reaching out which has made Little Goose grateful.* I caught myself before uttering the words. Ahfen didn't need me to tell her that. She, too, had been on the other side.

"Thanks to the protection and blessing of the Goddess of Mercy, I have come across so many who have good heart," Ahfen muttered as she offered more goodies to my foreigner husband.

I told her to say thanks for me and my family. For the role model she has carved out of her porcelain statue, I added silently to myself. I want to live like Ahfen, to never forget that you cannot contract love from even the most filial of children and the most faithful of husbands if you won't take the risk of loving each in the way he or she wants to live. At 50, I am still having trouble getting outside the story of investment, debt, and returns when relating to those I love: *I owe you one. I did this, so you have to do that.* I'm still caught in the quagmire of prerogatives we have been taught to expect from family members. However, when things did not work out between Ahfen and Yinyin, Ahfen managed to turn this setback in her life plan into a lesson on motherhood: No deal — adoption, marriage, or child-bearing — can buy her a place in anyone's heart. It is the element of risk involved in the giving and taking which keeps the heart going.

I wondered if that was why she recently turned down the government's offer to qualify her as a citizen-without-immediate-family-members. Not just because she didn't need the benefits such a qualification would entitle her to: she has her savings and she has Yinyin, her grandchildren and us. But also because she felt that, at 80, she was not too old to work on her place, even if that might not look like a "family" according to government surveys. So much waiting for her at home: so many more out there to meet, to lend her ears to and to receive their good hearts.

Ahfen was having too much fun expanding her household.

My second return to Shanghai was coming to an end.

I glanced at the little alcove above the Goddess in which, as Ahfen had proudly showed me earlier, she housed her disciple's certificate wrapped in a handkerchief. And I thought about the tablet my sisters and I had just arranged to have set for Ahfen in the temple in the suburbs of Shanghai.

"Bloody superstitious fool," the Papa in me scoffed. "Hundreds of yuan for the certificate, 10,000 for the tablet. Couldn't she see that those Buddhist temples are run like big corporations?"

Earlier during the afternoon, on the way to the temple's administrative section, I had peeped into one of the worship halls where two teenaged children were kneeling at the altar. A bypasser informed me that it would have cost several thousand to have a memorial service for their deceased father done by a table of six monks. I noticed one young monk on the left reading a newspaper and another on the right whispering into a cellular phone. With open boredom, they waited for their cue from the chanting monk to chime in, now and then, with the musical instruments and their *amitabhas*.

"Bloody fools," the Papa side of me raved some more.

"Not so rash," the Mmma in me warned.

"Bad institutions have produced good practitioners," the Haopo side of me chimed in.

I knew it was not superstition alone which had led Ahfen to want her tablet set in the temple of her choice: not just any temple. Definitely not the temple in her village, as Yinyin had implored her to, so that Yinyin and the kids could go and pay respect regularly. Long before we got to the temple, Ahfen had a clear idea of where her place inside was going to be. Not in just any hall, she told the clerk handling the transaction, nor the newest, the brightest, and biggest one being built as we spoke. Instead, she handed him a slip of paper with the name of the hall written on it — the hall where she wanted her tablet to rest. Before handing the slip to the clerk, she had used the writing on the paper to locate and inspect that hall. *There, on the second row, that's so and so with whom I did. . . . Here, this place on the third is reserved for so and so I know from. . . .* She pointed to the tablets for her friends as she read aloud their names carved in black (for the dead) or red (for the alive) at the front. *It doesn't matter*, the beam on Ahfen's face reassured me. The monks assigned to chant for their spirits on the first and fifteenth of the month might not be sincere, merely daydreaming about how to get hold of a watch like the one their colleague was sporting. The spirits of Ahfen and her friends would do their own lessons together, in the same manner they had developed through the years.

"She had other reasons for wanting her tablet in that temple," I reminded the Papa in me, taking note of the work Ahfen had put the clerk through to earn the right to house her spirit.

First, there was the question of how to address her on the tablet. Deciding on the wording for the inscriptions on the lefthand lower side was simple: respectfully set up by . . . (the Chinese school names of my sisters and me).

But what did we want put on the righthand upper side, above Ahfen's name? The clerk asked, brush in hand. My beloved late-wife, -mother, -daughter . . .? He ran through the standard titles to give us a jump start.

No, no, we explained. No blood relations but closer than family.

How about Auntie? Adopted mother? He was getting testy as he realized this transaction was going to cost him time.

Not really, we replied in unison. I thought to myself: Nanny, mother, friend, mentor. . . . But we were not allowed space for more than 18 characters. This is Shanghai, the clerk reminded us, where every inch was worth gold.

So we settled on Our beloved late Nanny, to acknowledge how it all began and, most of all, not to prematurely restrict where she might take us in the years to come.

Then there was the issue of how and where to bring in her late husband.

Husband first, then wife, from right to left running downwards, the clerk informed us. He was irritated, thinking he now had to rewrite the whole template, to move Ahfen's name towards the left to find place for the husband.

No, no, we tried to stop him.

"They don't know him," Ahfen explained, "he died before I came to Shanghai."

We concluded after careful deliberation that the most accurate appelation would be the Late Husband of our beloved Nanny. And how about putting his name to the left of hers, since he was the spouse and she, the one who had entrusted us to respectfully set up this tablet in memory of her and her life?

"It'll look weird," the clerk warned us. "But," he added grudgingly, "it's your money."

Ahfen seemed to like what we were getting at: she raised no objections.

Her silence made me ponder what she had meant when she told Yinyin that it would not make sense to have her tablet set in the village since *Shanghai is where I have been the last 50 years.* What was she trying to say with her selection of the two photos to be framed above their names on the tablet: A faded, black and white picture of a 20-something man and a full technicolor photo of an 80-year-old woman. No returning to the 20-something self sitting next to her beloved husband in the photo from which she had cut out his face for the tablet.

Come and join me, I heard her calling out to him, *where so much awaits.*

My second return to Shanghai was coming to an end.

I talked about my worries, what keeps me awake at night when I have my daily post-operation-menopausal hot flashes.

"So smart, so busy," I said of my daughter. "I'll be lucky if she'll have time to visit me once a year when I lose the ability to travel."

Ahfen's reply? She showed me the electric fan, carefully wrapped in a plastic sheet for the winter. My daughter had bought it for her last summer after spending an afternoon helping Ahfen make and eat shrimp wontons.

"How did she find it, so much more powerful than my old one and yet takes up so much less space!" Ahfen marveled. "So thoughtful. . . ."

Middle-aged post-tenure crisis. I tried to explain the term when describing what a lot of people in my foreigner husband's situation were going through in the States. "Pray for the protection and blessing of Mercy," Ahfen urged me. She's shown me what the willow branch and the trickling water could look like. I just have to learn to trust myself to forge them for myself.

"Thanks," I said as I turned to take one last look at her.

As the cab pulled away from the Garden Lane, I worried about what would happen to Ahfen when the final time comes. Who would (and who wouldn't) be there to take care of her and send her on her way? Will I have another chance to hold her hand?

"You worry too much," I heard Ahfen whisper in my ears: "while so much awaits."

3

Mmma

姆

媽

(1915–1976)

(A Victim of) Evil Doings

I've saved Mmma till last because I love her the most — so much that I censor my thoughts before finishing them.

"How can you even think such thoughts," I hear Mmma asking without words, with a twitch of her left upper lip.

I plead: "My daughter is 26. It is time I let her grow up. So long as my dreamscape remains frozen where you left me, I'll always treat her like she was still three."

"Help me say good-bye," I implore.

But I can't fathom Mmma's reply behind her Mona Lisa smile. I remind myself I haven't had a bad dream with Mmma in it for a long time. Certainly not this week, probably not even this month.

"There, there," I notice a quick twinkle in Mmma's eyes. It says: She's been doing her part. I just have not been listening carefully.

Then night comes and I have this dream again. Mmma is standing by the window with her back turned to me. I notice her shoulder blades poking at the Chinese style lavender lace evening robe hanging limp down her hip. I think to myself, it had fit her so perfectly in the only photo I have of her taken before the Cultural Revolution. I know what's aching Mmma. The other woman, my stepmother, has moved in. . . . Now I am punching, tearing, biting at someone's limb. Whose? I don't know. I don't care. I just want to provoke a scream of pain. But my nails and teeth tell me I'm dealing with a rubbery mess, like the meat of overcooked octopus or those stress toys so popular in the States a few years back.

The next morning, I get up and try writing some more about this woman who is always giving me such a hard time.

A Good-Looking Daughter

"Good-looking from the start!" Eldest Aunt and Number Three Aunt always said before launching into a fight over who took better care of Number Eight, my mother, during her childhood.

Eldest Aunt told of the many pretty things and tasty treats she bought Mmma from the biggest downtown department stores. We had all heard about those open accounts Outside Grandpa had set up there for Eldest Aunt, known as "the other good-looking daughter." We understood that, having been betrothed at 16 to the eldest son of the eldest son of a Catholic family with even more money and longer standing than my grandfather, it was my aunt's duty to comb the department stores to fill up the cedar trunks that would be paraded through the city on her wedding day.

Then, Eldest Aunt would launch her attack by turning to Number Three Aunt: "Anyway, we all know why you were able to close in on Number Eight after I left home."

Indeed, we knew the reasons well. Number Three Aunt was a Nobody Wants Old Maid well into her 30s. Number Three was also the first daughter to have finished high school. But I would have to wait for a different conversation to hear that story: Number Three had wanted to attend college. She had to stay home instead because there was no Catholic college for women.

Mmma always said: "Unlike the rest of us lazy bunch, Number Three certainly had the brains and diligence to excel in college."

By the time I turned ten, I had sat through enough of Mmma's lectures to know to include myself among the "lazy bunch." I also learned to fear for myself when others called me good-looking. I knew Mmma had been called the same, which had only made her lazier. I understood this to be the reason Mmma insisted that while I might be cute, I was far from good-looking. With the same gusto with which she called attention to her asymmetrical eyebrows, single dimple and eagle-beaked nose, she taught me to recognize my too-sharp chin, thick lips, flabby nose, faint eyebrows, and long forehead.

Other than causing vanity, I wasn't exactly sure how being considered good-looking would make a person lazy and thus waste her potential. Nevertheless, I was convinced it could and did. Mmma taught me this with that anxiety dangling from the nostalgia she showed on the few occasions she joined her sisters in their reminiscences. She had me listening for the waste within those tales of a golden time, when everyone was wealthy, healthy, smart, and good-looking. And so, stories of wasted lives are the only ones of my mother's youth I have to pass on.

Last night, I asked Mmma permission to tell of that fear of wasted potential she had passed down to me. But all I got in reply was Mmma's smile.

I reasoned: "You've taught me well to understand that dreams can be squashed before even taking conscious shape. But I want more. I want my daughter to be vigilant but not fearful."

But Mmma kept her silence.

I never met my Outside Grandpa, who died before I was born. Even at 60-something and after a stroke, he cut a striking figure on the steps of the Cathedral in my parents' wedding photos. He was a *chijiaoren* — a person who eats the Church, as we call Catholic converts in Shanghai dialect. I never completely understood the exact nature of his affiliation with the Church, other than the fact that he himself attributed his worldly success to his ascendance within the inner circle of Chinese Catholics.

It was said that at some point my grandfather made a smart move: he took a nine-month crash course in English. Working as a middle-man between foreign and Chinese merchants, he soon established himself. He married wisely, choosing a devout woman from a humble background similar to his own. It turned out to be a solid deal: she took care of matters of devotion, freeing him to funnel more in and out of the Church. He bought a huge Chinese-style mansion in the Old City just for its location: three doors away from the Cathedral. Every dawn, rain or shine, his wife marched all 12 of the offspring he had dutifully procreated to six o'clock mass for confession and communion. Judging from the number of children, property deeds, diamonds, and gold bars eventually filling the house, staying close to the church paid.

There was the story of my uncle's frustration when his father refused to move outside the Chinese City into one of the many Western style houses he also owned in the French Concession, with indoor plumbing and paved streets wide enough for a Rolls Royce to drive all the way to the door. "May this house be struck by a ball of fire from heaven," my uncle was known to have cursed. He got his wish, although not from the god he had in mind: the Japanese bombed the City and burned the house to the ground.

My mother told of her father's refusal to leave the house on the morning of the raid. I pictured him doing his daily exercise of tai-chi in his rock garden as airplanes circled overhead. I heard the sound of wheels racing through the cobblestone streets and the panicked voices of parents and children filtering through the ten-foot tall brick wall. His wife scurried around the house, stuffing diamonds and gold jewelry into everyone's pockets, while his son pleaded with him to hurry.

"We barely made it!" Mmma used to say as she stared into a vast emptiness known only to those who have seen every single object from a whole period of life disappear within 24 hours. The bombing was the reason we had no photos of my mother before she met Papa. "Stupid old man," my father used to say as he chuckled over his father-in-law's shock at finding out that his God had no jurisdiction over the Japs.

Predictably, even the Japanese bombers could only grant my uncle half of his wish. My grandfather moved the family into a block of row-houses he owned, houses which had, yes, indoor plumbing, but also lanes so narrow that no decent automobile could sail through. He had chosen the houses because they were an appropriate half minute's walk from the biggest church in the French Concession.

My maternal grandmother never knew me, although she lived until 1956. She had been "not all there" since the late 1940s. Also a fortune, her daughters believed: it spared her the pain of knowing more and more of her sons, son-in-laws, and grandsons were being *indisposed* by the People's government because of their allegiance to the Vatican.

On her better days, my grandmother called her youngest daughter *Auntie*, mistaking her for the blind aunt who had raised her by working as a professional chanter at funerals. She complained about the imaginary lice crawling on her scalp and between her fingers, and got agitated unless at least one part of her was slowly doused in warm water. Some days, she saw naked babies frolicking in the oak tree outside her window and sent her maid, with blankets and food, to cover and feed the cherubs. The rest of the time, she found herself surrounded by Satan's tempters. She had names for the more regular ones: the white-faced fat devil (my Aunt), the yellow-faced and triangular-headed devil (the maid), and the oil-mouthed little devil (my cousin). She had no name for me or my sisters. I surmised it was because, not having been baptized, we had no place in her world.

From stories of her younger days, I pictured a very different grandmother. At age 16, my grandmother was said to have overheard an exchange between two brothers from the rich family which had hired her aunt to chant rosaries. She could tell they were talking about her, but in a tongue foreign to her ears. She carefully tucked away the sounds, which, two decades later, she asked her son to decipher for her. Turned out the brothers were conversing in French, saying that although her features were not bad, she was far too short. Still more years later, when one of the brothers came to ask for the hand of her daughter for his eldest son, my grandmother asked quietly if her daughter might not be too short for his boy. Obviously not. The wedding was a big event, so much dowry paraded through the streets that the groom's family had to hire the police.

They said she kept her country taste for clothing and food. More comfortable in the cotton top and pants worn by laborers, she was so clumsy in her brocade, embroidered, floor-length two-piece dresses that, one morning, on her way up the aisle to receive communion, her skirt slid to the floor, exposing to full view the black cotton pants she wore around the house. She was also notorious for forgetting the whereabouts of keys and valuable objects, and for forgiving lazy servants who were known to drone around her like flies to rotten meat.

From her blind aunt, my grandmother memorized numerous local recipes for curing aches and pains. My mother told of my grandmother hovering over a charcoal stove in the semi-tropical summer, stirring the ointment for swollen joints or heat-sores. She dispensed it freely to anyone who knocked at the back door. To prevent her clothes from sticking to her sweat-drenched, round, and slightly hunched back, she tucked a big palm-leaf fan inside the back of her white linen top. I hope this image of a woman engaged in healing will be of some use to my daughter the gynecologist.

From family gossip, I gathered that my grandmother never cared much for Papa after he refused to baptize my sister — as he had promised when asking for my mother's hand. I had noticed the awe my elder uncle tried to hide as he talked about Papa's thriving practice in the foreign circles, his Rover (*One of the half dozen privately owned cars registered in Shanghai after 1955!*), his house in the (*priciest part of the*) Concessions. Even my grandfather was said to have valued Papa's medical opinions over those of my younger uncle. But not my grandmother. She believed that promises were made to be kept, no matter how prestigious or humble one's family or education.

With the help of my fifth-grade history textbook, I named Mmma a child of "China's aborted democratic revolution." She was born in 1915, about four years after the end of the Qing dynasty and the beginning of internal war among warlords. She was 11 when Chiang Kai-shek installed the Nationalist government in Nanking.

I dreaded history because I had always been terrible with dates. I memorized the whole chronology of modern China by matching it with Mmma's life which, being a nosy child, I found much easier to keep track of. I knew that no matter how nervous I got during exams, I would always remember the year of my birth, 1946. So I developed this golden formula: Subtract 31 (the age difference between me and Mmma) from 1946, add Mmma's age at the time of the historical event I was being tested on, and *voila*, as Mmma would say, I had the correct answer. Mmma turned 21 (and met Papa) just before the Second Sino-Japanese war broke out: 1946 − 31 + 21 + 1 = 1937. The date 1937 was an important one for history, since it also marked "the crumbling of the Nationalist government." Luckily, I didn't have to worry about what happened following 1937 until after the midterm exam.

For my exams, I learned to link Mmma's first birthday with China's joining the Allies, and her third with the end of the First World War — the "Western betrayal of Chinese interests at the Versailles Conference." But I knew, even as I memorized these lines, that very different stories were probably told inside the gates of my grandfather's mansion and the wrought-iron fence surrounding the Cathedral just a few doors away: The World War was just another manifestation of God's having stood by his flock — the French — after having momentarily punished France for its sins.

According to my history book, Mmma came into adulthood in the heat of the Communist Revolution. I knew that the year Mmma turned 6 was also the year of the "birth of the Party," when the first National Congress of the Communist Party was held in a girls' parochial school in the French Concession. When Mmma turned 11, Chiang Kai-shek "stole the fruit of revolution from the coalition" between the Communists and the Nationalists under Sun Yat-sen. But it seemed that none of these events had much significance for Mmma's people. Chiang Kai-shek, Sun Yat-sen, Nationalists, or Communists were just names in the long procession of warlords coming into and leaving Shanghai. In the meantime, life went on as usual. There was money to be made through and out of the foreigners — the saved or the heathens — if your father were smart and knew how to maneuver the roads crossing through the City, the French Concession, and the International Settlement.

Chiang Kai-shek, though merely a Protestant, was a gift from God. So much money was made that diamonds, jade, and rubies had to be bought as protection against inflation (so that later they could be unfairly distributed among the children, causing lots of heartburn when various aunts and uncles had to sit and watch various others flashing them at birthdays and wedding banquets). In the meantime, Chiang Kai-shek's notoriously crude manner, his volatile temper, his Ning Bei (*coarse, low-class*) accent, his false teeth, and, of course, his splashy Shanghai wedding with the Soong girl, furnished my elders with colorful topics during many chats over roasted peanuts, chestnuts, and seeds from all sorts of melons in varied flavors.

As for the Blood-Sucking Imperialists of my history book, some were simply saviors sent by the Lord our Father in Heaven to spread his wrath and save our souls. The French from the nation of *fa* — law, institution — were naturally to be trusted more than the English from the nation of *ying* — outstanding, handsome — or the Americans from the nation of *mei* — beautiful, excellence. But if you were smart, and attended church regularly, there was money to be made out of all of them. Those foreigners sure knew how to make and sell the best food, clothes, funeral services, gadgets, movies, drugs, cars, houses, female bodies, medicine — the list never ended.

I was all ears toward anything relating to Mmma's childhood, partly because, compared to Haopo and Papa, Mmma had always been so reticent about her past. However, I often came away thinking that the world of Mmma's childhood was indeed narrow, and her people, shallow. I borrowed my conclusion verbatim from Papa, who was in the habit of passing it out freely, beginning: "Daisy, you've got to admit. . . ."

Enlightened was the word Papa used to distinguish us from Mmma's people. Mmma's people belonged to the dark ages, blindly eating up the church doctrines as they ate up its wealth and power, denouncing desperately as *devil talk* anything having to do with the pursuit of knowledge.

What is left in life, Papa wanted to know, when they wouldn't allow you learning and inquiry?

Mmma always nodded and then swallowed even when she was not eating and drinking. This made me think that one side of her fully agreed with Papa while another side felt that there was more to the story. I was never quite able to fathom the more part, which my mother seemed determined to keep to just herself and her Madonna. But I did learn to distrust my hearing even as I puzzled together the pieces I gleaned from my elders' reminiscences.

When I tried to picture Mmma's childhood, I saw her days starting with that infamous 6 A.M. mass, the bare mention of which still brought involuntary shudders to my 50-something Eldest Aunt. Mmma never faked sickness, not even in the deadliest of the winter dawns. At the cathedral, she patiently rubbed her numb toes, right ones against the left ones, inside the cotton-padded shoes Outside Grandma had the servants put on her. She had not yet learned to be vain like her sisters, who braved the sub-freezing chill in their silk stockings and paper thin Western-style leather heels. Then I watched my grandmother troop Mmma and her siblings back to break their fast over congee and dim sum bought by servants from foodstands I knew would never have passed Papa's hygiene standards. I longed to taste some of those goodies, especially since my elders assured me that no one knew how to make them as well in post-communist-revolution Shanghai.

I followed Mmma, squeezed between Number Nine Uncle and Number Ten Aunt in the family pedicab, through the Chinese City to the parochial school in the French Concession. "Stay away from those non-Catholic children," Grandma warned. I noted to myself that those children would include students like Haopo and Papa's sister.

"Is that girl from a Good Family? Are her clothes uncouth?" Her older sisters inquired after Mmma's new acquaintances.

When I sat in the classroom with Mmma, I did not once see her punished by the nuns' rulers or knuckles. Mostly, all Mmma had to do was to keep her eyes modestly downcast and flash her dimple when spoken to. Only she (and I) knew, although the nuns should have noticed, that she never paid much attention to what she was learning by rote. She retained even less. A bad habit passed down to me, Mmma liked to point out.

Back home, I didn't hear anyone ask Mmma what she had learned that day, nor if she had any homework. I peeped into the Chinese-style parlors and dining rooms on the east wing of the ground floor and the Western-style rooms on the opposite wing. I saw a lot of mahogany furniture, brocade on wood painted gold and white, antique Chinese vases and bowls, valuable scrolls, Dresden porcelain, Swiss clocks, Venetian glass, and silver from whichever country was supposed to make the best and most expensive. Upstairs, I found a long corridor of bedrooms: mahogany beds, wardrobes, marble washstands, and square tables with marble tops piled with nuts and seeds of all sorts and flavors. I looked around just to make sure that, as I had guessed, there was not a single desk, nor bookshelves, nor reading lamps in any of the rooms.

Other than a pocket-sized leather-bound book of prayers that Mmma carried to church and kept by her pillow, I did not expect to find any reading materials. I had seen my mother cringe at the sight of Haopo leafing through a Bible: no Catholic would be so impertinent. No novels either. I had seen Mmma's breathing as she sat with a rose petal perched on her upper lip and a Jane Austen on her lap, in the same way I imagined Eve pulsed after she took her first bite off the apple. No newspapers or magazines. Unlike Haopo, who was always chuckling and munching as she skimmed through the evening papers, Mmma studied the *Times* Papa brought home from the consulates to improve her English and follow party conversations. She never touched the local papers: too full of Communist propaganda.

Being the other Good-Looking Daughter, Mmma was always welcomed by those gathered around the table in the room she shared with my Number One Aunt. From there, Mmma learned everything about anyone worth knowing — who and what was in or out, and why it was all right for this person to have done that, but not for that person to have done this. She also learned to swirl a fistful of watermelon seeds around in her mouth and then, while retaining meat, spit out the shell

of each, perfectly cracked through the center into two whole halves —
a talent passed down to both my sisters but not me.

When I tried to enter Mmma's mind, I heard her chiding herself
for vanity and carelessness. She took to heart the warnings against her
sins. She had seen the beggars huddled on the steps to the Cathedral and on the sidewalks by her school. She knew her elders were not
lying when they said that God could put sinners like herself out there
with the snap of a finger. Mmma tried hard to show compassion for
the poor but also to remember it was not her place to ask why some
people had to suffer like that. "God's punishment," her elders always
said at the news of someone suffering sudden bankruptcy, accidents,
or unspeakable diseases.

When the old priest pointed his fingers at those turning the church
into a competition for who could come to mass in a new outfit for the
most consecutive days, Mmma listened and vowed never to let herself
grow into her eldest sister. She worked hard at detaching herself from
earthly desires: trying to care less about the many new robes, the gold
chains, earrings, and bracelets her elder sisters were always fighting to
have her mother get for their favorite little sister. I figured that had
to be the source of Mmma's other problem, her carelessness toward
worldly possessions. I too was the one who was constantly reminded to
care less about such things, and then scolded for having been so
careless with them.

Vanity got Mmma into all sorts of trouble as a child. There was that
time when Mmma was eight and waiting for the family pedicab to pick
her up from school. A nicely dressed woman approached to compliment Mmma on her dimples and stylish brocade robe. Then the lady
offered to help fasten those pretty earrings which were hanging loose
on the Little Sister's exquisitely shaped earlobes. That night, Mmma
noticed during toilet that her solid gold earrings had disappeared.

The incident caused Mmma many occasions for repentance: That's
the way with sins, one leads to another until you can hardly pull yourself
out. It started with vanity, which had caused her to be fooled by the

woman's appearance and compliments. Then came deceit, when she tried to hide the theft from her mother. Not a difficult task! My grandmother never cared much about jewelry. More deceit followed when her sisters eventually noticed her naked earlobes. Mmma pretended she had merely misplaced them when washing her face. No problem selling that story. Everyone knew how careless Mmma was. Besides, who would be foolish enough to think that servants could be trusted. So a new and better pair was promptly ordered.

But Mmma was smitten with remorse. You can fool others but never your own conscience, Mmma always warned me. I knew she would have put *God* in the sentence, right next to *conscience,* if I had not just so vehemently declared myself (in third grade and to Papa's great delight) a believer in *science.* An announcement partly prompted by her having forbidden me to become a Red Pioneer, a Communist organization condemned by the Vatican.

People do not grow from a child into an adolescent in one day. But in my mind, I always pictured this happening to Mmma during a family banquet. "What a pair!" I heard guests exclaim at the sight of my mother sitting next to her eldest sister in identical robes cut to the latest fashion. I watched my ten-year-old mother dutifully flashing her dimple as relative after relative complimented her for being so good-looking, just like her Number One sister.

I dig my right thumb into the soft of my left hand, for I don't like the way my mother heard the compliments. She dutifully cautioned herself not to fall for such Satan talk, as Eve had. Instead, she concentrated on reminding herself of all her weak features. I fear for my mother because I think it was not the words "good-looking" but rather the word "like" about which she should be wary. "Like" is the word which would eventually seal my mother, in her own mind, for many years, in the shadow of her good-looking sister. I want my mother to have realized then and there that she was called "just like" her

good-looking sister because she had not yet become my Eldest Aunt.
This could have let her concentrate more on things she might do to
avoid becoming that woman in the identical robe sitting next to her.
But I don't think that was how my ten-year-old mother heard the
compliment. Everywhere she turned, she saw more reasons to fear for
her reputation as the other Good-Looking Daughter.

To begin with, the propitious marriage of Eldest Aunt soon turned
sour. Having come to their money and standing a generation earlier,
her husband's family was more experienced in the art of dissolving
the conflict between the teachings of the Church and the temptations
of the flesh. They fulfilled their church duties: attended (only!) the
special services, kept in close touch with the bishops and foreign
priests, made substantial contributions to the parochial schools and
orphanages, and gave lavish church weddings and funerals. They had
been in God's grace long enough to know that there was no sin which
could not be redeemed with generous donations accompanied by the
right number of rosaries, rosaries one could always pay to have said in
one's name.

Number One was ecstatic to have found this heaven on earth. No
more 6 A.M. masses. So many places to go in the family Rolls Royce
to gratify one's Mouth Fortune, Ear Fortune, and Eye Fortune. However, it didn't take Number One long to notice that even in this newfound bliss, the sons still had more places to go and things to do than
the daughters-in-law.

So she had many occasions to stomp and scream: "He did, why
can't I?"

They said that when Eldest Aunt was still the new delight of her
rich son of good family husband, she got him to take her places where
no woman from a good family should ever be seen. She knew how to
get to him: nagging just after he had his first whiff of that opium his
parents were always so eager to supply to keep him home, away from
the casinos and bordellos. "What a scandal for a daughter and wife, to
be seen at the casinos busily sampling the free food and wine!" To make

things worse, Number One was eager to freely tell all to all: "Father liked to play high stake Mahjong, so did Number Two Brother-in-law. Number Six, on the other hand, always went for roulette."

To slow her down, her in-laws offered the magic potion. I understood that was why she looked as if every muscle in her body was knotted up, perpetually waiting for that whiff of opium she had not been allowed to have since the communist Liberation. Husbands took mistresses. So she, too, found herself a lover. (I think she used the term "soulmate," with the same catch in her voice I noticed in Haopo when she talked about Dada.) After her husband died and against the counsel of both families, my aunt and her lover got married. He was 12 years her junior, which made my aunt the only other Chinese woman I personally know to have fallen in love with a younger man.

My aunt was still in her 20s when her first husband died. At the funeral, she refused to cry. The world never forgave her for that. "I had my pride," I once overheard her say to Haopo: "Why should I waste tears on him when he was so indifferent to me so soon after the wedding?" I registered the hurt in my aunt's hoarse, smoke-steeped whisper.

When her father-in-law died, Eldest Aunt shocked the world by taking her late husband's family to court. She asked that the estate be divided five ways: one for the mother-in-law, one for the brother-in-law, one for his son, one for herself, and one for her daughter. The family wanted it divided four ways, with one portion shared by my aunt and her daughter. She won but never saw much of the money: the gangsters providing the legal service sent their bill. All agreed: "God's punishment for keeping bad company." Eldest Aunt told it differently. She reminded Haopo that she wouldn't have had to listen to the gangsters if good lawyers like her high-powered, French-trained brother-in-law would have seen her point and had been willing to represent her.

Number One's behavior upset Mmma's family. There were things you do on a night out with friends that you'd just rather your wife, daughters, or sisters did not know about! How would her sisters be able to hold up their heads in front of their husbands and in-laws? What about the ones still at home? What family would be willing to take them now?

When her parents tried to set her right, my aunt asked: "He did, why couldn't I?"

This question put Mmma on a roller coaster of awe, sympathy, shame, fear, and anger. I know. I'd seen how uneasy Mmma got when Eldest Aunt's past was mentioned, almost as if she were upset at herself for failing to be either as gleefully condemning or as indifferent as some of her other siblings.

Number One's behavior pushed Mmma closer to Number Three, who was also good-looking, though this was a fact few besides Mmma were in the habit of observing. Number Three was the studious one. She longed for a bite off that fruit from the tree of knowledge which was served daily on a silver platter to a brother who seemed far too busy with the other prerogatives of sons to care. It rankled my Third Aunt to see the look of approval on her parents' face every time her brother remembered to send for his pedicab to take him to the university.

She, too, had wanted to attend college.

"Where?" her parents wanted to know. There was no college in Shanghai for Catholic daughters!

Number Three had in mind a women's college which trained teachers, run by those other missionaries, but very strict and hard to get in.

"She had the grades to get in," Mmma always said.

But her parents cried: "A teacher!? That's for orphans and daughters of poor families."

So Number Three had to stay home and help with the household. She turned 20, then 25. Her eldest sister's reputation continued to frighten off prospective in-laws. But her parents remained unperturbed: "Maybe Number Three could join the convent and do the

family proud. Arrangements could easily be made for her to teach in
the convent school. That's what she wanted, wasn't it?" Number Three
thought otherwise. She wanted to study literature. She wanted to see
the world.

On most days, my aunt went about the house doing what was
expected of her. She placed orders and made purchases for her mother
whenever they required picking up the phone or venturing beyond the
gates of home and church. Like her mother, she had no use for chit-
chat over nuts and seeds. Whenever she could, she too hid in her room.
Except she devoted herself to books she had bought with money she
took for household purchases and from stores no one else in the family
cared to find.

Then, once in a long, long while, Number Three would stay in bed
for a few days with the mosquito net down. "Off again," my elders always
said, winking and tapping their heads. Ever since I read *The Count of
Monte Cristo* at 14 and found out that my aunt had also read and liked
the book, I imagined Number Three, on her off days, mistaking her
mosquito net for her prison cell. She laughed scornfully when others
suggested that she lift and step out of the net. She sat huddled over
her books, scribbling ferociously while mumbling to herself that she
had to study harder, to figure out what and who got her here, and how
to get herself out of her life sentence.

"A female scholar! A female scholar!" Third Aunt always said this
of herself in beat with the rhythmic nodding of her head, her rebuttal
when her siblings made fun of the poetry she was always scribbling on
toilet paper and matchboxes, which she carried around in her pockets
and was in the habit of furrowing out at family gatherings. (At the sight
of me buried in a novel, my aunts always warned: "Don't let this one
turn into Number Three.")

My grandparents did what they could to contain my aunt's "off
days." They had four more daughters in waiting. They knew that the
reputation of having an eccentric old maid in the family was infinitely
less damaging than that of having a lunatic one. So they did not raise

objections when Number Three began to frequent the lectures organized by Protestant missionaries. When she bought herself a violin and started taking lessons, her mother turned a deaf ear to the scratching sounds my aunt made as soon as her father left the house. Then, friends with thick glasses, (*unshapely*) cotton robes, and stacks of books began to gather regularly in my aunt's bedroom. They drank tea, smoked cigarettes, and argued.

"God gave us a brain to use," Mmma always said.

I believe Mmma picked up that line from half-listening to the conversation between Number Three and her friends. They helped Mmma realize that there were other things she could focus on besides going to church, worrying about the big day, spending money, or keeping up with idle talk. If she were to avoid the self-abandonment and self-savagery afflicting Number One, she needed to figure out how and why people do evil things and how to stay out of evil's way.

When Mmma listened to Number Three and her friends, she was convinced that knowledge could buy her freedom. It could find her a job to support herself if she did not like that rich son of a good family everyone believed it was in her fortune to marry. She let herself hope. Maybe, just maybe, when she graduated, her parents would have realized the mistake they had made with Number Three and would let her attend college. She tried to apply herself more at school, to think more about what she had been assigned to memorize.

That worried my grandmother: "Why would you need to tire yourself like that! Go get some sleep. The family does not need another bookworm, a second Nobody Wants Old Maid."

Common Sense said: With your looks and dowry, you do not ever have to worry about making a living.

— Do not become a bookworm and botch your chances of marrying that son of the best of good families.

— Work? That's not for you! Just follow one of Number Three's friends home one of these days. Go see for yourself what a job would buy you: a room the size of a square of tofu in a rowhouse without indoor plumbing and with 72 tenants.

— You like holding your sisters' new babies, don't you? (I know Mmma did. She always said when cuddling someone's new baby that she'd have a dozen more if only they would stay that way forever. One of my earliest memories of the solarium next to her bedroom is my mother seated on a mahogany-framed lounge, upholstered in golden and blue brocade, playing with a newly hatched chick with a piece of oil-cloth on her lap.) Well, common sense said, you need a husband for that!

Besides, Mmma doubted she could be studious even if she had wanted to be. "Bad study habits are hard to get rid of," Mmma always cautioned me. "I know from experience," she'd add.

The more Mmma tried to think through what she was only expected to learn by rote, the more confused she got. And if she kept at it, her brain began to hurt. There was no one there to say to her: "Congratulations, confusion is the beginning of real learning!" Confusion scared Mmma because she did not want to lose her mind like Number Three. Mmma was never quite sure how much of God's wrath against Eve was over her having disobeyed him, and how much over her curiosity. She knew it was arrogant to presume that you could fathom the divine scheme of things. And it was certainly not ladylike to want, hunger, crave for anything — liqueur-filled chocolates or book learning.

So, as Mmma was the first to admit with open regret and shame, she continued to be a mediocre student.

I took a half day off from work yesterday because it was the first day of the Lunar Calendar. Did some long distance calling. I started with Jing, a high-school friend still living in Shanghai. Jing was sleeping in to recover from all that noise from fireworks that kept her awake on New Year's Eve and all that food and company the next day. "All Shanghai is rushing to bring back the good old days," Jing reported over the phone. Food, gifts, fireworks, all on a scale Jing claimed she had only seen in pre-Liberation movies and at my parents' house during the early 1960s.

We reminisced about those amazing fireworks lit on our front lawn (the best of which, Jing reminded me, Papa always saved until the fifth day of the New Year — my birthday). Jing and I talked about the Evil Doings of wasting, as Mmma always said when Papa took us girls shopping for fireworks in the Old City. Then, we fussed over where China was going. She told me about this book called *China Can Say No* and promised to send me a copy, my birthday present.

I told Jing to get herself a bargain next time she went down to the antique mall, her birthday present from me. My way of telling her that I remembered what she had taught me about the art of living in the postmodern city of Shanghai. When I think of Jing using bargaining to figure out what she wants and how to live with the consequences of her actions, I am glad some would call me a daughter of this city, which is rushing to surpass that hybrid world which had nurtured Haopo, Ahfen, and Mmma. I asked Jing to go see Ahfen for me. I didn't want to drag Ahfen out to the public phone booth in this deadly winter weather, didn't want to make her cry upon hearing my voice. We discussed the gift Jing should buy for me, what Ahfen liked, might need. Jing knew Ahfen would ask when I was coming back.

Soon.

Afterward, I called my mother's sister in Philadelphia. We talked about staying fit and keeping one's figure (which she wanted to know if I was) after middle age. Buy real estate, no more stocks, she advised, as if I had money for either. I let on that I was writing something about Shanghai during the time she and Mmma were growing up.

"Were you allowed to read novels and see movies?" I asked.

"Yes, yes, sure."

"What?"

"Never was much of a reader myself. *Little Women* and maybe what's the name of that book starting with a *Jane*? But I am not sure if I ever finished it. Saw all sorts of movies though, *Gone with the Wind*. You name it."

I was shocked: "Outside Grandma let you?"

"Nobody said we couldn't, and I never asked. You know, there was this pile of rent money on the table in your Outside Grandma's room. I just took some whenever I wanted to go out with friends — girls, of course. Once, your Outside Grandma found all these stubs in my purse and said, 'What've you been doing with yourself, girl?' But most of the time, no one really cared."

This conversation made me doubt everything I've just written down.

I probed some more: "How come Mmma said she was not allowed? You were a whole six years younger, right, so things could have been different for Mmma."

"Maybe. Your Mmma probably went to a more exclusive Catholic school, you know, while I just attended the parochial one down the block. I remembered walking home by myself. But then, your mother had always been Outside Grandmother's favorite."

Then we talked idly about her children, my siblings, and various relatives: new purchases and promotions.

My Aunt said, "I am always telling my foreigner (meaning, American) friends about you girls: two MDs, two lawyers, and two professors. (Counting the husbands, of course.) Incredible!"

I noticed she did not say English professors, who make considerably less than other ones.

"Your mother must be so happy up there," my aunt assured me.

"Keep her in your prayers," I asked.

Then my sister called.

Something bad happened this morning: she had broken Mmma's blue-white plate. Nothing valuable, or she would not have been allowed to take it out of China when she left, 15 years ago. But precious to her: one of two things she had of Mmma's. She had wanted to give it to her child, to remember Mmma with.

Life is so fragile, my sister kept saying. Here one minute and gone the next. She worried that this was an omen, that she could hurt someone precious to her in the same way, with the slip of a finger and the swing of an arm. Irretrievable. Final.

I wanted to say: This is how memory works. Memory does not stay with things, it is triggered by them, by the keeping and breaking of a plate and the talk of its breaking. The plate wouldn't mean the same for the children even if you had it to pass down. But I knew none of my thoughts would come out right, not in English, not in the Chinese I use with my sisters.

I wanted to tell her that I am working on something, something which might capture some of my memories and, I hope, something a little less fragile than a plate.

But I didn't. I was not sure this thing I called our "family manual" was turning out to be what I wanted it to be. Besides, it wouldn't do my sister and her child any good. We were not the same daughters. Mmma was not the same mother to us.

So I said instead: "It's not a bad omen. Things are just things. The children will remember Mmma because you love her."

Then I left a message on my daughter's machine.

I knew she'd be at the coffeehouse, fighting to stay awake and jam in all that information for her exams. I just wanted to make sure that she didn't waste time fuming over our conversation the previous night. I'd been upset ever since I hung up, worried that she might have detected the fear I was trying to hide.

"Mom, I'm cramming for this one course I hope to honor in, which means I won't have much time left to study for the other courses."

"You'll pass the others though, won't you?"

"Oh, yeah. I have a huge buffer on all three. I just don't think — realistically — I have enough time and energy to try to honor in all of them. You know how I am with finals."

"Don't give up yet."

"Yeah, but I just can't worry about all of them right now."

A signal for me to back off, so I did.

But just in case she caught the reservation in my voice — how can she not? — I left a message to let her know that I trusted her judgement and was with her on this. I hoped she'd listen to it before going to bed, if she didn't decide to sleep over at her boyfriend's.

Then I had this dream. I am standing behind Mmma, my arms wrapped around her waist, facing a mirror I only sense but don't see. She looks about 40, gorgeous. Her hands feel warm and supple in mine. But my heart is heavy: she has cancer and is not happy about how things are with Papa. She says while looking at herself: I'd always hoped that somehow, you'd have better memories of me. I notice that she speaks in English, in a voice I do not know. I think I am talking to her spirit. I say: But Mmma, I do. I just sometimes hoped you had not been always . . . so . . . unrelenting.

I take note of how carefully I am wording what I say.

Then I am opening my purse, and there is a stack of bills with Sun Yat-sen's face on them: thin, yellowish paper bills twice the size of the ones I've handled. Now she's alive. We are in my parents' old house. But I know this is after the Cultural Revolution. And I am who I am now. I pull out four bills with the numeral 200 on the corners and stuff them into Mmma's hands. Buy yourself something, I say, as I rush for the toilet. I know how much she hates spending Papa's money.

I am sitting on the white porcelain toilet with the mahogany and brass seat and I hear her saying behind the bathroom door: You know that I don't keep secrets from your father. So I start to fumble some more in my purse, searching for two more 200-dollar bills: So she'll have enough left for herself after giving him half. But the paper bills have confusing numbers: 28, 143, 76, 195. . . . I try various combinations but cannot come up with the right sum, no matter how many times I shuffle through the stack.

I woke up, waiting for the break of dawn.

Is this dream Mmma's way of reminding me to listen for other meanings to my stories?

I had a purse and I had money to give. If this were Mmma's dream, there would be a purse. There would be money, but she would not feel it was hers to give: she knew that, in the eyes of others, she didn't earn any of it. She had no rights over it.

I have money to give because I am my mother's daughter, because she has taught me to fear the fate of being a Good-Looking Daughter.

The Courtship

Papa always claimed that Mmma only attended a third-rate university to scout for a husband. Mmma never said anything to deny it. True, times had changed. Mmma got to attend college because a degree in home economics had come to be considered an asset, even for Catholic daughters in waiting.

True, if Mmma had been really serious about learning, she could have studied some more and tried again after failing the entrance exam to the national university in Nanking.

True, Mmma had met Papa through another student attending the third-rate university.

But I'd seen my mother rearrange herself in her chair enough times when responding to Papa's claims to know that she knew she had other goals in mind. From lectures on the sin of — her past and my pending — wasted opportunities, I pieced together Mmma's list of goals when she hopped onto the family pedicab on the first day of that fall term. Number Eight wanted to be studious and conscientious like Number Three, but feisty like Number One. That, I believed, was why she chose education as her major. My mother hoped to absorb as much knowledge as her mediocre self could without, she prayed, having to end up half-crazy like her third sister. And unlike her eldest sister, she was determined to try out only those ideas and activities which were good and right. Mmma always said: "You don't stoop to the level of the devil to get even."

Mmma never mentioned these goals to refute Papa because she knew as well as we that Number Eight had not pursued them as hard as she had planned to. Halfway into the term, Crazy Frances — a fellow student in one of the introductory courses — taking note of Mmma's looks, took charge. Crazy Frances was interested in her cousin PJ, a medical student at *the* St. John's University and Papa's roommate since high school. Crazy Frances was tired of having young Eddie tagging along whenever she got PJ to take her places. So she decided to find Eddie a girlfriend. And she just knew that Eddie would fall for this girl with the big dimples sitting quietly at the back of the classroom.

Frances began to follow Mmma around, into the Ladies, out, and through the campus as Mmma rushed from class to class. What's your name? Where do you live? Do you have a boyfriend? Want to come to a movie with me, my cousin and his roommate on Sunday?

Mmma was embarrassed. She was annoyed. She realized that she would never get rid of this crazy woman until she agreed to see a movie, *just once.*

"You were curious, even hopeful," Papa wanted to believe.

"No, no," Mmma insisted.

After much prodding, Mmma would concede that she was delightfully surprised when Papa showed up. She had expected the roommate to be either crazy like Frances or just plain dumb.

Who wouldn't? My sisters and I used to joke that we only learned to walk so we could run away from Frances's sausage-sized forefinger and her broken record of "None of you girls would have existed except for me! Don't ever forget or let your parents forget that!" But then, of course, we always stayed to show our gratitude to the crazy woman for bringing our parents together.

There were many stories of my parents' long courtship. Five whole years passed before Eddie became the chief of residents and was in a position to provide *decent housing* — a two-bedroom modern apartment — for his good-looking fiancée.

One story had it that when Mmma first took Papa home for dinner at her father's mansion in the Old City, all Outside Grandmother wanted to know was: "Is he Catholic? Will he convert?"

"No problem!" Eddie readily vouched. My aunts recalled that my father appeared so smitten that he had them all convinced that if Outside Grandma had asked him to go to hell and back to marry their Number Eight, *no problem* would still have been his answer.

"He's not very . . . handsome," Mmma's younger sister observed from behind the door to the dining room. Afterward, Outside Grandma chided: "Silly girl, what does a man need looks for?"

One brother asked if anyone else had noticed the clear signs of wear around the young man's shirt collar: "Not another of those poor students!"

"So what!" My Outside Grandpa liked what he saw. Eddie reminded him a little bit of his own younger days: alert, pleasant, diligent, and ambitious. Outside Grandpa understood the value of a degree from St. John's University, the alma mater of T.V. Soong, that young banker brother-in-law of Chiang Kai-shek.

"Extremely good-looking," Eddie's sister reported to Haopo after running into the young lovers at a movie theater. "None of that arrogance put on by so many daughters of wealthy families."

Haopo told of how lucky it was that on the day Japanese bombs hit downtown Shanghai, an emergency case had delayed Papa, so my parents missed the movie at the theater they had planned to go to. I had had enough history courses to know that those were actually bombs dropped by the Nationalist Army on what they mistakenly thought was the Japanese section of the city. But since the Japanese were the cause of the mistake, we still called them Japanese bombs.

Haopo learned of the bombing over the radio. It was reported that the walls of the theater Eddie was planning to take his fiancée to were covered by legs and arms, stuck to the surface. Haopo knew about the plan because Eddie was short on cash. After slipping him a few dollars from the grocery fund, Haopo had helped him pick a show at the theater which would give the young lovers time to make it to an early-bird dinner afterwards.

My parents missed the movie but caught the early-bird. The restaurant, along with the whole city, was buzzing with news of the bombing. But even the thought of Haopo and Dada worrying to death over the life of their Eddie did not keep the lovers from lingering over their hard-earned privacy at the corner booth.

So young and careless, Mmma always added.

I knew what she meant by calling herself careless for acting so carefree. Around the same time, Outside Grandpa's mansion in the Old City was burnt to the ground. He lost a lot of other properties and had a stroke. But all Mmma could think of was how to help Papa find time and money so they could go out and have fun and eventually move her out of the third-floor room she now had to share with three sisters.

One aunt recalled a model fiancé: so good-natured.

She told of Eddie crawling underneath Number Eight's bed to dig out the high heel matching the one Mmma had in hand and was in the process of putting on. Of course, my aunt was talking about that period after my parents had become formally engaged. Before that, Eddie had to wait in that dark, chilly parlor with its mahogany panels and marble floor, and Number Eight had to bribe her younger sisters to do the crawling.

It was in that parlor where another aunt recalled watching Eddie help his fiancée with her studies, going over the material repeatedly even though all could tell that his feet were itching to race out. Their stories made me think of a dog we once had, after his expatriate owner was shipped home by the People's Government: the way it looked when waiting for the treat he knew would follow after obeying our commands to fetch and sit. I'd seen that look on Papa's face when he half-listened to the after-lunch yet before-siesta conversation on Sundays, with his arm lightly wrapped around Mmma's waist as he watched the shadows of the trees caress the glass panels to the French windows. I always wondered if his sinus-stuffed nose was also trying to sniff its way past the scent of Yardley soap on Haopo's skin, of incense steeping Ahfen's hair, and of his own Tsingtao beer and Lucky Strike cigarette-spiced diabetic breath, searching for a whiff of Mmma's flesh where the neck meets the collar bone. Her neck was so soft, supple, and warm when I nestled against it, on one of those afternoons when I played sick from school and she let me nap with her in that bed where the Stranger had taken my place.

I knew of my father's impetuous faith in novelty, believing, as Mmma put it, even a night pot to be fragrant during the first three days of its use. I had heard story after story proving my father's all time ravenous appetite for things highly priced and just beyond reach, his cunning doggedness in securing and then, discharging them. But it was on Sundays like those that I realized what my mother had known from the beginning: My father courted her with the passion of someone capable of loving her anew even after the world — the Vatican or the People's Government — had deemed her rightfully his to take and keep, till eternity.

When I listened to my parents talk about the *qiong kai xin* they had during their five-year courtship, I calculated 1,825 evenings of movies, dances, and dinners. In Shanghai dialect, *kai xin* (open one's heart) means being happy and having fun and *qiong,* "being poor" or "in extreme." So I understood that dreamy look such talk always brought into my parents' eyes as meaning: They were having extreme fun in spite of being poor.

I pictured the young lovers holding hands at the matinees, he stealing a kiss on that soft spot behind her ears, which always made Mmma gulp for air. At the early-bird dinners they managed to squeeze in between his hospital schedule and out of his poor student pocketbook, with occasional help from Haopo, she listened with her Mona Lisa smile while he spelled out the many later-but-better times her presence had conjured up in his mind.

"Foolish," some said before going on to list the names and dollar value of each son of the many wealthy Catholic families which Number Eight could have married.

Others dared to differ: "It'll pay off. This young man will far surpass all those sons in wealth and fame. And he'll stay faithful if Number Eight makes sure he never forgets that it was she who had helped put him wherever he was certain to reach someday."

"You are one of us now," Haopo said after the engagement. Whatever *best* education was provided for Eddie and his sister, it should now also be made available to their future daughter-in-law. Haopo and Dada would come up with the tuition, though only God knew how, if my mother's father wouldn't.

So, out of Eddie's list of English names, Number Eight picked Daisy. "A white, exquisitely shaped but unpretentious flower," Mmma always said when translating the meaning of her name for non-English speaking friends and relatives. Then, Daisy took crash courses in English and found herself retaining quite a bit of what she learned. "You have to really *want* to learn," Mmma always said when I would read "lamb" with a "b" and write it without the consonant. *Want* had always been my problem. My parents wanted me to work on my English. But all I wanted was to join the Red Pioneers. Why would a young Pioneer want to learn the language of Western imperialists? However, I understood why Daisy might want to pick up 12 school years' worth of English in a year. She wanted Eddie, didn't she? So she had better speak *his* language.

After a year, Daisy mustered enough English to try out at the real universities. As luck had it, St. John's decided to go coed that very fall. Outside Grandpa footed the tuition bill, counting it as part of Number Eight's dowry. Then Eddie got his promotion to chief resident. So my parents were married just two terms before Daisy got her degree from a *real university.*

"Didn't learn much during the last year," Mmma was always the first to point out. A lot of distractions: new marriage, first pregnancy, Dada's death, a world war and the Japanese occupation. But I knew that their hearts were young and it was another year full of *qiong kai xin* — Extreme Fun — for my parents.

It was Eddie's enthusiasm for living which initially swept Daisy off her feet. I know well the medical student with whom my mother had fallen in love. I am the daughter of the man who taught me to swing to Satchmo's *you are alive, so come and show it, such a lot of living to do.* First in my bobby socks, stepping on Papa's toes, and later, in nylons and heels, with my closest male friend sandwiched between Papa and me to give the boy a sense of how to lead, with his hips.

When I envision Eddie wooing Daisy, I hear Louis Armstrong singing "A Lot of Livin' To Do." I picture Daisy sitting with her head slightly tilted and turned to the left, as he caressed her right hand while rattling away: medical school, residency, surgical training abroad, private practice . . . so successful that neither his wife nor his mother would ever have to worry about money again, and his children could have the best of everything — education, toys, vacations.

When she watched him getting mesmerized by his own words, his eyebrows flying while his short, burly neck stuck more and more forward from that hump of flesh at the tip of his back; her heart raced in beat with his "got to move, time is wasting . . . Satchmo's got a lot of living to do."

This was the tune, these the words I imagine Daisy hearing on their dates. I don't really know if she had actually come across the song until the early 1960s, when someone from the British Consulate gave my father the Armstrong album. But I had heard Papa humming "A Lot of Living to Do" on those long Sunday mornings when, thanks to the Anti-

Rightist Movement, there were no more churches in Shanghai for Mmma to attend. Papa would swing across the room after putting the song to replay on the hi-fi sound system, the only one owned by a local, Papa was assured by the radio repairman. Papa would utter the notes and words without ever removing his cigarette, which dangled from — glued firmly to the inside of — his thick, moist lower lip. When he stooped to blow my mother a kiss before settling back to his coffee, she would twitch her nostrils ever so slightly to inhale the smell of his chest hair bursting through the open neck of his silk dressing gown. And I knew that no matter what had happened between them during the week or in the world outside (about which Papa would only trust the barely audible voice of BBC passing through the People's electronic intercepter to inform him), Eddie had made Daisy believe, yet once again, that there was "wine ready for tasting, Cadillacs all shiny and new, music to play, places to go, people to see, everything for you and me." She knew it was her cheeks which were "ripe for some kissing" and which he had in mind when he said "I mean to kiss me a few."

You too would have fallen for that magic if you'd been in that room with us that day in 1972, merely two hours before Nixon was scheduled to arrive in Shanghai. All afternoon, Haopo, Ahfen, my sisters and I had been standing behind that window facing the entrance to the lane to catch the sight of Mmma bringing Papa back to the one-and-one-half-rooms which had housed us for the past six years but into which he had never yet set foot. A maze to step through, as the government had just returned without notice everything the Red Guards had confiscated in 1966. So we had to stuff the place with the most compact and practical of the most valuable but the least visibly damaged pieces of the furniture my parents had spent the first 25 years of their marriage accumulating, selling the rest to a secondhand store.

Everything's going to be fine now, we reiterated to one another as we clung to this man whose return we had prayed for for so long and whom, now returned, we had to learn to know all over again. He didn't have my father's face. Deprivation had sunken the cheeks and bleached away the color. There were 80 pounds and a whole inch lost between this man and that body which had shouldered me around its burly neck and turned round and round the living room, leaving our reflections all over the parquet floor, leather sofa, lacquer piano, circling the chandelier which Mmma was so sure we were going to knock off the ceiling any minute.

I dug my right hand into the soft of my left hand as I watched this man twist his vocal cords to replicate, without success, the resonance with which Papa used to pronounce things *bloody*. To remind ourselves, no more tears, we brought him a half bowl of clear chicken broth slow-simmered for hours in an earthen pot from a whole succulent hen, a chunk of the driest of aged ham, and the tenderest parts of dozens of bamboo shoots which had taken Ahfen days to gather from the market. No more than a few mouthfuls for now, we said and he agreed, to give his stomach time to come home with him. Too soon for the real talk, how he survived the solitude of his three-by-six dark cell and what we did outside it. We talked instead of all the food we'd got stored in the bathroom we shared with a family of eight living below us. All his favorites, so many because our memories could not agree on what he truly liked.

We suggested: this for breakfast tomorrow, that for dinner.

He said: No, no, that for lunch and this, for dinner the day after.

My father was back: *Satchmo's got a lot of livin' to do.* I could literally see the lyric ooze out of my father's ears, which appeared disproportionately large as they sat atop a long, thin neck I never knew my father had. And I watched Mmma inhale, ever so slightly with a twitch of her nostrils, as if there were a whiff of coffee in the air and she had finally admitted to herself she had a craving for a sip.

And I wanted to leap and hug this man for making my mother fall in love, just like that, all over again.

But the mother who raised me did not just fall in love with, nor was she merely smitten, by Papa's enthusiasm for doing-living. She courted and loved with a fierce deliberation I've seldom seen in others. When I ask how my mother learned to love like that, I find myself returning to that evening when Eddie finally took Daisy home, after Haopo had had time to repaint and redecorate their living-dining room to do justice to that good-looking daughter of a wealthy family who had stolen Eddie's heart.

When someone else, usually Haopo, recalled that first visit, my mother's only comment was: "Never saw anything like *that* before."

I knew Mmma's *that* stood for the love between the four: Haopo, Dada, Eddie, and his sister. My mother taught me to covet that love through the vehemence with which she supported Haopo's devotion to the well-being of my aunt — my father's *less fortunate sister* — and my aunt's two daughters. "Let's help out," Mmma would suggest to Papa at Haopo's slightest hint that my aunt was having difficulty providing for my cousins what my mother deemed necessary for me and my sisters. "She always favored my sister over me, now her daughters over mine! Always watching out for them, what *they* are not getting," my father would complain. At moments like this, I felt it was not so much that Mmma never had her own doubts over Haopo's claim that all her children — her daughter, daughter-in-law, and granddaughters — meant the same to her. Rather, ever since the first time my father took her to meet his family, she had simply chosen to always think of Haopo's love for my aunt as also an expression of something deeper: principles I've since learned to call Haopo's appreciation for the world's "not much to look at's." My mother was working hard to ensure that my father stay in touch with "that" — the love and the principles behind it — because she wanted the same for herself and us.

No one who had heard my mother talk about my Dada could miss her affection for Haopo's Old Good Person. Opened his heart — as we say in Chinese of someone who appeared happy, content — was how Mmma always described my Dada's state of being around Haopo and the children. I think it was my Dada who first ignited Daisy's desire to partake in *that* love she had never seen the like of before. Takes one to know one, as Mmma liked to say. When I imagine my mother watching my Dada open his heart on the eve of her first visit, I see her taking note of the subtle ways in which he looked after and with — rather than merely at — the three better educated and more capable members of his family.

I believe it was through Dada that Daisy first got her calling: conceived a clear sense of the kind of "living" she and her Satchmo might do. The closest metaphor I have for describing my mother's sense of her newfound career is that of an ensemble, a sort of chamber music or jazz group. Through Dada's relationship with my missionary-certified Haopo, Daisy perceived a place for herself in an ensemble where she would be the least known but no less central contributor to this making of real love. The world might not respect nor reward her as much as it would the other members of the ensemble for the particular temper she would bring to it, nor the way she might temper it. But other members of this ensemble would know and never lose sight of the central part she played to sustain the magic. They understood that it was only with the concerted efforts of all involved that they learned, through subtle improvisations, to rely on the best of each to bring out the best in each.

When I return to the evening of Daisy's first meeting with Eddie's family, I see my mother arriving with a template of married life she had forged out of her love for her Number One and Three Sisters and of her fear of succumbing to their fates. She wished to be the wife who accompanies her husband on trips to historical sites, lectures, plays, and concerts. This wife finds time to take lessons on French conversation and piano between her pregnancies. She reads books sitting at her desk in her boudoir and never falls asleep after the first few pages. On birthdays, anniversaries, and saints' days, her husband would court her like the lovers in movies, with flowers, poems, leatherbound volumes, and diamonds and rubies. She keeps the flowers, poems, and books as symbols of natural, spiritual beauty, not of his infatuation, but begs him to return the jewelry and send the money instead to the orphanage, for food, clothing, and a better library.

But above all else, this wife is pure and lofty: upright, refined, and noble. Like Outside Grandma, she remains pious and generous to the poor. She despises people who gauge all their thoughts and actions according to the dictates of earthly powers. This wife never has trouble telling the good from the bad, the right from wrong, for she stays in touch with her conscience, a concept Mmma liked to point out that we Chinese wisely spell out as "good, instinctive heart." When I heard Mmma say that, I knew she was thinking of her porcelain Madonna. I thought that explained why the Madonna stood hugging Baby Jesus to her heart with one arm, with her face half turned away from the world. That was how the virgin mother protected her instinctive heart! Looking at the Madonna, I knew Mmma once hugged me as she did our relatives' new babies, before I lost my instinctive heart to vain praise, trinkets, toys, and *communist propaganda.* That was why Mmma always averted her face when Papa kissed her, even though the throbbing of that blood vessel in the front of her neck told me she secretly liked it: to retain her good heart in the face of earthly desires.

When I picture Daisy returning from her first meeting with Eddie's family, I notice she left with a new template, one with the rougher but richer lines of Haopo and Dada's love-making superimposed on the one she had forged out of the fate of her first and third sisters. Daisy still imagined herself and Eddie occupied by the same activities pursued by her dream husband and wife. But she had shifted her attention from what each of them would or would not actually do to how they would understand, appreciate, enable the other's part in that "living" which Haopo and Dada had just helped her conceive and which she now prayed was the same "living" her Satchmo was ever eager "to do . . . such a lot of."

"God gave us more than looks, he gave us a heart, an intellect, and a conscience," Mmma was always reminding us: "And God meant for us to use what he gave us."

In Mmma's revised template, the dream couple used all that God had given them to help each other in the making of love. Together,

Eddie's enthusiasm for living — which sometimes sounded suspiciously similar to her Number One Sister's *why couldn't I* — could complement and be complemented by Daisy's effort to hold, tightly, on to her native, good heart. Together, they would make sure that Satchmo's "a lot of living do to" would involve more than "wine ready for tasting, Cadillacs all shiny and new, music to play, places to go, people to see, . . ." "Got to move, time is wasting . . ." they'd urge one another: "knowledge ready for inquiring, hearts to unfold, conscience to guard, patients to heal, . . . a lot of work to do, . . . for you and me." The world might pit her Madonna against his Darwin. But, like Haopo and Dada, they would forge a cord to string together the best of both. Others might call her the dependent and him, the provider. But, like Haopo and Dada, they would never forget the work she put in to keep this "living" on track.

After she met his family, whenever Eddie updated his ever newer and bigger plans for their future, Daisy, the queen of understatement, would add: "Like Haopo and Dada."

"Sure," Eddie agreed without stopping to find out exactly how Daisy intended them to be alike.

"Like Haopo and Dada but better," he quickly added. He pictured a virtuous mother and wife just like his mother but more content, since she would not need to work outside the house. And a husband and father just like his equally beloved father but much, much more content, since he would have all the career, money, and fame any man could ever want. That sent Eddie scurrying, like an ant on a hot pan, to secure the diploma, the job, and the Gold House to Hide His *Jiao*, as we call good-looking and pampered brides.

For his part, Eddie memorized the catechism with the same speed and fluency he did anatomy. He dutifully accompanied Daisy to the big masses, baptisms, weddings, and the birthdays of patron saints. Anything to be around his fiancée! To please her and his future in-laws!

Besides, Eddie just loved all that fabulous food Daisy's family put out after the church ceremonies, especially when his hospital duties exempted him from the church part.

For her part, Daisy steadily took advantage of the fact that Eddie's string-bean budget required several evenings at Haopo's instead of at the newest Hollywood movies, reasonably priced good eateries and respectable clubs Satchmo just knew were waiting out there for the two of them. Daisy carefully absorbed the art of living, of love-in-the-making, which Haopo and Dada kept on improvising even through Dada's stroke and ensuing paralysis.

When Daisy looked from one to another of this family gathered in that modest living room, she saw a room so much smaller in size and flimsier in build than the mahogany-paneled, marble-floored one her own family had been reduced to after that infamous Japanese bomb. But she saw a room furnished with so much more loving care, in slip-covered sofa chairs and pale apple-green painted wood furniture. She heard Haopo and Dada say to each other and to Eddie and herself: we are all God's children.

Daisy set herself on fire.

Ever after, nothing could keep my mother from stoking that fire with the ferocity I was later to fear, yet desire.

A Virtuous Wife and a Good Mother

"A perfect couple: a man of capacity and a woman of beauty!" People often concluded when admiring my parents' wedding pictures taken on the steps to the big cathedral.

Such remarks and tales of the Extreme Fun my parents had during their courtship made it even more confusing for me on Papa's birthdays, when we heard his anger piercing my parents' bedroom doors, breaking the sweet anticipation of Haopo and us girls as we waited in the second-floor small dining room, drenched in mid summer morning sun, each holding tightly on to our beautifully wrapped birthday presents.

"Why couldn't Daisy just, for once, wish me a happy birthday, like a normal person?" Half an hour later, my father would wail to Haopo over coffee and the (by then) cold sausage and French toast.

We knew but did not dare to answer him: because good Catholics celebrate the birthdays of their patron saints. Because you did Mmma wrong by revoking your conversion.

I wished to myself that Mmma had not been so uncompromising and thus ruined the breakfast we had spent weeks planning.

Hearing others call my parents "the perfect couple" always filled me with not only anger (at my parents) but also fear and shame (toward myself). But I did not fully understand why until recently, when my younger sister brought up an incident I'd completely blocked out.

I was around ten. It was after midnight. My parents had a big row upon returning from a party and woke up the whole household. Afterward, Mmma came upstairs to spend the night in my younger sister's bed, moving my younger sister in with my older sister. I lingered by the door to the bathroom between our bedrooms, hoping Mmma would change her mind and crawl in with me instead.

"Go back to sleep now," Mmma kept telling me.

Then I heard Papa stomping up the stairs, his full-lipped mouth foaming as tears boiled down the creases between his bulby nose and ruddy cheeks. I watched as he tried to drag Mmma, in motions which appeared ten times slower than actual time, back to his bed, which he kept asking if she now thought she was too bloody holy to share with him.

I wanted to be that child who would cry: "Leave my mother be!" Then I would rush to her side and pull at her other arm to lend her support, just in case that fire shooting out of her dry eyes should fail to melt down the steel filling Papa's grips. Instead, I remained as dumb as a block of wood. I waited for that look of horror to take over my father, after he had caught sight of himself in her consternation. Without words but unequivocally, her eyes returned the same verdict Papa reserved for all those rich Catholic sons from whom, he liked to remind us, he had rescued Daisy: "How unenlightened!"

Then I watched Haopo's shaking swollen-jointed hands and wobbling bound feet lead her son down the stairs to wait quietly for Daisy to find the strength to forgive and come back to that bed he was so afraid to get in without her. I was breathing again, the cold tiles hard against my bare feet. I knew he knew that he had done something shameful, like when he had resorted to his fists to settle an argument during school recess and torn the uniform which had taken his mother nights of knitting to pay for. Papa's receding back announced his remorse: This time round, no amount of sobbing promises from him and forgiving hugs from Haopo was going to fix things.

And my numbed feet told me it was time to get back to bed.

After my sister mentioned this event, memories of other fights came flooding back. A dozen or so times, when a push or shove clearly harbingered the eruption of this physical violence always lurking underneath my father's "enlightened" outlook. Reliving those moments, I wonder if my anger towards my father was the only reason I blocked the fights from my recollection. It was probably also my own fear of violence, which made me fear for Mmma. But most of all, it was my way of dealing with that fear which had frightened me.

Why can't she just stop provoking him! I always thought just before he raised his arm. Fear made me blame Mmma instead of the aggressor for making me watch and fear. To forget my shameful reaction, I blocked out the acts of violence leading to or following it.

But, as Mmma always said, bad habits formed early are hard to break. I thought the same thoughts all the way through the Cultural Revolution, when my mother persistently fought the Red Guards coming to humiliate and steal from us. By then, I was 20 instead of 10, and had been hoarding too much for too long. So those later memories kept on creeping out at night to lock me securely inside that dreamscape.

"Don't provoke them!" I am still yelling at my mother when I have my Cultural Revolution dreams, sobbing and kicking until my husband wakes to hug me back to the home I now share with him in the U.S. midland.

For long enough, I had fooled myself into believing Mmma was the keeper of this dreamscape. Suppressing memories of my mother's fights with my father and the Red Guards had not served me well. I am no longer a 10-year-old torn by my love for two people who loved, in very different ways, one another and me. Neither am I a 20-year-old trying to protect a mother from Red Guards she refused to fear. Ugly fights are what my mother left me and what I have to work with. If I cannot dump them, maybe I ought to scavenge them for lessons on love, on how to work on it in *ensemble*.

Even during the most tempestuous of my parents' fights, I had always known that they loved one another. I just wished their love had been more like the one I pictured Haopo sharing with Dada, a wish both my parents would (separately but repeatedly) express to Haopo after each fight. I blamed the world for the differences ripping at my parents. I held the Vatican responsible for the splinter in my parents' hearts, festering in their disagreements over matters of faith and spirituality. Communism took away my father's ambitions as a surgeon. The frustration it caused made my father do things which brought unforgivable injuries to my mother's heart. The Cultural Revolution robbed us girls of all chances of reaching Mmma's expectations, leaving her with nothing but despair at the end.

My conclusion: like everyone said, Mmma had indeed been the victim of evil doings.

Yet, I am too much Mmma's daughter to overlook the double entendre she was sure to detect in such a remark, if anyone had been foolish enough to have called her a victim to her face. "A victim of whose evil doing?" My mother would have asked while flashing the dimple on her right cheek. I am too much her daughter to be deaf to her rebuttal: "Yes, the world had indeed done us ill. But what about the things I did in return? I am not afraid to take responsibility for my own actions!"

I have to reckon with this Daisy until the Mmma of my dreams can let me go.

Daisy would have me begin by contemplating why, in a world where saving face dictated every thought and action, she — the most private and proud of all people — would rather lose face in front of servants and relatives than avoid a fight with her husband. I did not comprehend the scope of Daisy's choice until I realized in crossing the Pacific that the training of women to put up with, cover up, and take the blame for being the targets of aggression knows no national borders. In spite of such a trans-national heritage, this woman, who had never lived a single day outside the city of Shanghai, had nevertheless tried to leave her daughters a different script for living.

My sister's chagrin during last Chinese New Year, when she broke Mmma's blue-white plate, triggered memories of the little things Daisy did to daily ready herself for battling the script handed down to virtuous wives. Like my friend Jing, Mmma went regularly down to the antique market. For every few valued pieces Mmma bought, she would bring home something flawed like that blue-white plate, where the petals of a few lotus flowers stretched with just enough vigor to break the perfect symmetry a connoisseur would have expected from an authentic version of its kind.

I used to think that my mother bought the flawed pieces for the bargain they offered. Lately, I wonder if she bought them also for their potential. In the midst of the chicken-oil-yellow bowl and the pig-blood vase — all authenticated with dates and places of make — I recall

Mmma had displayed on an equally gorgeous teak stand the plate my
sister broke recently, or a cobbler-blue urn with a dent on the edge, or
a goblet with an intricately carved stem leading to a wobbling base. I
remember the time Mmma spent arranging and rearranging her ensemble of flawed and authenticated pieces until, when she removed
the dented urn, neither the texture nor the color of the authenticated
pieces could ever appear the same again; until all the certified pieces
appeared to be working in concert to tease the most stunning of the
blues out of the flawed urn. These memories make me suspect that
Mmma bought the flawed pieces to test her faith in the infinite potential of *damaged goods*, as she jokingly called herself and us when admitting to the many bad habits she had passed on to us.

My mother had studied my Good Old Person Dada — another
damaged good in the eyes of his contemporaries — and my Exceptional,
missionary-school certified grandmother file and temper that love they
had mined out of an arranged marriage. She understood what it was
like to be deemed less than perfect, what it took to work on, fight for,
a love which would not compromise the potential of all involved.

My mother left me memories of her enigmatic smile on those
occasions when she would bring home a flawed piece and set herself to
arrange and rearrange it along with the more prized pieces on her
mantel: a visual representation of the magic of concerted loving and
living my father had fired her to long for. Her smile prods me to wade
through my dread over the sight of my parents fighting and to ask,
instead, why she had chosen to take on the fights and how she had
steadied herself through them, for as long as they needed to go on.
Her smile prompts me to probe how my mother worked to keep her
longing in sight.

It has taken me a long time to realize that when my parents fought
over religion, they were having lovers' quarrels over one another's style
of dealing with differences. As a point of marital contention, religion

for my parents was no holier nor any less serious than any other irre-
concilable differences driving other couples to distraction and divorce.

When I think about the fight over my sister's baptism (which all
agreed was the source of my parents' marital problems), the fight appears to be like so many fights with new couples, so entirely unnecessary, and yet so inevitable. I'll wager that it was just as possible that the
actual fight might never have taken place, and my sister might have
been duly baptized with great fanfare, if any one of those mundane
details crowding our lives had passed over my parents on that particular
night. I'll also wager that to have avoided this infamous fight would by
no means have kept them from quarreling just as persistently and passionately as they did throughout their marriage.

In my script of that critical fight, Eddie came back from the wards,
late, after a long shift cleaning up the mess left by some surgeon too
bloody old to be holding the coveted position. The braised ham Haopo
had been trying to teach the new maid to cook had too much sugar in
it and was burnt on one side while sitting on the stove for Eddie to
show up. The baby had awakened as soon as rice was brought to the
table and refused to be calmed by that *dumbbell of a little maid no other
mistress would have hired.*

Daisy said: Maybe we should go ahead with a quiet baptism instead
of waiting for your bonus.

Eddie said: What's the bloody hurry?

Daisy would not humiliate herself to repeat again: We Catholics
believe that. . . . So she stared, silently and intensely, into her food.

There was nothing Eddie dreaded more than Daisy's silence. He
liked good food, good laughter, and good conversation, all at once and
all the time. Besides, Eddie had his reasons for wanting to wait on the
baptism. He liked to go all out on all occasions, birthdays, weddings, or
funerals. And he did not like to be reminded of the mismatch between
his pocketbook and his appetite. That kind of talk reminded Eddie of
the humiliation of having to go to one's wife's relatives for advances.
Daisy should have known that Eddie, too, had his worries about making

those payments left from Dada's passing a week after the baby was born, especially since the damn Little Japanese and that stupid World War were putting all Eddie's career plans on hold. For how long? He had to wonder.

When Eddie heard Daisy's "We Catholics don't. . . ." resounding in her silence, he didn't remember to include himself in that "we." Instead, he heard her saying *my people*, which he pictured as herded under the whip of her sister. Eddie just knew that now that he owed the bloody woman some money, she presumed she could lord it over him and his family too! So there could have been only one answer for this We Catholics talk: No one tells Eddie when to baptize his daughter.

My sense of realism tells me that Eddie didn't speak his mind just yet. Vivified by the sugary meat and Johnny Walker, he remembered that tomorrow was another day. So Eddie reached over to kiss Daisy behind her ear, sliding his hot palm softly down the side of her back until it rested on the curve, from where his full lips were quivering to take over and move beyond.

But Daisy breathed on, steady. And anxiously I wait for my mother to gulp involuntarily for air, as I had waited along with my father on many other occasions while growing up. But I know there could have been no such response that evening.

Daisy had too much on her mind. She had just been reminded, yet again, of her inability to make herself make sense to Eddie. She could not think of any other way to help raise money than go out and find a job, which both Eddie and Daisy had decided was bad for the baby and for Eddie's career. So, instead, she had decided to help by showing Eddie that his wife was *proud* but not *pampered*. Two very different words in written Chinese even though they shared the same pronunciation, *jiao*. Too bad Eddie's written Chinese was so elementary. Otherwise, she might have explained that although the two words shared the same symbol on the right side, *pride* had a horse symbol on the left because horses stood tall and brave going into wars. *Pampered* had a woman symbol on the left since women were supposedly the only ones guilty

of such a state. Well, Daisy was not one of those women! She wanted to
plan with her Satchmo a baptism with no new outfits, food, or guests,
to show him that they did not need to wait for his bonus. But she did
not know how to explain any of this to Eddie. And she was mad at
herself for not knowing how.

Daisy had too much on her mind. So she breathed on, steady, to
Satchmo's urge to *move, time is wasting, such a lot of livin' to do.*

So Eddie got mad at Daisy for refusing to come with him just because her mind was stuck on some stupid Catholic ritual. She should
know by now how long his next shift could last, how precious time was
for him! Eddie decided two could play this refusing game. He yelled
with whiskey-fumed tears trickling down his flushed cheeks: "That's it!
Forget about baptism or confirmation or the whole bloody Catholic
business! I am not going to subject any child of mine to *you people* and
your stupid dogma!"

A statement so haphazardly arrived at, yet so irrevocable in its consequences. I grew up watching my parents lick the wound it opened,
for neither knew how to drain the pus festering there.

They fought over Catholicism because it pitted Daisy's contempt
for the dictates of worldly trends against Eddie's three-step pragmatism, which taught that, if one wanted something, and if the world said
one could not get it unless one did this or that, then one should just
do this and that. Eddie converted to Catholicism with the same
enthusiasm with which he had earlier become a Protestant: to obtain
something he valued. Church was where Eddie was told he was not
good enough for their scholarship dollars, nor their daughters, unless
he became one of them. Out of this personal history, he developed a
profound impatience with all religious institutions. Add to it a pinch
of Eddie's stout reverence for scientific knowledge and one ended up
with the absolute skepticism my father held towards matters of faith
or spirituality.

"Men evolved from apes! Jesus was an historical figure! There is no life after death!" To Papa's delight, I learned to chant these as soon as I began school.

Eddie could relate to Haopo's Protestant church goings, which in his mind remained nothing more than a big social club for open-minded wives and mothers of Western-educated men to gather, bake, knit, sing, read, and raise or dispense funds. This social-club view of Haopo's Protestant faith made sense, rested snugly within the logic of Eddie's own conversion to Catholicism, made only to secure the sanction of Daisy's parents to their marriage. Eddie's pragmatic approach to religion made Daisy's Catholic faith all the more confounding, especially since she so openly shared his disdain for the social net woven by generations of inter-marriages among wealthy Catholic families like her own. He would have understood her faith better if, among the things offered by her church, he had been able to detect anything they could not have obtained from somewhere else. But he hadn't. So what was the point of returning, Sunday after Sunday?

Daisy, on the other hand, believed that Eddie should never have made a vow to anyone, God or her, about anything he did not believe in. She felt insulted that he had not trusted her with his true feelings toward religion before their wedding. She took it to suggest that he did not perceive her as capable of working with him, as Dada and Haopo had with one another, through their differences. Rather, he had thought their love would need a seal of marriage obtained through false vows to survive the forces dividing them. Furthermore, Daisy held suspect any action which suggested that whatever the world said you should do, you would. She had nothing but contempt for expediency. She always warned: "Listen to your conscience. Never to the clamor of worldly trends."

Eddie just had to laugh at this nonsense: "How would you know what to listen to when you could not even study that conscience business as you might the physical world or historical trends?"

Daisy swallowed in disdain.

Eddie retaliated with more scathing ridicule of her Catholic nonsense.

I, their child, dug my fingers into the soft of my hands.

I sensed that lurking behind my parents' fights over religion were two very different views and attitudes towards reality. Both their styles frightened me, although I often understood the nature of his better than I did hers. I felt my mother was in the right but usually found myself wandering over to my father's side. I found particularly convincing his complaints against her willful indifference to reality, which made me recall times such as the evening before my first Labor Day parade.

I was nine. I had been worried ever since my teacher instructed us that we must all dress for the parade in white shirt tucked inside blue cotton pants. No ugly blue Communist clothing allowed by Mmma in my ten-times-too-extensive wardrobe! So I had enlisted Haopo's help. But weeks of prodding only moved Mmma to borrow a pair of blue cotton pants from the son of a family friend, pants that buttoned in the front rather than on the side. I was devastated, anticipating the derision — even Haopo and Ahfen couldn't deny — I was sure to get from my schoolmates when they saw me, my frilly linen shirt tucked inside a pair of boy's pants.

"Maybe no one will notice," they kept on suggesting in as convincing a tone as they could manage.

"Better not let your Mmma hear you," they cautioned, and I nodded in agreement between my sobs.

We knew how much it would have irritated Mmma to see her daughter so eager to accommodate the instructions of her communist teachers. Why waste money on new pants just because the world said you had to wear them, when you have all that good stuff sitting in your wardrobe? The Papa in me wanted to scream: But I was the one, not my lofty mother, who would have to face the world tomorrow morning! The Mmma in me would not let me forget that it was this same world that had unfairly persecuted her people for remaining faithful to the Vatican. And I reminded myself to never cave in to such a world even as I tried without success to curb my tears.

I don't know if my mother ever realized the remorse her unrelenting disdain for my father's and my three-step pragmatism unfailingly produced in either of us. To recover from my shame, I joined Papa in insisting that Mmma did not know what she was talking about. She was too bloody naive, completely unrealistic, out of touch with the world outside our house on HengShan Road. She could afford to be so righteous only because she had the good fortune to have been the *jiao* — lofty and pampered — daughter of Shanghai's most respected Catholic family. She never knew what it was like to want something you could only get in return for yielding something equally precious. She never had to! What did she know about wanting a scholarship from people who classified your father a heathen and an illiterate? What about a red-pioneer tie which required that you struggle against your parents, the Lackeys of Western Imperialists?

My defiance did little to ease my sense of guilt because I had a hard time denying that what Mmma wanted me to do was also important for the good of my self and the world. This became even more evident in junior high, after I survived numerous self-criticism sessions especially devoted to the improvement of my bourgeois consciousness. The sessions made me wonder (in words I did not have then) if, as my mother had insisted, whenever people like myself and my father tapped our three-step pragmatism, we had indeed made life a little easier for those with the clout to sway reality. The more we tried to follow their dictates, the more we helped to clad in steel the reality they desired, and the more we cast out those people — ourselves and others — they feared might corrode their reality. I sensed without full articulation that my mother was after a conscience which would be vigilant toward the dictates of all realities but not fearful of any. It lived for a reality to come, one which did not stack people in discrete slots, one on top of another.

Unfortunately, this nascent understanding only intensified my fear:

I could never be strong like my mother wanted me to be. I did not feel I knew how *not* to fear the dictates of worldly trends. Fear always seemed so much more tangible and compelling. I loathed the smell of it perspiring from my three-step dance. The feeling that I had turned out to be more Eddie's daughter than the daughter Daisy had wanted made me more fearful. In fright, I rehearsed her contempt and then, his defiance. And back. And forth.

Decades later, while doing my graduate work in the U.S., I found a different vocabulary to figure out yet another reason for my parents' fights over religion. I suspected that a part of Eddie loved Daisy with all the anxiety and benevolence his missionary school teachers had earlier showered on him. He wanted to Enlighten her memory and imagination. He desired for her a complete assimilation into that world he believed to be best for everyone at all times and places.

To Eddie, the Catholicism practiced by Daisy's family was a configuration of the worst of all Pre-Enlightenment worlds, one entrenched in everything that was local, feudal, and unscientific. He desired for her, as he had for himself, a smooth crossing into a brave new world. A passage which severed all umbilical cords to the past. From his own teachers he had learned to fear that the slightest attachment to the old worlds could not only immediately forestall her induction into but also slowly contaminate the purity of the new world he so desired for her to enter.

But Daisy at 25 was too mature a thinker and too determined to change her old habit of facile learning to become the kind of student Eddie had in mind. She was willing to — had always been the first to — admit the hypocrisy of some priests and members of wealthy Chinese Catholic families: their dogma, scare techniques, and lip service. But she was not ready to dismiss the good she also sensed in her faith: it gave her the desire, will, and energy to temper Eddie's "Satchmo's got a lot of living to do" with the refrain of "What kind of living? How?

Why?" It emboldened her to deliberate over how to work some soul into the tune of Eddie's Enlightenment, which often appeared no more than a medley of things — scientific knowledge, diploma, private practice, fame, mansions, servants, places to go, people to see, wine, Cadillacs, kisses — to be had and enjoyed.

My mother's deliberations frightened my father. I'd witnessed him dress his fear in arrogance whenever Mmma asked him to explain the rules of English grammar behind the strange way a word had been used in a book or conversation.

"Look it up in the dictionary," he always replied shortly.

I cringed at Papa's impatience. I wanted to be the child who dared to answer back: "She had!" I understood how confusing dictionaries could be. They gave you more unknown words for whatever you didn't know to begin with. So many meanings to choose from, and all those rules for using it and for breaking other rules. Why did he have to be so mean, hoarding his command over English and humiliating her by implying to us all that she, a grown-up, still had not learned to use a dictionary?

I could not hear the panic in Papa's arrogance until, years later, I offered a seminar for training native English-speaking tutors of non-native English speaking tutees. One after another native-speaking tutor complained after their first few sessions: "I know what sounds right and what sounds wrong. The rules seem clear cut. But the more I try to explain a rule to my tutees, the less it seems to make sense. As one of my tutees pointed out the other day, if the 'she' in his sentence already signifies the third-person singular, why does he need an 's' after the verb to restate the obvious? Why add an 's' on the word 'apple' when the word 'five' preceeding it has already established the plural case?"

The complaints of the tutors taking my seminar made me wonder if Eddie was irritated by Daisy's questions about the rules of grammar because he, like my native English-speaking student tutors, didn't know how to explain any of them. Her questioning forced him to think, carefully, about the rules he had merely learned by rote. That got him confused. He couldn't resort to native speaker status. So her questions made him doubt not only his grasp of grammar and the art of teaching it (as had the native-speaking tutor taking my seminar) but also his command over English. And that had to be scary for Eddie. As all knew, English was the gold to his rice bowl.

But I would not come to these thoughts until decades later. Instead, I suffered with and for Mmma every time I watched my father dismiss her questions concerning the rules of the new language or the rules of the new world he so desired for him, her, and their children. I did not understand that her faith made him nervous. Her probing brought subtle but complex aftertastes to the fruits hanging in the tree of knowledge he had learned to feast on throughout his missionary training. In re-sentiment, he named her faith a tree of ignorance, a tree bearing nothing but stupid questions and yielding a sap responsible for duping her into the kind of student his own teachers had taught him to dread.

Papa always claimed that Mmma only went to Sunday mass and prayed daily in front of her porcelain Madonna out of habit. Mmma never objected, since she saw him as partially right. My mother went to church in search of that smell of incense, wood polish, marble chill, melting candle wax spiced by the scent of old female bodies which had not bathed since summer and by vegetarian breaths from lips feverishly moving for the advent of hope in a tongue foreign to one's ears. It was a sensation you could only long for if you had grown up with it, when accompanying your mother, as I once did, to those midnight masses before Easter Sunday in the big cathedral.

When I watched Mmma inhale that air with a slight twitch of her nostrils, I could tell she longed for Papa to be there, next to her, to share this living he didn't know he was missing. Not to experience it in the exact same way as she had — she learned from her own efforts going into his world to not expect the impossible. Besides, she loved him too much to want simply to convert his imagination. She loved him enough to want him to try to know her past as she had known it and as she was learning to know it anew. She wanted him to travel back with her, in the same spirit she took when going into his world. She longed to hear him say: I'll do it even though the whole thing seems so ridiculous. And she wanted him to tell her afterwards that it was all worth it, even though he'd hated every minute of it. Worthwhile because she had asked him to, and because he could tell how much she had pined for those — to him — mysterious sensations.

I imagine this to be ultimately not much different from my occasional longing to hear on Sunday mornings Satchmo trumpeting "all that living to do." My way of inviting my husband back to the place I have come from, to meet him over Janis Joplin and Tim Buckley on this side of the Pacific. I need to be told that he is willing to tread down that path with the same sensitivity and willing suspension of disbelief my mother had taught me to strive for when I fumbled my way around his 1960s East Coast suburbia. The world we live in might never let us forget that it does not rate equally our mutual ignorance about the other person's past. It has different names for our pasts. His is standard, mine, peculiar. But we have vowed not to rely on those tags when tripping back into both lanes in order to move forward.

It had to have hurt Mmma to hear Papa belittle her efforts to attend church and pray. It hurt even more since his derision was in tune with the hymns of a government which had systematically locked away every grown male in her family. To make a point, she withdrew on his birthdays from the hint-guess of gifts, the elaborate drawing of cards, the ordering of favorite food for breakfast, lunch, tea, and dinner, and the happy birthday wishes upon waking up which he loved and she had graciously taken part in at the beginning of their marriage. She wanted not to hurt him in the same way but to illustrate her hurt. I know because, after his release from prison by that same government, I'd watched her methodically reenacting all the birthday rituals he had by then learned no longer to expect.

I doubt my father ever realized that churchgoing and praying were habits Mmma had steadily maintained with the kind of critical distance you could only have when you had deliberately moved yourself outside your native environment. Daisy went to Sunday mass and prayed as Eddie's wife and the mother of their children, the keeper of a love which did not divide and rank. She did so because she was no longer Number Eight and required to by her parents, nor the nuns at school. Because she wanted to renew her vow to believe in, search for, and join forces with, the good of the world. I see her spending most of her time at church musing over how far she had moved away from that good-looking daughter who used to warm the same benches. She reviewed why that daughter had to be replaced by this Daisy, who had now come back to seek courage and energy so that she could go home to fight for this love Eddie had dared her to conjure up but she knew only her conscience could help her sustain.

I think my mother tripped back in search of what others have called reverse cultural shock, shocks Shanghai immigrants like myself experience upon returning after 15 years in the States. My mother went to recharge herself with the shock of how little and yet how much everything — one's self, friends, relatives, and the city — had changed. During their returns, immigrants often notice things they didn't know were there, things they now realize they can use in the new place they now called home. Many also run into things which did not use to irritate them, things they now can't help wanting to criticize and change. So they take off again, energized not only by the tastes, smells, or sounds they had missed so much (things which had initially brought them back) but also by a firmer grasp of what their current selves and lives are all about. And they try to pack and smuggle across as much of this realization as they can, to help them keep track of what works, what needs changing in the new place they now call home.

As I try to imagine my mother at church on those Sundays of my childhood, when I alternated between feeling guilty for having not been there next to her and feeling angry at her for having left me with this cranky Papa across the breakfast table, I see a woman returning to her past to recharge her commitment to a new way of living. Mmma had more reasons to go back: she was let down more often by the people with whom she was trying to build a new life, people for whom she had voluntarily exiled herself from a past to which she now needed to return, Sunday after Sunday, to confirm her faith in the choices she had made.

Yet I doubt my mother ever put any of this into words for Papa. Instead, she stated (before clamming up) that she simply needed to, her conscience told her to. Like so many who were private with their own thoughts and who had developed a knack for intuiting the inner-most thoughts of others, Mmma probably just assumed that anyone who truly loved her and who was as verbally articulate as Papa would — should have been able to — perceive what was going on in her mind. My guess is that Papa, who loved the challenge of depicting with sound and color every minute thought crossing his mind, and who deemed every one of his thoughts worth sharing, just assumed that there was not much going on inside Mmma if she was not telling him and the rest of the world about it. I should know. I am more my father's daughter in this respect, and I live with someone who could easily have been a child raised by my mother.

So my parents fought on.

Mmma said: I need to.

Papa diagnosed: Pavlovian conditional reflex. Catholic guilt. Idol worship.

Mmma swallowed and took care of her need with renewed vigil-ance, methodically gathering from her faith that love medicine for which he had helped to create the need but the prescription for which he had not been taught by either St. John's University or Johns Hopkins.

Because I had spent so much of my adolescence collecting the shards hinting at the events surrounding my infant brother's death, it is easier for me to understand why my parents continued to feud and hurt over this tragedy than to take note of the things they did to fight their way out of it. From the idle talk of various servants, family friends, and relatives, I had heard different details mentioned, all pointing to a range of conclusions. Some emphasized my father's initial dismissal as silly both my mother's observation that the baby screamed during and after feeding and Haopo's prodding to have the baby X-rayed. Others stood by (or denied) with equal vehemence the famous specialist's diagnosis of a knot in the baby's lower intestine, a disagreement among experts over whether an operation was necessary, the success of an operation promptly performed by the best surgeon in town, nature's surprise — the surgery revealed intestines which had straightened out — or the baby's post-surgical pneumonia and the impossibility of finding penicillin during World War II Shanghai under Japanese occupation. Yet still others insinuated the questionable status of the soul of an unbaptized dead baby, the irony of hiring a best surgeon for an operation your son turned out not to have needed, God's punishment for Papa's fake conversion and for Mmma's compliance with his heathen parenting style.

I swallowed with my mother as her dimple hardened at any hint of my brother's death. And I blamed my father for my mother's grief. I had seen his desperation, trying to make amends after having rashfully and wrongly dismissed her opinion. I knew of my father's obsession for quick fixes. I had noticed his arrogance when singing the praises of the miracle of surgery. And I knew Mmma's feelings toward Papa's fake conversion, their fights over our baptism. Assuming that all of these spoke for Mmma's understanding of the tragedy and the source of her silence, I wanted to punch, bite, tear at my father for the pain he had caused my mother, on his chest, where his flesh was the supplest, as I had learned from trying to grab it underneath his chest hair when I floated astride his stomach in the pool at the French Club (the *best* pool in Shanghai and soon to be reserved for Our Great Leader Chairman Mao's private use when he honored the city with a rare visit).

Lately, I've come to wonder if my parents' silence over their son's death signaled less their grief and anger over the baby's death and toward one another, but more their regret over not having ever mourned, together, their loss. I see the two of them on the night of my baby brother's death, lying on their twin beds always arranged side by side to form a larger than king-sized one.

Not speaking.

Nor touching.

Apart from one another.

He wanted to reach over and weep tears of fear and remorse into hers. But her eyes were dry. So he rehearsed instead the numbers forming the basis of his decision: the age of the patient, the symptoms, the ratios of success with the operation and of cure without the operation. He reminded himself that he could not afford to personalize the outcome. The nerve of a surgeon was the foundation of his golden rice bowl. He had a whole family to support.

He was glad he had not had a chance to really know the baby. Yet he regretted not having loved his son as he knew she had. He realized nothing he could say or do now would appease the pain she was going through. If there was ever a time my father had regretted his refusal to baptize his children, this would have been the night. He would have wanted to have done it for her, just to ease her worry over the boy's place in heaven.

Earlier in the evening, he had watched her talk, dry-eyed, to her porcelain figurine. It angered him that she had chosen to share her sorrow with an idol and not him. At the same time, he wished as he never had before that she'd make some sort of gesture to invite him to join her, as she used to when they first got married. But she didn't. And he told himself that it was just as well. The opium of religion could be addictive. This conscience business could lead him astray from the world of knowledge and inquiry.

She wanted him praying by her side more than anything else. But she didn't ask. If there ever was a time in her life when my mother did

not feel she could trust herself to fight his derision of her faith, that
would have been the night. I wish my father could listen with me to my
mother pray. I know she prayed for the living as well as the dead. She
needed courage to go on loving her surviving child with the same
intensity with which she had loved her infant son. She wanted for my
father the strength to continue his commitment to medicine, which
she understood was lit by the same spirit she sought in her conscience.
She prayed for strength to disregard the idle talk of her relatives. And
she prayed that when she woke up the next morning, she would have
the courage to get up to pray again, for love.

I don't know for how many nights after my brother's death my
parents lay in their bed without speech, nor touching. But I know it
went on for some time. I had watched their fights escalate because
neither of them would make the first move to tell the other what each
had earlier willingly admitted to Haopo, he weeping and she, dry-eyed.
But I also know that they loved one another enough to eventually sur-
mount the rift left by their separate mourning of their son's death.

Papa knew that Mmma would never blame the death on his decision to operate on the baby. She had given him permission to make
the call, and she would not be afraid to take responsibility for having given him that vote of confidence. Mmma knew that Papa lived for
the same love she would continue to fight for with the strength she
gained from the praying he refused to join. And she was determined
to fight him (and with him) every inch of the way to keep that love
on track.

Sometime during the month after my brother's death, my parents
made passionate love. And I like to believe that I was the product of
that night. I wish I had been there to jump into their bed that morning
after, as I had when very young and on those rare Sundays when my

mother did not go to church. I would zoom in uninvited as soon as I heard the slightest move behind the oak doors to my parents' rooms.

Make a tent, make a tent! I'd beg while bouncing up and down with half of my butt on each of my parents' pillows, firm and stacked high on Papa's side and soft and flat on Mmma's. And I'd scream *here I come* as I crawled under the tent my parents made of their blankets.

I just know that if I had been there on that special morning after, I'd have found, as I often had on other Sunday mornings, my parents' fingers tightly locked underneath the tent. And I'd sense that I had got myself where I both should and should not have been. I'd inhale, quietly, that scent which I thought at the time was pouring from the open pores of those legs so lovingly holding up the blanket for me. And I'd try to figure out what it was about the way my parents held their hands to make me feel that those legs longed to be wrapped around one another. And what it was about the way they held their hands to make me believe that they wanted me to come out, in between their legs, in just the way I was slowly crawling my way down.

I know the strength of that love. For I had seen those fingers lock as often as I had seen them separated. They stayed linked throughout the six hours we stood, me next to Mmma and Haopo next to Papa, with our backs pressed against a wall in my parents' bedroom. It was the summer of 1966. Of all the rooms we were able to find the keys to lock ourselves into, as the police had advised us, this bedroom was the only one which had a wall space in between the two doors wide enough for the four of us to stand against it and, we hoped, stay outside the view of those Cultural Revolutionary Red Little Soldiers wandering in from the street, looking for Anti-Four-Old-Elements Cultural Revolutionary action.

"Where are the Rotten Nine Category owners of this house?" we had heard one group after another ask as they tried to spot us through the stained-glass panels above the bedroom doors. We listened hard to

the revelry on the other side of the hallway, in the upstairs small dining room and the storage room leading down to the pantry: the
slamming of cabinet doors, the smashing of Anti-Revolutionary foreign
goods in bottles and cans, and the shouts of children and adolescents
drunk on chocolates, beer, nuts, liquor. We prayed we had enough
supplies to keep the party going, to draw away the attention of whoever
was pushing at the doors to the bedroom in search of the Rotten Nine
Category owners.

From time to time we gave one another's hand a gentle squeeze to
remind ourselves to put strength into my 70-something Haopo's bound
feet, so that she could press with the rest of us, for the wall to let us in,
make us invisible to those outside. We could hear and smell violence
through the oak doors and guess what would be waiting out there for
us if we were found.

We squeezed one another's fingers to say, fear not. Even if we were
to be found, we would be there with and for one another to go through
it all. In the meantime, let us focus our hearts on holding up for as
long as we could.

I know that soon after that incident, it was the memory of this
linking of fingers which sustained my parents through their six-year
separation across the prison walls. My stomach churns at the memory
of Mmma's shoulder blades poking through the back of her grey
cotton top, which she wore as a shirt in the summer and a jacket during the other seasons, as she stood staring in front of the window,
huddled over the hot water she cupped in her hands: that dreadful
greeting I knew I could always depend on when returning from a date
in the apartment building where my first husband and other Patriotic
Overseas Chinese lived, and where my dreams for a new life in the old
way seemed still a possibility. I felt instead I should have been standing there with my arm around Mmma's bird-framed body. So frail that
I worried that if I hugged too hard I'd break the bones, and yet so

strong that I feared I might humiliate her by suggesting she could use my support.

Late at night, I would reach out for my mother's hand when waking to her moaning, which she muffled into the pillow next to mine on my parents' twin beds. The Cultural Revolution had reinstated me temporarily to the place I had never forgiven the Stranger for usurping. Except I knew then that my mother wanted my father, not me, by her side. And I wanted that for her, with her. So I locked my fingers into hers, gingerly, to let her know that they were not meant as substitutes, for no one's could, but as a reminder that his were out there, locked behind bars but alive (we hoped), groping for hers.

Years later, I could tell from the way my father held on to my mother's hand as she walked him home on the day Nixon arrived in Shanghai that he too had daily fed himself with the sensation of her fingers in his to survive his prison cell. The sensation made tangible his worth in the eyes of many besides her before this cruel turn in his life. It reassured him of her faith in him and their love. He knew she knew that they would both live just for the chance to fight one another one more time, for no more than an excuse to lock hands again when making up.

When I picture my father nourishing himself with the sensation of my mother's fingers in his, I wish I could claim that it was the knowledge of Mmma's love alone which had sustained Papa through his incarceration. But the world of romance has had little use in our family history. I know there were other sources of renewal for Papa's faith in his self worth. Papa always said, when recounting his numerous brushes with death in prison, that he could tell all the guards and doctors knew who he was: He was No. xxx, the Johns Hopkins-trained doctor of Western bankers and diplomats whom the authorities wanted to keep alive. So whenever Papa felt himself driven to the edge of sanity by the solitude of his confinement, he would complain about his health in medical terms he knew his guards would have to consult him to comprehend. On at least two occasions, Papa was able to save his own life by diagnosing his own condition and dictating his own prescriptions. More than once, doctors in the prison hospital came to seek his opinion concerning their own health.

His short stays in the prison hospitals were truly a boost for Papa's body and ego. Yet Papa understood the danger of crying wolf once too often, of thus not being taken seriously when a serious attack came and then, not making it to the prison hospital on time. To restrain himself from overusing his medical knowledge to get the treatment he often needed more for his faith in himself than for his diabetes, Eddie injected himself daily with the memory of Daisy's fingers in his. Soft but firm, silent yet pregnant with promises.

I have one more picture of those hands to give my daugher and husband, for them to give back to me when I need it. 1976. My father gently squeezing my mother's morphined fingers as he chanted and sobbed into the prayer book he had asked Mmma's sister to send from abroad during the last stage of my mother's illness. Papa kept at it for hours, long after the interval between the feeble puffs wafting from her lips — lips which had not moved to form a word for over a month — eventually stretched into infinity. His way of telling her that he would be with her this time as he had not been over the passing of their son.

I cried for this man who had to rely on a prayer book (she had shown no sign of missing hers after the Red Guards took it) to join her, because he had never listened carefully to her praying before. I cried because to send her on her way, he nevertheless tried, clumsily and so late in their marriage, to sing for her yet one more time in what he hoped was her language the song he knew would set her on fire: *you are alive, so come and show it, such a lot of living to do.* And I cried for the passing of this woman who never gave up on her praying and on him, in spite of his resistance until the very, very end to try it her way.

But I also cried for my 30-year-old self, my 5-year-old marriage, and my 3-year-old daughter. I could no longer deny what I had never admitted to myself: the love of my parents scared me because I didn't know if I could ever love like that.

I wanted my mother back to answer the questions I did not have the courage to ask her before she passed away. I wanted her to confirm my suspicion that when she had told me before my marriage that my first husband and I were not meant for one another, she did not have in mind, as I told myself at the time, the differences in our backgrounds and temperaments. She was asking me to search my heart for that fire to love and fight for that love which she had seen in Haopo and Dada, which she had guarded in Eddie and herself.

Watching my parents make their last love, I realized that I had known all along that my mother had warned me to probe the nature of my feelings for my first husband before our marriage. I had chosen not to hear her because I was too busy denying to myself and to others my three-step pragmatism. I yearned for life to go back to where it had left me that summer afternoon in 1966. I heard the world say, you might find it there in that apartment building where the Patriotic Overseas Chinese lived. You could only find it there, with him. For you did not have the wits nor the resources to make it back on your own. So I tuned my mother out and got married.

Watching my mother depart, I realized how much she had made me covet that love she had for my father. That was when I ended my first marriage, even though I had to wait eight more years and cross the Pacific to end it legally. During those years, question after question pulled me back: "Why work when you didn't need the money?" "Why try graduate school when you might lose your Shanghai residency and make him lose face for having a lesser degree?" "Why go abroad before he had a chance to go and settle down?" But the memory of my father squeezing my mother's drug-numbed fingers as he prayed by her side prompted me to ask: would my mother think it right that I could not find the heart to fire back any Why-nots to redress these questions simply because the idea of fighting with and beside my first husband into eternity did not fire me up? Would my mother ever want me to have my daughter grow up with parents who were too scared to love?

News of my decision to break my first marriage brought more advice: "Stick to him, for the good of your daughter." "Your Mmma would never approve, see how loyal she was to your Dad." "Be realistic, your marriage is a whole lot better than most." I knew my mother would expect me to take full responsibility for both the marriage and the divorce, for everything I had done to get myself where I was. But I also felt that she would never want me to live a life where I had to focus all my heart on accommodating a reality I knew needed changing. She had left me too many memories of her at work, ferociously stoking a fire which heats up without burning down the yearning to rely on the best in one another to bring the best out of one another.

I once heard my mother tell Haopo that she knew her infant son was with Dada. I hope it was my brother's death which eventually pushed my mother over her worry concerning our unbaptized, unconfirmed souls. She would continue to voice for her relatives the doubts on their minds, which I took to speak for her mind as well. But I am beginning to think she only did that to show herself and the world that she was no longer living under the tyranny of idle talk.

When my mother said she believed her infant son to be with Dada, she probably had in mind Dada's answer to Haopo, when Haopo asked if he cared to join the Protestant church along with her and the children.

Dada's answer: "Mother, from what you've been telling me about your God, I don't think He'd separate me from you and the children just because I have not been baptized."

Dada knew he would belong to the kingdom of Haopo's God if he kept working on his Old Good Person's heart. He did not need to join her church to do that. He also knew he would not have fit in at her church, as he had not at the bank, even if he had joined.

I think the thought of Dada watching over her children comforted Mmma. It helped her focus less on our baptisms and more on how to make sure we developed a good conscience. If there was a heaven Dada

could not enter, her children would not be missing much staying outside of it. Mmma knew she belonged where people like him had gone.
She would fight to cross over, if her baptism were to place her in a
heaven with no room for the likes of Dada.

I want to leave my daughter this image of my mother and Haopo
discussing death, a rare heirloom in this culture we live in, where we
take seminars to talk about such matters. A believer of no life — as we
know it — after death, I am still haunted by the idea of what-if. I long
for the possibility of revisiting in death those I've loved while alive. Even
though a side of me is fully aware that such meetings, if possible, would
have to take forms beyond human imagination, another side of me
carries this picture of an electrically-wired fence separating those with
baptism cards from those without. It makes me list the names of my
loved ones with the right passports for Heaven — my daughter, husband, Mmma, Haopo, . . . even Papa. Then I panic, as I used to during
my first year in the U.S., whenever I thought of my eight-year-old
daughter behind the Bamboo Curtain. Twelve years after my naturalization, I still dream about being back in China and being denied a
permit to leave and reunite with my husband in the States.

At times like that, the conversation between my mother and grandmother reminds me that, if there were such a border in death, I would
want to stay on the side where goodhearted men and women like Dada,
Ahfen, and many others — Jews, Native Americans, Marxists, Darwi-
nians, transcendentalists — were placed. And this is the side to which
my baptized loved ones would find a way to cross over. For haven't we
all lived with the hope of composing a manual of love which does not
rank and divide? Isn't that why my husband and I had taken our
daughter to that Episcopalian church when she turned 12?

We thought it was time for her to explore the relation between
religious organizations and faith. I hope we chose the right place for
her to think through the meaning of religious vows, bar mitzvahs and
confirmations, celebrations to which she was being frequently invited.
We found a tiny Episcopalian church where the priest talked about the
difficulties of faith in modernity without resorting to either scare tech-

niques or euphoria, where she could sit without fear or shame between her Methodist-raised stepfather and her unbaptized mother and with the consent of her biological father in his West Coast Chinese-American Christian church.

We wanted our daughter to be multilingual in probing how and why faith is something you would have to work on every minute of your life. It is not, as I once thought, anything you can have by the mere joining of any religious institution. Yet in all these institutions and outside them, there are places of worship and persons of faith to sustain you as well as places and people to impede your search for it.

I am still not quite sure why our daughter decided to get herself baptized and confirmed. Peer pressure? Passage into mainstream U.S. culture? Gifts, a party, and lots of attention? A little bit of all of them, we figured. But also, we hoped, an understanding that the ceremony symbolizes a vow of commitment, not the attaining of either a certificate to the ownership of a good conscience on earth nor a passport to heaven afterwards, if it exists. I like to think that with or without baptism, we are together, in spirit, as Dada and Haopo or Mmma and me.

Unfortunately, what I believe and how I feel do not always go together. So occasionally I wake up in the middle of the night and wonder, what-if? And I panic.

I know I will panic again when it comes my turn to leave this earth. I saw fear in my mother's eyes when she died. And if I am lucky and my daughter and husband are there to sustain me, I hope they know to remind me of what my mother said when she and Haopo discussed death.

In the meanwhile, I must face the fact that the lessons on love my parents left me with their fightings over religion have taught me more about how to detect the absence than the presence of love. I think I have it with my husband, but I am never sure. It just seems that our differences are so mundane. Even as I pray we will never have to negotiate some of the crossroads the world had dealt my parents or grandparents, I worry about whether we will have the fire to sustain us through any we may happen to encounter.

Sometimes I believe that, with the kind of love I have in mind, no one can ever know for sure they have it. Only the fact that you have not yet stopped wanting it and wanting it with this person you call your life partner. Other times I worry about what I have with my husband. I worry about the kind of model we have been setting for our daughter.

Here is a question I've been meaning to probe with my daughter and husband: are we making love when, before setting the table every evening, he asks what I want — plate and silverware or bowl, chopsticks, and Chinese porcelain spoon? Are we, when we settle down at our mission oak table across the candlelight I love and he hates, me slurping soup and shoveling rice with chopsticks against a bowl heaped high with a motley of dishes and he, working through the vegetables, meat, rice — arranged in separate piles without touching — one at a time, always in that same order, cutting everything into pieces while letting the juice — the best part — drizzle wasted onto the plate, and ruining the texture and flavor of rice by smearing it onto his fork?

Such a trivial scene, and yet one which has taken us so long to arrive at.

When we first started out, it used to be always plates and silverware. Mine and his preference. Didn't make sense to eat rice and big chunks of meat on plates with chopsticks, not for people like us who had both been brought up to never take bites off the meat except with finger food. I reassured him that many in China besides my sisters and I were also strictly forbidden to shovel rice into our mouths, and to make slurping sounds when drinking soup. Only Hollywood actors impersonating Asian characters do that!

But lately, I've been having this urge to occasionally eat like a coolie — as my mother would put it — or like a real Chinese, according to Hollywood. I don't know if it is because at 50 the repressed child in me is finally coming out. Or maybe after 15 years in the USA, I have caught the nostalgia for a Chinese-ness I never had. Or my liberal academic guilt is edging me to find some tangible way of acting out my rebellion against my upper class background. A little bit of all, I suppose. Whatever my reasons, I do so now and then.

I do so deliberately, knowing full well the visceral reactions my slurping and shoveling involuntarily evoke in my husband, as they had in my mother and as they still do in myself when others do it in public.

I do so knowing also that both my husband and I understand the strain such actions and reactions had — can still — put on our relation.

When we eat facing each other in our separate ways, we know that the noise and absence of noise makes us edgy. A casual remark about the Bach or Davis we both love. A passing comment on whether he should read or would like Toni Morrison. A side observation over us not talking about anything at all. Any one of them could erupt, launching us both right back where we find ourselves sitting and watching one another think, say, do things which reveal prejudices neither of us can believe the other still has.

We've been there before.

We are still nursing one another over the injuries left from moments like these. So unnecessary yet so inevitable.

But we have also learned to risk these eruptions, having realized from all these years together that there is no avoiding moments like that if we are to stay and move forward together.

So he asks: what do you want, a plate or bowl?

And I say: chopsticks. If I am in the mood. And with as little defensiveness in my voice as I can manage.

I like to think that we do things like that for the same reason my friend Jing and my mother visited the antique mall, to whet our appetite to bargain for the living we are trying to do together. A prelude for our joust in the next 24 hours.

But I worry about the crossroads waiting ahead of us, about our not being ready when the big test comes. And I am back to the question with which I began: are we making love when we sit over bowl, chopsticks, porcelain spoon, and steamy tea across from plate, silverware, and French wine?

I guess I'll never know until the day I sense, for sure, we are not. I hope that day never comes. And I hope that, trivial as it is, a scene like this is enough to make us adequate parents for my daughter.

Working Woman

On the family registration book issued by the Public Security Bureau, Mmma was classified as a Household Woman. In the China I grew up in, that stood for *women who do not work*.

My mother knew she had worked as hard as my father and for as many hours to make possible that life she wanted so much to change. The reputation of a Virtuous Wife was the wage she earned for the work she did. But my mother wanted more. She wanted recognition of her share in every step he had and had not taken in his career. She held herself responsible for failing to dissuade Papa from becoming a generalist and oftentimes an exorbitantly priced interpreter for Western diplomats and bankers who were themselves stuck in the no-action Shanghai of the early 1960s for reasons one would be better off not knowing. She would not excuse herself from the moral ambiguity surrounding Papa's later contacts with the Public Security Bureau, impersonating in his own mind a Graham Greene's "Our Man from Havana" type of agent in order to continue his lucrative general practice.

Mmma made her position clear during the Cultural Revolution, when she along with other Relatives of Anti-Revolutionaries were ordered to sweep the street at dawn and dusk under the self-righteous cruelty of preteen Revolutionary Red Little Soldiers. She never once complained. Not because she thought the People's punishment for her husband or herself was fair, but because she did not think it was fair for the People to punish him more for a life for which she was not afraid to claim equal responsiblity. To acknowledge her labor in building that life, she met with a befuddling eagerness her penalty as a Parasite of the Nine Rotten Categories.

Every dawn and dusk, Daisy marched on to the street with a lofty air, in the same way we knew she would have walked into prison if she had been allowed to accompany Eddie past the Public Security personnel guarding the gates. Even as I wished my mother would put her

lofty air aside so that I did not have to fear and watch the extra pun-
ishments it brought her from her zealous child overseers, I sensed
without wanting to admit to myself the declaration it sent: Daisy wanted
full credit for all the work she did and did not do to make possible the
Anti-Revolutionary life for which Eddie alone was imprisoned.

No one, least of all myself, ever knew enough to call her a working woman to her face. Never before, during, or after her street-
sweeping ordeal.

For decades, my mother tried to convince herself and others that
she had the strength to be the one to start a new life outside China, to
work at helping my father get his surgical aspirations back on track. I
knew this to be a subtext to her fights with Papa over his affair with
Miss F, his U.S.-trained surgical nurse. But while growing up, I understood better Daisy's right to be the jealous wife than her indignation at
my father's reluctance to move beyond the life they had worked so hard
to establish and gotten so settled in.

When Miss F came to visit, everyone watched.

No one could miss my father's attraction to her, which he openly
displayed as he did around any female friend he found appealing. The
extreme caution Miss F exercised in her movements and words, I always
thought, was what gave away the intensity of her feelings for him. The
rise-dip of my mother's first words before she managed to streamline
them told me that Mmma shared my observations. Haopo, however,
watched the rest of us watching these three so that she could supply
answers to all the questions on our minds when telling her stories.

Haopo traced the source of idle talk concerning an affair between
Eddie and his head nurse to a family friend who had spotted the two in
an ice cream parlor one Sunday afternoon. To correct the impression
that Eddie was seeing his nurse behind Daisy's back, Haopo pains-
takingly furnished details (to both the creators and receivers of idle
talk), details no one else, least of all Daisy, could be privy to. Haopo

vouched that, on that particular Sunday afternoon, Eddie had used a stroll in the park with my sister as an excuse to shop for a wedding anniversary gift for Daisy in one of the nearby boutique stores — the ones right across the street from the French Club, the ones all knew to be the most exclusive in the city. An ingenious ruse, Haopo reminded us, since Daisy was too pregnant to want to take part in any park outings.

It was May and sunny. The flowers were budding, and everyone was out. Not surprisingly, one of the people Eddie ran into at the entrance to the park turned out to be Miss F. To recuperate from the exhaustion of heat and walking, Eddie treated his daughter and nurse to an ice cream in the parlor across from the boutique stores. There, he and his nurse chatted freely with my sister sandwiched between them along the counter, as any two colleagues would have when bumping into one another in the U.S. These two were merely following an old habit, developed when finishing their post-graduate surgical training.

You know our Eddie. So . . . Westernized!

Haopo taught us to filter talk of similar rendezvous through the lens we had used when we admired the photos displayed in our family album documenting Eddie's years abroad. In one of them, he was standing ankle deep in snow beside his new car, with his arms around two young Caucasian women wearing identical red wool coats, crisp nursing caps, and huge smiles. Haopo superimposed onto the idle talk images of a man whose daughter had to undergo a self-criticism session organized for the sole purpose of helping her to struggle against an Imperialist Lackey father who had been seen by a classmate walking down a main street with his arm around his wife's waist.

Eccentric but harmless!

Haopo then led us to put the affair back to its collegial setting, to see it as a special friendship between people who had to spend a third of their day and half their waking hours working closely together. We had seen that among colleagues of the same sex and accepted it as normal. What was so shocking, then, about seeing it between a man and a woman? Besides, we'd all seen the affection Haopo and Grandpa

Wong — the husband of Haopo's Small Sister, my Fanatic Haopo — had for one another. We could tell how very close they had been and from how far back by the way they grabbed each other's hands after a long absence, reminisced about their school teacher past, and exchanged their thoughts on new books. Yet we had accepted their intimacy as natural. Look at Cook and Ahma, who were always jabbing at one another because they both admired a sharp tongue and enjoyed a cup of rice wine after a hard day's work.

So why this fuss over Eddie and his nurse? Haopo asked without asking. Who could better understand Eddie's surgical anxieties, aspirations, and triumphs, not to mention his memories of the States? Could there be any wonder that his nurse would enjoy Eddie's company in return — Eddie, the rare son and brother of two equally open-minded working women?

Even as I accepted Haopo's rendition, I waited, with irritation at both my grandmother and mother, to see Mmma's dry-mouthed swallow. Haopo's subtle rebuttal echoed Papa's raving against *all this bloody Chinese fuss about nothing*. He would not have to be so secretive about their outings if those bloody locals — *ignorant and backward bastards all* — would just stop whispering false accusations.

The rendition of Haopo and Papa pitted Mmma against herself, asking her to celebrate a relationship inspired by an ideal she upheld — a friendship daring to transcend the dictates of local codes which had erected thick walls between friends and colleagues of opposite sex. It asked Daisy to consider if that hurt rising from her groin to clutch her heart at the mere mention of the name of her husband's nurse could have been caused by her own entrapment in the very social code fanning the idle talk she loathed so much. Was she indeed under the sway of petty jealousy, consumed by her envy of women who could hold their own when talking with men like Eddie about work, books, or the West? If Daisy really loved Eddie, she should not grudge him that pleasure just because she herself did not know how to give that. She should instead join forces with people like Haopo and Eddie in defense of such friendships.

Seeing Mmma's dry-mouthed swallow, I sensed that the duet her husband and mother-in-law sang parched Mmma's throat, turning her anger into a white rage. I don't think Daisy disagreed in principle with anything Haopo or Eddie said. Rather, it was the partiality of their rendition, what they had left unsaid, which infuriated her.

She wanted them to also consider: "What about Miss F's love for Eddie? What about his abuse of that love?"

"It is not moral to play with someone's heart," Daisy always said before withdrawing into silent contempt.

Daisy was just as adamant in publicly disputing rumors concerning the sexual nature of Eddie's affair with his nurse. Not because Eddie had sworn his innocence. Not because he had denied ever having even fancied it. Nor because she was trying to save face by willfully turning her back to reality. But because she trusted her own understanding of the integrity of Miss F's love for Eddie. Daisy refused to overlook the depth and scope of Miss F's love. ("Takes one to know one," as Daisy liked to say.) And she would not let him forget that she disapproved of the way he had fed and fed on that love in the name of work.

Daisy could live with the fact that Eddie took pride in his catholic taste when dealing with women as well as in other matters. Go look it up in the dictionary, he was always saying, "catholic" means being broad in sympathies or interests. I'm much more catholic than any of your bloody church-going relatives. Daisy could understand the appeal for Eddie of Miss F's steady hands and her cool presence in and out of the operating room. She could see why he might fall for those bony, long fingers as they brushed back the shoulder-length permed hair from that square-jawed, full-lipped, fawn-eyed face. She could imagine his thrill upon hearing his nurse toss her "Rs" in her husky voice when she switched to English for terms neither she nor Eddie had the Chinese words for.

She would have tolerated his infatuation, as she had his infatuations over many other things in other women: a gorgeous body comfortable with itself, an analytical mind capable of intimidating high-ranking diplomats and bankers, or a daredevil spirit raising eyebrows in all quarters. After Eddie ended his brief affair with the wife of a family friend, Daisy had sighed an implicit agreement to Haopo's *men were weak like that.* The woman friend had been lonely and angry with her husband, who had been sent to work in another city because he refused to collaborate with the Public Security people as Papa had. Mmma had nodded when Haopo suggested that part of the thrill for Papa might stem from this woman friend's open contempt for her husband's idealism, especially since Mmma had herself been so hard on Papa for selling out. Besides, the woman was certainly not shy to show her affection, Haopo pointed out. A stunning figure too, Mmma added. I remember thinking I knew what my mother might mean. This woman always made me think of the nude caucasian women in the two plastic thumb-sized viewmaster keyrings Papa kept locked in his bedside table, which I was definitely not supposed to have secretly looked at.

Papa's affair with this woman friend hurt my mother both during and after. But Mmma seemed quite willing to let it go once it was over: a sexual affair was all that both Papa and the woman friend had wanted, and that was what they had. But Daisy would not let go of Eddie's affair with his nurse because she was convinced that Miss F loved Eddie as no one besides Daisy had loved him. I trust my mother on this. And it was the way Eddie loved back that angered Mmma.

"It was not moral to play with people's hearts," Mmma insisted. We could follow the logic of Mmma's argument on behalf of Miss F: she was wedded to him by a love far more complex and deeper than he could ever expect from any other colleague or friend. In reducing her to just his right hand at work, Papa could wallow in her love without the obligation of ever having to acknowledge or return it.

"Why worry about Miss F? Focus on Eddie and yourself!" Haopo advised, and Mmma swallowed.

Haopo's advice made sense to me because I, too, would do anything to stop my parents from fighting. So long as Miss F knew what she was getting into, so long as Papa kept his promise to treat her as no more than his right hand at work, what did it matter to the rest of us if she was still in love with him?

Haopo reminded Mmma that the story of why-men-keep-concubines was also a story of why-wives-(in-the-past-have)-let-their-husbands-have-concubines: no wife could humanly fulfill the multiple needs of any husband. Luckily, we did not live anymore in that Confucian world where friendship between the sexes was strictly forbidden. It was better for Eddie and Daisy that he was able to find someone who could simultaneously satisfy his needs for a reliable right hand at the clinic, a pair of sympathetic ears to absorb his grievances against their hypochondriac banker diplomat patients or the Communists forestalling his surgical practice, and a pair of nostalgic eyes for reviewing his postgraduate glories in the States.

Mmma's reply: "Find a friend who wanted to stay a friend, a nurse who wanted to be just his nurse."

"What difference would that make to *you*, so long as she stayed just his friend and colleague in action!" Haopo would sigh and ask.

It took me years to grasp why it hurt Mmma so much to hear Haopo say that. Not because she asked exactly the question Mmma had been wrestling with, but because of the answer Haopo's sigh clearly implied: "Not much." Mmma was aware how persuasive Haopo's tacit answer could sound to the rest of us. As long as we held on to that answer, we would always render Mmma's position suspect.

I have enough memories of the timing of my parents' fights over Miss F, and enough memories of Mmma's last statements before clamming up, for me to believe that, in her mind, Papa's relationship with his nurse was more than a simple love affair. It was another example of his greed for tangible rewards and his fear of losing them. Therefore, when I return to Haopo's question of what difference his treatment of Miss F could possibly make to Mmma, I hear Mmma replying with her dry swallow: "It would make all the difference in how we and our children learn to love and live."

My father loved being loved. And he loved being loved simultaneously by his wife and head nurse. He believed he needed both: He did not want his wife to work outside the house, for he wanted more from her than what he remembered Haopo was able to give to himself and his father. But he wanted someone who could love him just as passionately by his side, at work, for and with him, all the time. He believed he needed both because he had seen how well similar set-ups had served some of his friends and heard the envy behind idle talk of their affairs.

Daisy knew well Eddie's greed for — and thus, his fear of losing — things coveted by other men — things he had grown accustomed to having and could not imagine living without. She saw his relationship with Miss F as another instance of his impatience to catch a living confined by things he only believed he had to have: an exorbitant income plus a stay-home wife and a right-hand nurse, both deeply in love with him. She refused to let herself, Eddie, or Miss F be pigeonholed by Eddie's greed and fear. Daisy believed that both women loved Eddie enough to labor with him, to pose a refrain of "what kind of living" to his "time is wasting, got a lot of living to do." It pained Daisy to watch Eddie swaying to a medley dictated by his greed for immediate and tangible rewards.

So she insisted: "Make a choice, her or me!"

Eddie claimed: "I already did. You are my wife, I love you more. She is my right hand at work. And she seems to be fine with it."

"Choose again," Daisy persisted: "Her *or* me, not me *and* her."

Mmma would not let Papa off the hook. She reminded him of the fundamental unfairness of his choice to everyone: Miss F, herself, himself, and us. Mmma wanted us to join her in asking that he choose again: "Her *or* me. Not me *and* her."

It seems that Daisy would rather risk losing Eddie to Miss F than remain an object of his greed and fear. Instead of letting Eddie cling to what he thought he needed — a stay-home wife *and* a right-hand nurse, both deeply in love with him — Daisy demanded that he learn to love with the trust that together, he and his lover (Eddie and Daisy *or* Eddie and Miss F) would work out where they needed to go, even though all they knew at this moment was that what they had was not good enough, and that venturing further meant risking everything they had worked so hard to achieve.

"She or I, not me and her" was Daisy's improvisation on Satchmo's "got a lot of living to do." It was her way of daring Eddie to pause and reckon with the living into which his enthusiasm for three-step pragmatism had locked them. She wanted that for him but also for herself and their children, for she understood that the same greed and fear which had held him hostage in his dealings with the women who loved him was also steadily derailing his aspirations as a surgeon, keeping him from probing with Daisy the work she might do to get their life back on track.

"Let me try," Mmma urged in 1961 after the government turned down Papa's application for an exit permit. By that time, my 40-something father had already been retired for several years from his surgical practice.

During the late 1950s, the People's Government began to buy out all private enterprises, including the hospital Papa used for his private surgical practice. So Papa had to choose between working as a surgeon in a People's hospital or staying in private practice as a generalist. Papa chose the latter. He had a family to support, he reminded us. He would not work for the Communists. His foreign patients seemed to approve. They promptly offered a generous package, making it worth his while to maintain a clinic serving exclusively their general health needs and those of their Chinese employees.

Mmma insisted that money should not have been the deciding factor: except for Haopo, who deserved all the luxury she desired, the rest of us could and should try to live on less, deal with whatever pay cut my father might have to take to pursue his surgical practice. At the same time, she fully endorsed Papa's refusal to work for the Communists. So she accepted Papa's choice as a reasonable temporary measure until they figured out a way to get my father out of China through Hong Kong — the only possible route at the time.

When my father's application to leave China was rejected in 1961, Mmma reasoned that they might work instead to get her out first. It had become common knowledge that the government seldom granted permits to persons who had been classified (like Papa) as High Ranking Intellectuals, whom it also titled National Treasures. The government seemed much more willing to let go of their stay-at-home wives. Mmma thought it made sense that we follow the route taken by many family friends: let her apply for an exit permit first. Once she got out and settled in Hong Kong, the rest of us could then apply to reunite with our newly titled Patriotic Overseas Chinese mother.

"Let me go and get settled first."

"On your own?"

Not entirely. My parents had some foreign currency hoarded away, enough to get her started. She could look for a job teaching school or clerking, like several of her college friends were rumored to be doing in their downward mobility in Hong Kong.

"Don't be ridiculous. What would we do without you? Besides, you'll never make it out there. What do you know about work?"

The rest of us let Papa speak for us.

Too many hard facts to support our skepticism, to be used to cover our fear of the long years of separation between husband and wife, parents and children. We made mental lists of all the children and wives dumped by Papa's former classmates and colleagues who had not returned from studying abroad. "Started a new family with someone else," we'd heard it rumored again and again. What if women, virtuous wives and good mothers like Daisy, were also capable of such gradual changes of heart? What if irresistible men like Eddie could also be found *lacking* by their wives after they crossed over, as so many of Papa's former classmates and colleagues had concluded about the wives they were about to dump?

Too many hard facts working against Daisy, facts Daisy could not, nor would, deny in good conscience.

Fact One: Daisy had not wanted to accompany Eddie abroad in 1946, the year of my birth. We had all heard Mmma admit to her dread of living abroad: no servants. No friends. The need to speak English all the time. The same would have been true in Hong Kong, if and when she made it across.

I suspect other reasons led my parents jointly to the decision that Mmma should stay behind in 1946. They had openly admitted to how politically naive they had been before the Communist takeover. The war was just over. Along with everyone else, they thought that, with the Alliance back, Shanghai was heading back to the good old days. Who would want to hassle with living overseas unless one had to? Besides, it cost less for a single man to go and live in the States. The money saved would ensure that Haopo did not have to wait any longer for the good life she rightly deserved. It would leave Papa money to return with the expected car and the gifts and savings to set up, quickly, a good practice. Furthermore, Daisy was too young and proud to doubt her husband's fidelity. She refused to be one of those wives who tagged along just to keep an eye on their husbands.

But when Mmma suggested in 1961 that she apply to leave for Hong Kong, no one, least of all her, mentioned any of these reasons for her earlier decision to stay behind. Mmma was too honest to shirk her share in that decision. She could not be certain she would have accompanied her husband even if they had had the money or if he had urged her to. She recalled her difficulty in imagining leaving the kids behind, which everyone had insisted was best for the young ones. She too had assumed that she could never cope with the kids, not she who had never even had to wash a diaper. She had agreed she could only be a financial burden rather than any help to Papa while abroad:

given her English and lack of work experience, who in the U.S. would hire her? The world had called Eddie a man with capacity and her, a woman with looks. And she had readily agreed: why work when your husband did not need nor want you to?

Fact Two: Mmma had not joined the work force during the Great Leap Forward of the late 1950s. All over China, cadres from the lane organizations were going from door to door to persuade in-laws and husbands to help Liberate Women from the Shackles of House Chores. My parents instructed servants to fend off the propaganda teams by announcing that the young mistress was indisposed. When the movement lasted longer than expected and hiding began to interfere with my parents' social life, a medical certificate of a heart condition had to be arranged.

Eventually, Papa had to pretend to hire Mmma. So, for about half a year, we watched the two of them leaving for work together, Papa with his black leather case and Mmma, a cloth bag holding her book and knitting. As the movement went on, fewer and fewer female friends and relatives stopped by during the week. They had become teachers, shop assistants, and clerks. One, tired of her husband's infidelity, took off with her two sons to teach high school in Inner Mongolia. Once every few years, this friend brought back more parched but ruddier cheeks along with tales of hardship, such as learning to wipe yourself with the stalks of plants we had never heard of.

When we reminded Mmma of her earlier dread over partaking in her friends' adventures, she seldom mentioned the real reason that had held her back, a reason she knew never to mention except in the privacy of home: after what they did to her people, Mmma had vowed to never work for the Communists. But she did not remind us of this reason because she did not feel she could deny in good conscience the many other points Papa was making. Daisy was not like any of her women friends, not the ones who had joined the People's work force during the Great Leap Forward nor the ones now holding jobs in colonial Hong Kong.

She had been more pampered as a daughter.

She was too idealistic and difficult to get along with.

Her English was not as good.

She was better looking, which could cause hazards when dealing with lusty bosses and colleagues.

Mmma was too honest to deny that work — meaning paid work outside home — had remained an intimidating mystery to her. So she worked harder to prove to herself that she had more self-discipline and fewer personal needs than anyone thought. Food became too rich for her to digest unless it was obvious that no one else upstairs was going to touch it. Underneath the custom-made silk robes by the head tailor at Bond Street — the most exclusive clothing store in downtown Shanghai and the only appropriate place for the wife of someone in Eddie's position — Daisy wore her few changes of raggedy underwear. Every morning from 9:00 to 12:00, you would find her at her desk with a dictionary, ploughing through the complete works of Balzac, Dickens. Then she'd join Ahma or whoever was assigned to wax the floor. Polishing the baseboard became Mmma's specialty. "Good exercise for stomach muscles, and patience, and precision," Mmma would claim as she pulled on the surgical gloves my father no longer needed to protect her manicured hands.

Daisy worked quietly and steadily for five more years to build up confidence in her ability to find and hold a job in Hong Kong, if and when she got her exit permit. But the Cultural Revolution caught her before she filled out her application.

I was too young — and busy with my fear of losing the mother I loved — to record any of the things Daisy did to expand her work record. Looking back, it seems that one such entry could be set during the summer of 1961, when my parents made serious plans for Papa to leave China and reestablish himself in Hong Kong.

Volume after volume of hardbacked books with photographs of

body parts sliced, clamped, or sewn up arrived from England. To study for the board he would have to pass if and when he got his permit to leave for Hong Kong, Papa made arrangements to take the afternoons off for a whole season. When I return to that summer, I see Mmma spending her mornings quietly plodding over the pages he had gone through the previous day, so later in the afternoons she might mentally follow the graphics when he reviewed, aloud, the surgical procedures he had memorized from these pages. At the end of the review, she could reassure him with her dimple if not actual words that, once again, he had got it all down. Only the occasional slight twitch of Daisy's fingers folded on her lap gave away her excitement as she listened to Eddie calling out the names of one instrument after another and watched his long, soap-bleached hands making incisions and knots in the air. It was almost as if she could barely keep her right hand from reaching out to touch his, as it stretched in her imagination to hand him the tools he needed.

By the end of this summer session, Mmma personally organized a surprise party for Papa. She encouraged us to draw a diploma modeled after the sheepskin he had earned from St. John's. She let us all chip in for the leather case which my lofty mother had to ask a foreign friend to smuggle in. And she arranged to have us skip school so that we could get all dolled up and wait in sweet anticipation with our carefully wrapped gifts at the upstairs small dining room for him to return home for lunch.

Unfortunately, I don't have a happy ending to this story. Papa never got his permit and never got around to applying a second time.

Another entry for Mmma's work record would start in the following winter, when a *Bastard* important enough to require bodyguards invited Papa to a banquet in a section of the Peace Hotel closed to the public. This Bastard, as my father called all the plainclothes men from the Public Security Bureau, laid out a deal Eddie did not feel he could afford to reject: a weekly report on who said what in his dealings with West-ern diplomats and bankers in return for a tacit promise that the Peo-ple's Government would never close down his clinic and that he could with impunity continue to have his patients channel abroad local cur-rency and bring in merchandise he fancied but could not get in the People's market.

My parents were not entirely surprised by the offer. They had always speculated that the Public Security Bureau had let Papa and a few others continue to work for the Western diplomats and bankers only because it needed them to cover the real agents it had planted in the consulates and banks. Unfortunately, death had recently claimed one of the agents, thus turning Papa and a few of his friends into possible candidates in the eyes of the Bastards.

"Might as well," Papa sighed. The political risk of refusing their deal was too great. He would be out of work. He could become the target of one of those movements which the Party was always cooking up but from which he'd so far escaped.

Mmma disagreed.

"Make yourself useless to them," Mmma urged: "Show them you are a doctor, so politically naive that you do not know how to take the hint on what the Bastards want passed on to your patients. Show the Bastards that no one ever cares to talk politics with you, that all know you only hobnob with them for their money, wine, and food."

But Eddie was never the stereotypical doctor. Eddie was a man of catholic taste, an avid reader of history, philosophy, politics, as well as Graham Greene and Le Carré.

"Let them close down the clinic," Mmma argued: "We'll sell the house and live on our savings."

But what would Papa do then? There was nothing he dreaded more than boredom. What was life without parties and books, which he was sure to lose without foreign connections? He'd have to give up his car, head nurse, . . . no more eating out at restaurants, nor trips to scenic places because there would be no money to keep it all up.

"Maybe," she suggested hopefully: "after the Bastards finally realize how useless you are to them, they will let us leave China."

"Don't be naive," Papa argued.

He was probably right, she agreed. But it would still be worth trying. Even failing would be better than cooperating with the Bastards out of fear of losing things you only thought you needed.

Easier said than done, Papa countered. Have you ever been poor? Do you know what it is like to be a nobody? What it was like to work to get where he stood!

Daisy swallowed and fumed. She worked harder at proving how little she needed to live on, how much this slow self-killing out of fear was costing us all.

A third entry for Daisy's work record brings to mind the many Sundays Eddie spent reminiscing about his medical glory. My mother taught me to listen for the nervous tap of Papa's fingers on the cigarette which, at the first mention of the word "surgery," he would automatically peel from the inside of his lower lip where it ordinarily dangled. I love those long, soap-bleached fingers, soft and strong as I've only seen in a few pianists and artisans. *Sexy*, I remember thinking once, long before I'd come across the word, when watching my father stitching up a cut on someone's knee. Thirty-some years later, the same fingers looked so ready for action, folded underneath the white sheet when the man at the funeral house pulled it away. The thought of these fingers still jolts me into a panic: what if, in spite of the autopsy, my father was still alive when cremated?

I think the tapping on his cigarette reminded Mmma of that hole in his heart left open by his idle surgeon's hands, a hole he tried in vain to fill with women, food, wine, watches, cameras, hi-fi speakers, hair dryers, anything and everything others could not get from the People's market but he would — with the help of his foreign patients and out of that generous raise they had promptly offered for his service as their family physician. It reminded Mmma of that noise Papa made on his Underwood typewriter on Sunday mornings, two white sheets sandwiching a piece of blue carbon paper so that he would have a record of those conversations with his diplomat or banker patients he was diligently fabricating, impromptu, for the Bastards from the Public Security Bureau. *The work of a genius,* he claimed, admiring the pages of "information" he'd concocted to bait the Bastards. None of it, he reassured Mmma, could bring real harm to any of his diplomat and banker patients.

I learned the contour of my mother's thoughts from watching her grind her own often freshly lit cigarettes into the ashtray as she watched Papa tap, chase, buy, and type. It was almost as if his idling made her fingers burn for work. And yet she felt that, given her work record, she had no option but to stub that urge out as fast as she could.

Years later, standing daily in front of the window, clutching a cup of hot water and waiting against hope for the return of my father from prison, my mother blamed herself for not having worked harder against that fear orchestrating the tapping and typing of Papa's fingers, for having too quickly stubbed out her own urge to live according to the dictates of her conscience.

So she set herself to work. She took in a 6-month-old infant and provided 24-hour care for it for the next 5 years. She earned 25 yuan a month — two-thirds of what she herself had paid Ahfen but the same as Ahfen's wage from her new, Revolutionary employer. She used the money to buy the vitamins and medications she prayed the prison guards would accept on Papa's behalf on the 15th of every month. This was the only way for her to know for sure, from his signature on the receipt the guards handed back to her, that he was still alive, and might survive yet another 30 days. She developed a complicated system for soaking, brushing, and bleaching soiled diapers, which all three of her daughters would later use for their children. She swapped new tricks with Ahfen on laundering and housecleaning so that after Papa was politically rehabilitated and there was again money and needs and government consent to hire servants, she would tell them quietly that she preferred to do her own, in her own way.

She did more.

I see my parents on the first nights of Papa's release from prison, their fingers locked across the twin beds pulled tightly together, as they relived the ritual interrogations Papa had to undergo each time the power behind the Shanghai Public Security Bureau changed hands during the years of the Cultural Revolution. She burned with him under the glaring spotlights designed to keep him awake for 48, sometimes 72, hours at a stretch. She cringed with him under the weight of physical blows never delivered, never needed because of the unspoken threat that they could, at any minute, issue from any of those able-bodied men taking shifts to loom around the stool to which he'd been shackled. She pressed his fingers to both help him along and pull him back, as he fabricated, retracted, refabricated, and re-retracted under pressure his dealings with the former Chief of the Public Security Bureau.

During those first nights, Daisy lived through every single one of those interrogations with Eddie, without the help of his usual eloquence as a storyteller, without any of the colors and sounds he had taken such pride in supplying when recounting his childhood, post-doctoral days, and surgical glories. Instead, she let the random words he managed between his sobs lead them both back through his ordeals. With empathy and patience, she enticed him to go further back so that he might eventually come out with an account where things made relative sense and from which he could emerge with some dignity and hope.

After the initial shock of homecoming, my father always claimed that the real ticket to surviving his time in prison was his ability to fabricate and then destroy evidence of his "multiple services" to foreign government agencies under the "prompting" of the former Chief of Shanghai Public Security Bureau. This made sense; it was common knowledge that the faction working for the Gang of Four was intent on punishing the former Chief for keeping a file containing evidence of the risqué, third-rate movie-star days of Mao's wife in the Shanghai of the 1930s. Papa's potential for bearing witness to the *evidence* he produced against the former Chief made him valuable to the cohorts of Mao's wife. His power to dispute the *evidence* he had himself fabricated made him equally valuable for the foes of Mao's wife in their struggle to regain power and reinstitute the Chief.

With bitter sarcasm, my father named his six-year incarceration a "People's witness-protection program." Neither were the other ironies of his incarceration lost on us. On the day of his release, the People's Court had Papa sign two pieces of paper, both hastily issued to give his incarceration an appearance of legality: a warrant for his arrest and a prison sentence for illegal exchange of foreign currency and purchase of foreign goods. Irony One: Papa was punished for the very things for which the Bastards had originally led him to believe he would enjoy immunity in return for his weekly reports. Irony Two: the People's verdict made no mention of his connection with the Bastards, even though Papa could easily have been persecuted for having offered them false reports on his foreign diplomat and banker patients during the pre-Cultural Revolution years, and even though his supposed connection with the former Chief of the Public Security Bureau was obviously at the heart of all the interrogations, all conducted with equal rigor and violation of human rights by all the powers fighting to control the Bureau throughout the Cultural Revolution.

My father always claimed that the change of faces each time his *crime* had to be reexamined was how he kept track of the tide of political change going on outside the prison. It took all of his surgeon's training in observing and storing details for him to keep up with this perpetual revision of his crime throughout the six years. He had to remember all his *confessions* during the previous round until he could methodically undo them for the next group in power.

"It would have made a great novel," Papa concluded.

Watching my idealistic mother listen to Papa recount his prison glories, I often wondered if she would be busy stubbing her cigarette again, had she not quit smoking at the beginning of the Cultural Revolution. I knew that the sight of Papa's long fingers still made her burn for work. I also knew that by then, she had learned to imagine along with him many other possible uses than surgery for those hands. China had just opened its bamboo curtain since Nixon's visit, and my parents along with our relatives and friends all over China had begun to hope again. In one version, they pictured him typing a memoir, or a novel titled *Our Man in Shanghai*, while providing live-in care for the rich, old or young, in the United States.

I also knew that if my idealistic Mmma still had a cigarette at hand to grind, she would not do it out of her contempt for Papa's readiness to perform according to the dictates of political powers. I had seen my undemonstrative mother reach out to steady my father's hands when he described, with more colors and sounds at every recount, the ritual interrogations and the depth and scope of his fabrications. Her gesture said: no one, herself included, had a right to judge him until they had gone through what Papa had. She could only guess what she would have done in his circumstances and pray that she would listen to her conscience when the time came. She was grateful that Papa's three-step pragmatism had guided him home, alive. Instead of fighting him, she would fight for her own action, against her own fear that she did not have the strength to carry out what she knew was the right thing to do. Her way of taking responsibility: an invitation to him to work with her on what had trapped them previously.

I knew that if Mmma had a cigarette to grind, she would not do so through fear that she lacked ability to work for a living. She had earned a living for close to five years. She knew the work she had put in to help my father recover from the prison nightmares and to hum and swing again for *so much living to do*.

Rather, she'd grind her cigarette out of impatience for an opportunity to expand on this new work record.

"Let me go first," Mmma started to suggest again during the mid-1970s, as more and more friends and relatives began to obtain permits to leave for the States.

Our reaction: The same reservations. The same fears.

But this time, Mmma sat down and wrote her sister a letter. No more checks, no more packages of food and clothing, Mmma told her sister. Find her a position as a live-in caretaker instead. For proof of her will and capability, she enclosed a picture of herself with the child she had raised from infancy.

Mmma kept on writing and asking.

An invitation came from her sister for a tour through the States. Worry about work later, her sister said; no one would hire her until they had seen her in person.

But Mmma never got around to use the letter to file her application for an exit permit. A few weeks earlier, Mmma had to be rushed to the emergency ward. The doctors thought she had appendicitis. But cancer was what they found. I have often wondered if she would have spoken more about her *slight indigestion*, and if her cancer could have been caught earlier, if she had been less anxious to convince herself and us that she was physically fit to take up the challenge, if and when the invitation came and she was issued her permit to leave.

By 1974, we all knew that if my mother were to be given such a permit, she would have waved away all our reservations and boarded a plane within the week. Not because she did not understand the risks involved. She anticipated dire physical and financial conditions. But she understood more the cost of living without hope. I knew exactly how she had planned her new life once she crossed over. She would wash, scrub, make herself useful, hire herself out. I knew that was how she would fight my aunt's insistence that there was no need for her sister to do any of that work. And I knew it was this new life on which she had set her heart, as she stoically underwent all the therapies rumored to have worked, from monthly chemo which left her drained, in bed for days at a stretch, to consuming powdered dry seahorses or huge quantities of pureed asparagus which made her retch so violently that you expected to see her insides tumbling out after the yellow-green bile.

Mmma was determined to live for a chance to make it across, to work toward the day when Papa, then us, would be able to join her. She hung on for over two years, for a chance to prove to herself and the world her ability to find and hold a job.

My mother withdrew into complete silence about a month before she died. She could no longer trust her voice to hide the pain eating at every inch of her body, when she would wake for a few minutes from one dose of painkillers pumped through her veins and before the next could be administered.

When I think of that month, my memory is often crowded with the sight of her swallowing as she drifted in and out of consciousness. And I burn with the rage I knew was parching my mother's throat. My mother died knowing that, to the world, all this work I have just spent page after page writing about was non-work. And she died angry at fate for denying her a chance to set the record straight.

But instead of the paralysis of rage, I think my mother would have me ask: would all her daughters have struggled for an advanced degree and a career after turning 35 in the U.S. if we had not known at heart that we are the daughters of a working mother, not just the grand-daughters of an Exception?

I cannot help wondering: now that I've set some of my mother's work record in writing, am I any better prepared to help myself or my daughter work on a life which is not trapped by a standard medley on what constitutes good living and how lovers should go about living out their dreams.

I don't know.

I can hope and try.

My anger at fate for depriving me of a chance to call my mother a working woman, in person, is too deep in me to be squelched by the mere telling of a story. The guilt of never having realized in time to tell her about my understanding of her work before we parted will never leave me. I know both will come to taint everything I do and say around my daughter. But I also know that my mother would want me to fight back, to let myself and my daughter go.

Using her self as a template, my mother has taught me that the cost of living in fear and regret is too high. It seems that, with those dreadful memories of her fighting my father, she may have also left me and my daughter a manual of labor, on how to help members of a love ensemble let the best *of* one another bring the best *out* of one another. The latter is where she would like us to focus our energy, to listen more carefully. I think it is for this work that she left me her Mona Lisa smile with her single-dimpled, twinkle-eyed, slightly tilted face, turned to the left.

4

Yimin

移民

Telling Immigrant Stories

Writing about Haopo, Ahfen, and Mmma makes me think that to tell an *immigrant* story is to take up the challenge of explaining "what-happened" in the context of why we have often found it so difficult to talk about our experiences. It is learning to start with minute but attentive steps: weighing those questions which often appear so mundane yet so impossible to answer, probing how and why I remain dissatisfied with the ways I have been handling each question, and teasing out new possibilities, new answers. It is trying to proceed with the hope that maybe, just maybe, if I keep chiseling away at these questions, I might eventually find my way in, down, where I have scarcely allowed myself to tread, so that my loved ones can help me go back in order to finally move forward.

Where Are You From?

I get nervous when strangers ask me where I am from. I think I am supposed to say "China" and then add, "Shanghai." But I'm always reluctant to do so.

A side of me is still trapped by memories of the commotion my wool pleated skirt and white cotton knee socks had caused in the midst of a Shanghai winter and against a sea of pedestrians in padded coats and pants:

> "*A little Foreigner!*" *People would nudge, point and call out.*
> "*A little Soviet!*"
> "*A White Russian!*"
> "*A fake!*" *Some would conclude as I got close enough for them to observe, aloud, my too dark hair, eyes, skin.*
> "*A half-caste?*"
> "*A little Overseas Chinese?*"
> "*Not really!*"
> "*. . .?*"

Such reactions troubled but did not surprise me, for I too grew up seeing the world as a place populated by what mathematicians call natural
numbers. I imagined a world where each natural number stood for the
people from a particular country. According to Papa's schema, this
world looked something like this: No. 1 stands for Americans, No. 2 for
the people of Britain, . . . According to my school textbooks, the ordering would be the reverse: No. 1 stands for the Chinese, No. 2 for the
Soviets, . . . In this world of natural numbers, there was nothing more
devastating than being given the status of a zero, a negative number, a
fraction or a decimal: appearing UnChinese (UnAmerican) or partially
Chinese (halfway American).

Not Three Nor Four, as we say, in Shanghai dialect, of people difficult to classify and thus deemed lacking in authenticity.

I learned the tyranny of natural numbers by growing up in a city
historians have named the *Other China*. Whether it was during the Qing
Dynasty, the Republic of China under Chiang Kai-shek, or the People's
Republic of China under Mao's Bamboo Curtain and then, under
Deng's Great Leap Westward, the nomenclature — Shanghai — stands
for the not-China of China, a negative number if you will, or, at most,
a decimal of the Real China. The latest political joke in China goes
something like this: "Why is it that no one nowadays can follow what
is being said at the Central Committee meetings? Because all the leaders are natives of Shanghai and speak Standard Chinese with a heavy
local accent." My Shanghai friends tell the joke with equal parts pride
and worry. They can't but feel proud of the current political clout of
the Shanghai gang. They are nevertheless concerned because the voice
of History cautions: "How long will China let Shanghai lead it away
from itself?"

Even in this city called the Other China, I grew up seeing myself as
its most unnatural daughter. A number too irrelevant even to have
deserved the status of a decimal or the fraction: a Half-Caste or an Overseas Chinese. Only a "Not really!" followed by an even more puzzled
and disapproving ". . .?" Memories of my non-status in the eyes of my

fellow citizens make me nervous when strangers ask where I am from. Because I learned along with the rest of the world to count with natural numbers first, a side of me longs to be counted as one. I worry that to admit I am from Shanghai, China would only invite attention to where I might appear to have fallen short of others' expectations for what a person from Shanghai or China was supposed to look and act like. I dread having my so-called lack of authenticity exposed.

My first few months in the U.S. left another set of memories to make me nervous when people ask where I am from. When I arrived in January of 1981, there were just eight students from the People's Republic of China studying in the university I was enrolled in. (I got the number from a newspaper article after a reporter interviewed all eight of us.) We were frequently invited to talk about life in China under Mao at mini-conferences organized by the university, where we were often introduced as "ambassadors from behind the Bamboo Curtain!" My new designation turned out to be just as taxing as my old self-designation as the most unnatural daughter of the Other China:

"The Chinese do drink coffee!"
"No, they prefer tea."
"Actually, green tea, if you offer it. They are so polite, you know."

I imagined myself the direct cause of such conversations, conversations taking place simply because various people had seen me choosing a different beverage on the occasion each had met me.

I was, after all, the daughter of a man who took pride in his catholic taste, a taste which had caused him a great deal of trouble in China but a taste which I thought should help me thrive in the U.S. Indeed, instead of being (as People from the Communist Bloc are supposed to have been) overwhelmed by the sheer variety of options in the Free Market, I was delightfully surprised. Thanks to Papa's special connections with Western diplomats, I recognized enough brand names on the store shelves to sustain me through my first shopping trip: Maxwell (coffee), Carnation (condensed milk), Del Monte (fruit cocktail), Sunkist (oranges), Kraft (cheese), Quaker Oats (hot cereal), Lipton (tea). . . . Even as I put the familiar products into my cart, I vowed to expand my horizons and systematically sample all the available brands — within my budget, of course.

My rite of passage.

I loved going to Baskin-Robbins for the same reason, to celebrate the wealth of choice through its 31 flavors. Open-minded sampling was also how I managed my first term in the English department. I imbibed with equal conscientiousness the varieties of approaches offered by the professors. To 18th Century British Novels, I applied Marx's labor theory and the professor's constant reminder that "it was all about money." In a survey course on Contemporary American Literature, I learned to trace the rebellion of the id against the super ego. And when reading the metaphysical poets, I worked on my fluency at something called paradoxes.

Waiting to exit China, I had conjured up from years of diligently reading *Reader's Digest, Time,* and *Newsweek* a vision of the Mall of America where the very abundance of choice would somehow release me from having to deliberate over the political and cultural significance of my choices. However, my new designation as *the ambassador from behind the Bamboo Curtain!* made me hesitant to reveal my love for cheese, *Saga Bleu* — my mother's favorite. I was reluctant to order beef, let alone beef cooked rare — the way my father took his. I dreaded the comment my words and actions might provoke: "I didn't know the Chinese eat . . .!" I worried over the conclusions my performance at various graduate seminars might lead others to draw: "The Chinese believe in (have no use for) . . . criticism!"

I resented my duty as a stand-in for the Real Chinese, as people used to call the eight of us to distinguish us from students born and raised in Hong Kong or Taiwan. Being treated as the Voice of Real China (!) made me think of times as recent as the previous year, when, in 1980, I had to sit through a whole lunch watching five of my fellow graduate students at the Shanghai Foreign Language Institute convince a visiting professor from the States that I was "not really Chinese." ("Banana" — yellow skinned but white inside — was the epithet they would have used if they had heard of it.) A side of me found the whole incident farcical. I perceived their vehemence as yet another expression of their pitiful need to explain to themselves how and why someone like me — one of the two women in a class of 13 picked from the whole country through a month-long entrance examination and the only one without any undergraduate training — could deserve any grade higher than a C. I saw it as just another way of stating their rumor that it was my father — the foreign doctor — who had really written all my term papers or their reiteration to my face that it was my Westernized manner alone which had earned me my grades. Nevertheless, another side of me was perturbed by their vehemence: It saddened me to be reminded that so many of my contemporaries perceived me as so utterly UnChinese.

Memories of such occasions warned me to proceed with caution in my newly acquired authority to speak in the U.S. as the Voice of Real China (!): they reminded me that I could never in good conscience pass as a Real Chinese, nor speak for a majority of my contemporaries from Shanghai, China. I felt overwhelmed by my potential power to make strangers walk away from a brief encounter assuming that all people from Shanghai or China would somehow look, think, and act the way I had on that particular occasion. I was frustrated by my new mission: all I wanted was to act and speak as one person from China and to be accepted as no more, no less, than just that. But that seemed just as impossible here in the land of Individual Rights as it had been for me in the land of Communism.

A cultural shock for which no one had prepared me.

Because of both sets of memories, when asked where I am from, my first impulse is to reject both my old designation as a "fake" and my new designation as the "real" Chinese by saying something like this: "I am from the Shanghai I knew, which may very well be quite different from the Shanghai a lot of others have come from. In fact, in the eyes of these others, I often appear Not Three Nor Four. This is in part because I am from a long line of *immigrant* daughters intent on *yi* — fusing, confusing, and diffusing — the traditions upheld by many of their contemporaries who were also living in this city called the Other China."

But I seldom do. I doubt my reply, wordy as it is, would make much sense to anyone besides myself. I am more certain of my need to identify myself as an unnatural daughter of the Other China than of how to do that in actual conversation.

I want to acknowledge my dual alien residency in my home city because I am convinced that natural numbers — People from Shanghai or Real Chinese — are idealizations forged by a very exclusive group in their own images: mathematics has long illustrated the necessity of moving beyond the confines of natural numbers. I am equally convinced that, in spite of the differences between myself and some of my contemporaries, I am no less, no more, a person from Shanghai, China, than any of the Real ones. In fact, because I have been made so acutely aware of my differences from those who claim their own authenticity, I have come to know intimately the national norms they take pride in personifying. In this sense, I am the producer and product of at least one kind of Chinese or Shanghai experience, the experience of living under the tyranny of the nomenclature of the Chinese or the People from Shanghai. I am in part what I am because I once lived in Shanghai, China.

Yet, the precise answer, "I am from that Shanghai, China, where many considered me a Not Three Nor Four," would make no sense to others unless I flesh it out with concrete stories from my past. But how does one come up with the right stories?

During the earlier years of my immigration, I blamed my U.S. audience for my difficulties in telling stories from my past. Shocked by the eagerness of some to receive me as the Voice of Real China, I construed from their reactions a U.S. Audience just as consumed by an anxiety for "authenticity" and fixed forms as some of my fellow graduate students at the Shanghai Foreign Language Institute. I convinced myself that trying to tell a story against the grain of the stories told by and about the more "authentic" Chinese could be no more a simple matter here, in this land of freedom and opportunity, than it had been for me, my Grandmother, Ahfen, or my mother back in the Middle Kingdom.

My three-step pragmatism reminded me of my own adolescent irritation toward the way my elders had chosen to tell and not tell their stories: Ahfen's ghost walk, Mmma's dry swallows, and Haopo's refusal to give me the straight answer I was looking for. It warned me that my U.S. Audience would have the same impatience toward my effort to tell my experience as a Not Three Nor Four from Shanghai, the same inability to hear what I have to tell.

To prepare myself for the criticism I feared would soon be applied to me, my pragmatism urged me to listen carefully to my U.S. professors and fellow graduate students when they critiqued the writings they did not like. I made a list of taboos for U.S. storytelling: A writer who wears her differences on her sleeves, who has a chip on her shoulder, who does not know how and when to get to the point, who is didactic — telling rather than showing, who is dogmatic — arguing rather than seducing. . . . I watched every nonverbal expression made by my listeners to second guess the content of their silent critique.

But ultimately none of these deliberations seemed to make any difference to how I behaved whenever people asked me where I was from. It was almost as if my tongue knew something my mind did not want to acknowledge: I could no more be a Hemingway or an Emily Dickinson than be my Haopo, Ahfen, or Mmma. My tongue announced to me what I could not not-do for the sake of my sanity: I could not not-tell stories. My Haopo, Ahfen, and Mmma had left me too many stories of the cost of living under the dictates of natural numbers. I knew of too many situations where to tell a story admitting to one's having acted or thought like a Not Three Nor Four could incur severe political consequences. I had had to watch during one political movement after another too many Not Three Nor Fours suffer the humiliation of having to hide or deny thoughts and actions central to their sense of being and integrity. I could not wait until I had perfected my style of storytelling to begin telling stories about Shanghai's Not Three Nor Fours: I owe it to these people and to myself to tell more about that past.

My tongue went wild no matter how much my three-step pragmatism cautioned it beforehand and reprimanded it afterwards. It keeps on spinning out stories. Yet, hundreds of attempts afterwards, I am still struggling for a better way of telling these stories.

Through the years, I have learned not to let my projection of a generic U.S. Audience confine how I work on my answers. I realize that there are many in my life — my daughter, husband, new friends, and new relatives — who genuinely want to know more about that time and place from which I came before starting my life in the U.S. They and I both know that how I perceive and talk about "where I come from" has profound consequences for where our relationships might go. This is the audience I want to work with. They can help fire my desire to go back, if I learn to take seriously the questions they pose with words, gestures, and silences, so that together, we might move forward.

But choosing to work with people who care and therefore deserve to know more about my past has not released me from — has only put me more squarely face to face with — my difficulties. The question of where I am from is difficult to answer because it is always caught up in questions of where I am now, where I hope to go. I get nervous when asked this question because it tests my sense of the connections between who I was, who I have become, and who I aspire to be. Everything

I do here is informed by everything I did back there. Everything I think and say about back then is in turn informed by everything I think and feel about myself and my life over here. Every day, I have new thoughts on this life I'm building with my daughter and husband. Accordingly, I must constantly change my understanding of my past, of how I go about telling it.

Reliving my shock when Ahfen told me, in 1996, of her past as a smuggler during World War II, I wonder if the challenge of having to constantly revise how one recalls one's life is a part of the reward (rather than the burden, as I used to think) of immigrant life. It is a privilege Ahfen has worked hard to earn through her refusal to lock her life and my life at the point where we had last met. Telling me about her life as a smuggler had been Ahfen's way of reminding me of the changes which had taken place since I left China in 1981, changes making her ready to tell, and me ready to hear, this story. It was also Ahfen's way of reminding me that, in the years ahead, she expects new turns in our lives and thus, new needs for both of us to come up with new stories from our pasts for each other when we next meet. If I intend to venture into new crossings, I ought to actively seek out these needs rather than dreading them. Instead of trying to pin my answer down, I ought to review old answers to figure out new ways of seeing and talking about "where I am from."

Recalling my shock over my new designation as the Voice of Real China when first arriving in the U.S. has also made me understand that everything I do or say (do not do or say) concerning every ordinary detail of my daily existence — what beverage I drink or how I interpret and repeat the stories my relatives like to pass around — is always also a story about where I am from, where I am, where I hope to go. Instead of looking for a single, all-encompassing story to illustrate where I am from, I might start from the seemingly insignificant incidents of everyday life and try out variations and collages of little stories.

Let me try again.

Do the Chinese Drink Coffee?

Do the Chinese drink coffee? People were always asking after they found out I was from Shanghai, China and upon hearing me accept or decline coffee, especially when green tea was also being offered.

When I take this question to the lives of those Chinese I knew back in Shanghai, it seems that taste and distaste for coffee are often as much matters of economics and politics as of palate or habit. I have too many beverage stories to tell about the people from my past. I know too many people who see the drinking and not drinking of coffee, green tea, or hot water as essential to their sense of where they've come from and where they hope to be heading. Their lives suggest that, instead of asking "Do the Chinese drink coffee?" — which could only lead us in a mad chase after nomenclatures such as the Chinese, the Chinese beverage or the Chinese palate — we might try out some different questions: "How and why has someone in China chosen to drink or not drink coffee?" "How and why is someone from China interested in telling a story about that decision?"

In the household where I grew up, coffee was served on all occasions which involved my father — during breakfast and to his guests after dinner. On the list of things confiscated, the Red Guards counted six coffeepots: glass, silver, stainless steel, aluminum, electric, large silver. Papa had different names for them: percolator, drip, espresso-maker.

The only other beverage Papa and his guests would drink was tea, meaning, needless to say, black tea, which we called Red Tea in Chinese. Tea was never brought to us in a tea bag sitting by the side of a pot of lukewarm water. The tea I grew up drinking was steeped in linen-cozied porcelain pots pre-rinsed with — Please! — boiling water. Tea was mostly served in the afternoon with cake, cookies, or dimsum and poured into cups perched on top of saucers with milk added before and sugar, after. A tradition learned from movies, books, and missionary schools.

Coffee was sometimes politely declined, with a sheepish smile, by some of our Chinese guests. *The green tea drinkers*, we labeled them: people who admitted to "have not learned how to" drink tea or coffee, an expression we use in Chinese to describe things we don't eat or drink out of necessity or choice. We understood that people remained green tea drinkers often because they had "not learned how to" drink milk.

Green tea in our household meant Long Jing — new crop tender tips — the only kind Haopo drank. Never Jasmine or Ou Long: the former was just a sham using the scent of the flower to disguise the inferior quality of the tea leaves mixed with stems, while the latter is not even really a green tea. Neither curbed the fire element in your system like quality Long Jing. My sisters and I always said when laughing at the popularity of Jasmine or Ou Long in the U.S.: "What could you expect from these stupid foreigners!" Green tea, of course, was served in tall porcelain bowls with matching lids, bowls nestled inside the half inch deep hollows at the center of matching saucers with two fresh olives perched on the rim during Chinese New Year time.

Downstairs, they called coffee *that brown stuff*. Ahma, who never hesitated to sample anything brought down from upstairs, claimed that it smelt and tasted just like Chinese herbal medicine, which Papa called *mudwater*. Ahfen cautioned that coffee was bad for your body, added to the fire element! Ahfen said the same about fire element when I worried about my zits or came down with a cold: "All that coffee, tea, milk, and iced water you drink!" So I would, still do, switch to green tea whenever I have a cold. The tea Ahfen and Ahma drank was a brown, cold beverage stewed out of toasted wheat. That in the summer and hot water in the winter was what the servants had "learned how to drink," even though most of our servants came from the province renowned for its Long Jing and grew up in houses with tea bushes in the back. I did not realize the bitter irony of their choice beverage until after being assigned in school to memorize a classic poem in which the speaker lamented: When will it be my turn to wear the clothes I weave and sew?

I had to wait until I turned ten to be granted the few drops of coffee I had been watching my sister savor with great fanfare for the last four years. Like most kids who grew up with coffee-drinking parents, I coveted those drops, which grew in proportion with my age, for the status they brought. And for years I too tried to counter its bitter taste with inordinate amounts of milk and sugar. But mostly, I enjoyed this sweetened drink because of the aroma those few drops of coffee could add to that pint of milk I had to finish before I could leave the breakfast table. There was nothing I detested more than the odor of freshly boiled milk, the only kind served in our household out of concerns over pasteurization and over the local rumor that milk might have been diluted by water which was itself not safe for drinking unless boiled. Ahfen and Ahma taught me to notice the "beef stench" of hot milk from the way they held back their heads and held in their breath when pouring it.

My elders urged: "Drink up while it is still hot. Easier on your stomach this way!" They said the same about chicken broth, Chinese herbal medicine, or anything else considered rich or nutritious.

"Milk is good for you!" Papa insisted when I complained about being too old to need milk. I wonder what he would have said if he had known what I know now: I am lactose intolerant.

"Drink it down like medicine!" Haopo coaxed by setting the example every morning.

"So spoilt!" Mmma scolded when I got caught bribing my younger sister to finish my pint along with hers. Mmma then reminded us to think about all these other kids out there needing it, wanting it, but not fortunate enough to have it!

How could I not? I knew that Ahfen's monthly wage would not cover the cost of those eight pints of milk delivered every morning outside the gate. At the ice cream parlor where Haopo took us, I had seen parents sit and beam as their son, the little emperor, twirled the scalding milk around his mouth to figure out if this treat was really worth all that fuss. I knew I was supposed to consider it my double fortune that milk drinking was a daily chore rather than a rare treat for me and that I had coffee and sugar to turn this nasty but nutritious beverage into a real treat for my taste buds.

By 1961, I was old enough to have equal portions of coffee and milk, which, needless to say, now required three instead of two lumps of sugar. Every morning, I would dump in the sugar, knowing that there were no more than 12 such lumps in every four ounces, the monthly ration of every Chinese for years to come. Everything was rationed — rice, oil, cotton, meat, tobacco, toilet paper.

"I had this dream again," my mother would announce now and then at the breakfast table. Glad that my mother had yet another shopping spree — sans coupons — in her dream, we tried to guess from the depth of Mmma's dimple the variety and quantity of unrationed meat or sweets populating the stores of her dreamscape. I was often there to partake in the revelry triggered by Mmma's dream because I had figured out that thanks to the recent spread of hepatitis, "fatigue" had become the magic word for being allowed to skip school.

My mother had so many coupons to take care of that they required separate envelopes and a special drawer and careful inspection for expiration dates on every 9th, 14th, 19th, and 29th of the month. I read recently in an article that at least 30 million Chinese, perhaps even 40 million — "What is 10 million to the Chinese?" — died of starvation as a result of the Great Leap Forward to "Overtake Britain in per capita industrial production within 15 years!" A national famine prompting the Party to declare the nation under Three Years of Natural Calamities and to call on the heroic people of China to meet the revolutionary challenge of overcoming such natural calamities along with the betrayal of Soviet revisionists. Although I, along with the rest of the world inside or outside China, had to wait until after the death of Mao and the collapse of the Gang of Four to learn the number of deaths, I sensed the presence of that starvation as early as 1961 from the number of people eager to trade in their meat, oil, sugar, or cotton coupons for our rice coupons.

"Evil-doings," Mmma would sigh when staring at her drawerful of coupons. I knew she had in mind both the doings of government rationing and of us. We had surplus rice coupons because we had so much else to eat, thanks to the supply from Papa's foreign patients and the black market Cook combed with Papa's exorbitant pay. We ended up with so much of the sugar, meat, oil, . . . coupons *robbed from children with more dire needs* that on the day before they expired, Mmma had to sometimes send several servants to different stores to use them up so as not to raise the rightful suspicions of the shop assistants.

By then, milk became strictly rationed only to nursing babies, the extremely old, and the seriously sick. Because of Papa's special status, our family was permitted four pints each day. To my great guilt-ridden relief, my daily load was cut to half.

"Enjoy, enjoy!" Papa would urge as I sweetened my coffee/milk with lump after lump of sugar. I measured the depth of his love by the gratification he got from seeing his family escape the fate of the country which had been forced to join diabetics like himself in settling for the bitter, watery aftertaste of artificial sweeteners.

"Hot water for me," Mmma insisted with a slight burp-like sound to remind everyone of her *condition*. Her stomach seemed more and more averse to tea or coffee as more and more coupons from people in more need than us found their way into her drawer. I would not fully appreciate this change in taste until having first watched my mother go back to coffee and tea during the mid-1960s after China had officially survived the Three Years of Natural Calamities and then, witnessed her return once again to hot water during the Cultural Revolution years, this time to keep pace with the deprivation her husband suffered behind prison bars.

My Number One Aunt had her theory on why it was *evil doing* to consume strong coffee or tea in times such as this. She believed that the acidic drinks would wash away all the body fat only a few could still afford to maintain. She would savor the sugar sweetened hot milk I willingly surrendered from my portion — my ticket to heaven, she assured me — as she brought us up to date on the number of pounds different relatives had continued to shed and the new tricks they had come up with for stretching the rationed goods.

My paternal aunt had yet another story to tell, which furthered my sense of guilt about the amount of milk and sugar I was adding to my coffee. Hers took place during the beginning of the Natural Calamities. My aunt and uncle had just come out of an evening movie during a French or Italian film festival. Thanks to all those national cultural exchange treaties which required the People's Government to showcase occasional foreign movies in Peking and Shanghai, I had the opportunity while growing up to watch great classics like *The Bicycle Thief* beautifully dubbed by famous Chinese actors who matched their words to the shape of the lips on the screen. The movie was good but left my uncle and aunt hungry. My aunt had a few rice coupons in her purse which they had hoped might buy them a snack before returning home. They walked several blocks of the busiest street of downtown Shanghai and could not find anything on sale in all the stores, all brightly lit, open, and fully staffed. Then they decided to turn back, realizing that the walk farther down would prove just as futile and make them even more hungry. No food at home either. "I've had it," my uncle announced as he and my aunt gulped down their freshly-boiled water to tide themselves through the long winter night. The next morning, he went and filed his application to leave China.

But none taught me more about the meaning of my coffee/milk/sugar drink than the two-year-old son of Yinyin, Ahfen's adopted daughter. The year was probably 1964, so the three years of natural calamities heroically fought by the Chinese people in spite of the betrayal of Soviet Revisionists was officially over. But folks in the "country of rice and fish" were still starving, as we could tell from Ahfen's red-rimmed eyes every time she received a letter from Yinyin. Finally, Haopo and Mmma sent along money for train tickets and an invitation to come and help around the house. Yinyin arrived with the boy while her husband tried to make ends meet with his elderly mother at home.

Alert and cocky, we all agreed about the boy as he followed Yinyin around, flashing his late autumn chilled bare behind through the maroon corduroy open-bottom pants we had bought him. "Do your father for us," we'd urge and laugh before the boy even started posturing. "Now, do your grandma," we'd ask after he had impersonated his father. And the boy would lean back with his tiny hand softly draped over his forehead and moan in the voice of an old lady: "I'm feeling so dizzy today. I could really use a bowl of life-saving sugar water."

Because of these memories, I always feel funny when others ask me how I like my coffee. I take my coffee straight, which puts my taste in sync with most of my friends and colleagues. Yet, I alone know that I only started this habit 15 years ago, because I found the dishwater variety served at most places in the States a little more tolerable when taken without milk and sugar. I also know that 15 years of practice still have not trained my mind to keep in step with my taste buds. Saying no to sugar and milk still does not seem quite right. It brings to mind this friend of mine, a man in his late 40s, sent to the States during the early 1980s on a one-term exchange program.

Every day during his whole stay, my friend would pack down three hard-boiled eggs at lunch. When others asked why or expressed their concern over his cholesterol level, my friend would answer that he felt obligated to eat one egg for every person he knew in China, where, at the time, eggs were still rationed. A side of me feels that I should be doing the same every time I am offered milk and sugar. Take two lumps of sugar for every grandmother of a boy like the son of Ahfen's adopted daughter. A quarter cup of milk with my coffee for every baby born during the Three Years of Natural Calamities. Another side of me feels that I should be switching to hot water altogether.

I am torn every time I drink my coffee, even though I know the China in my and my egg-eating friend's memory is no longer there for most people we knew then. Mao's Great Leap Forward has long since been replaced by Deng's Great Leap Westward. None of the people I used to know in China have problems obtaining milk, sugar, or eggs in

China's new free-market economy. In honor of my return home last Spring, Jing, my only remaining friend in China and a lover of antique malls, prepared a meal she promised would take us all the way down that memory lane. When coffee was brought out, it came with a sugar bowl and sweetened condensed milk in its original can. I watched her fill at least one third of my cup with that thick, dark-creamy liquid and then dump in two full scoops of white sugar before filling the cup up with coffee. And I described for her and her family a Vietnamese restaurant my husband and I liked to go to, the only place I knew in the States where coffee was still served *our way.*

Jing knew I took my coffee straight nowadays. Making me coffee *our way* was her way of honoring the Lu Family Restaurant, Jing's nickname for the hospitality of my parents. We watched one another's taste buds absorb the aftershock of our once familiar coffee/milk/sugar drink. And we watched her 19-year-old son frown over the contradictions he had sensed in our earlier complaints about all the good stuff we now had to turn down in honor of our middle-aged bodies and this poison we were savoring with such nostalgia. And we smiled at one another right through him.

We knew not to expect the boy to understand us, as we would not have expected my daughter or my husband to, if they had been in the room. This was the same boy, our smiles reminded one another, who had asked earlier, when Jing and I were going through some photos taken at the time of the Cultural Revolution: why is everyone wearing the same style shirt? Same color too, greyish blue, we had to inform him, since the color did not show in the black-and-white photographs. When I wrote to ask if there was any gift he would like me to bring over, this same boy had asked instead, when I arrived, that I take him to the Hard Rock Cafe newly opened in downtown Shanghai. Jing and I smiled because we could not decide whether we should feel happy or sad to see our past becoming so incomprehensible to our children. We had not wanted the same life for them, neither for ourselves. So why this feeling of air swelling up our chests and dryness shrinking our mouth glands when our children's eyes begin to wander in response to what they call our effort to guilt-trip them with our never ending stories of past hardships?

I wonder what this boy would say when asked if the Chinese drank coffee. His Shanghai is not my Shanghai, his China, not my China.

When I first arrived in the U.S., the espresso craze had not yet hit the country. My sisters and I were always commiserating over the phone: "Look at this dishwater these foreigners drink. So provincial!" (We were our worst Shanghai Best Family selves when some native-born acted up, when we felt snubbed.) I liked to believe that my sisters and I knew about coffee because we were the daughters of my father, a man who took pride in his catholic taste. But I knew that my father's taste in coffee had itself grown out of the China and U.S. he had lived in.

The first can of coffee I bought in the U.S. was, of course, the *good to the last drop* Maxwell my father had taught me to worship from the gleam in his eyes when he surveyed the cans bearing that name, bought duty-free through his diplomat patients and saved strictly for special occasions. However, even before I had time to finish the first can, I found myself lured away from the familiar looking red can by the also-familiar hum of the electric coffee bean grinder and the aroma of freshly ground quality coffee wafting from down the aisle. I was forced to admit that despite my father's residual fetish for Maxwell coffee — a souvenir from his own post-graduate days in the U.S. — my own taste buds had been indefinitely corrupted by all that quality African and Latin American coffee in abundant supply at the People's market throughout the 1960s.

I was old enough to remember the exact look of the biggest specialty food store in Shanghai during the time when my mother was having her recurring dream of shopping *sans*-coupons and when a cup of hot water on an empty stomach had driven my uncle to leave China. The grace of the hardwood, brass, glass, and marble counters in that specialty store would make the original Marshall Fields in downtown Chicago appear merely familiar rather than spectacular when I actually set foot into the latter 20 years after having read about it in *Sister Carrie*. The only difference was that, in the Shanghai specialty store of my adolescence, I and other customers had found display after display cases filled with sample goods with not-for-sale stickers in Chinese. As I waited for the rich aroma of coffee beans being ground to Mmma's order to rise above the scent of sticky syrup oozing from dried dates, I tried to imagine the nauseating effect of this unique combination on empty stomachs caught in a national famine.

For an extended period during the Three Years of Natural Calamities, coffee beans and dried dates seemed the only produce available on the People's market. Both were generously supplied in great abundance by our Brother African and Latin American Nations, a family affiliation for which Mao coined the term, The Third World. Both were faithfully supplied in return for the foreign aid the People's Government continued to send our Brother Nations in rivalry with our Arch-Enemies — the Russian Revisionists and the Western Imperialists — and in spite of our own Natural Calamities.

The People opened its arms to the dates, working out imaginative ways to substitute them for sugar in all sorts of recipes. (Later, the country would regret and resent with equal enthusiasm its own ingenuity, believing that we had imported a hepatitis epidemic with the dates and thus incurred a national health debt for which millions are still paying some 30 years later.) But very few Chinese besides my father had any use for the quality coffee beans. Every time I poured sugar and milk into the dark coffee brewed from freshly ground quality African or Latin American beans, I was reminded of the hundreds of people lined up in front of the half-dozen state owned coffee houses in Shanghai. They were the fortunate few waiting for a tiny piece of the cream cake in limited supply which could be bought without any ration coupons if one would also order a cup of coffee costing ten times more than the cake and about one sixth of the monthly paycheck of a Revolutionary

Proletarian. Peasants who had never tasted, nor cared for the taste of, either whipped cream or coffee sat down, after hours of waiting, next to Capitalists and High-Ranking Intellectuals who had learned to love both cream cake and coffee on the sidewalks of Paris. The former paid with money they had just earned by selling vegetables on the black market to the likes of the latter. All ate the cake. Almost none touched the coffee. A rare consensus in taste, achieved by the dictates of empty stomachs, accompanied by pockets overflowing with the People's currency but depleted of rationing coupons.

So tell me whether I was being Chinese, American, or a Chinese American Immigrant when I turned down coffee when the dishwater variety was served, when I craved a cup of strong coffee on the rare occasions when liquor-soaked cake layered with fresh cream was offered. Hold your answer, though, until I give you my family's recipe for Cultural Revolution coffee:

One new thermos with tight cork stoppers (preferably with metal
    casing including screw-on caps)
one cheesecloth bag (8 × 1.5 inches)
eight tablespoons of finely ground coffee
a kettle of water

Place coffee in bag, seal tightly with string. Slide bag into thermos. Bring water to rigorous boil. Pour immediately into thermos. Close thermos with cork (and metal cap). Let steep for three minutes (drink might taste bitter if allowed to stand longer).

The winter of 1972, the first six months after my father's return from prison. What could bring our old Eddie back faster than a nice cup of coffee with sausage, eggs, and toast on a Sunday morning? Money was no longer an issue. All the accounts previously frozen had been opened as soon as my father paid the fine which was announced to him along with his prison sentence on the day he was released. Checks and packages poured in regularly and now officially and directly (rather than surreptitiously through friends in Hong Kong) from the U.S. by aunts on both sides of the family. All six coffee-making devices previously confiscated by the Red Guards had been duly returned with their owner on the afternoon Nixon arrived in Shanghai. Quality coffee beans, needless to say, continued to be faithfully supplied on the People's market in great abundance by our African and Latin American Brothers.

Yet brewing coffee with any of the six gadgets seemed risky, since we were not certain if Papa's recent rehabilitation also sanctioned a return to the old lifestyle. Foolish to make the eyes of our working-class neighbors red with envy over little things like coffee which they, after eight years of hard struggle, still could not afford. (No sarcasm meant. My family and I were fully aware of the unfairness of it all, and this was part of the reason I could not get over the futility of all this suffering my family had to go through.)

So we worked out this recipe, which was not as easy to follow in our one-and-one-half-room residence as one might have imagined. To boil water, we had to go down to the first floor where the gas range was sandwiched in the hallway between the door to our neighbor's bedroom and the door to their lavatory. We could not risk bringing the thermos with coffee bag inserted down to the kitchen, since the aroma escaping from the contact of still boiling water with the bag might give us away. Since we could not bring Mohammed to the mountain, we had to bring the mountain to Mohammed. One of my sisters was the designated boiling water carrier. The other sister would stand behind the door with her hand on the knob, listening for the footsteps of the water carrier racing up the stairs. (I could not be entrusted with the task. In my excitement, I might forget to close the door afterwards. No aroma could be allowed to escape to the hallway leading downstairs when we brewed and drank our coffee!) Papa, the most scientific, personally watched over the time. And we experimented week after week until all agreed that the result tasted as good as ever.

In fact, for me at least, it tasted better. Part of that was, of course, because Ahfen was no longer standing behind but sitting at the table with the rest of us. "Warms you up," Papa would urge as Mmma passed Ahfen the sugar and milk — their way of showing appreciation for Ahfen's having gone in the deadly winter dawn to queue for all those things Papa liked and others had difficulty getting.

Light on milk, heavy on sugar, that was how Ahfen fixed her coffee. I could tell from that and the way she sipped it that the thrill was not in the taste. I wondered if Ahfen was remembering my ten-year-old face when I was given my first coffee/milk/sugar drink. And I silently thanked the gods — Mao's Red Guards, Darwin, the Goddess of Mercy, and Madonna — for bringing us all together over this coffee made out of African beans steeped in a Chinese thermos.

So now you tell me whether I am acting Chinese, American, or American Chinese Immigrant when I crave a cup of good coffee after a long department meeting ducking verbal bullets from colleagues on the left and right? Am I Ahfen, who was finally served tea and coffee by the Young Master and Mistress? Am I Mmma, who had just returned from hot water to coffee and tea? Am I Papa, hoping to follow that familiar aroma all the way home? Am I my 20-something self, who loved them all? Or, am I all and none of the above? How am I acting when I sip my green tea when discussing the literary canon with my native English-speaking colleagues mulling over their coffee or with my students gulping down Coke at 8:30 in the morning?

I got hooked on green (Long Jing) and herbal (Chrysanthemum flower) tea during the winter of 1973. People kept on warning through-out the pregnancy: Stay away from anything which might add fire element to your body. Green tea is good for the baby's eyesight. So I quit coffee and black tea and learned instead to distinguish the tastes of tea steeped in pea green, new crop tender tips from tea brewed from forest green leaves mixed with stems aged from sitting in the store.

On Sunday afternoons, Ahfen always dropped by because all the girls, including my sister's two-year-old daughter, were sure to return home. And we'd hold a green tea party with Mmma and us girls sitting around the edge of my parents' twin beds arranged together. Ahfen, being the guest, sat along with Haopo and Papa in the three chairs squeezed against the wall in the space left by the bed and a chest of drawers we had saved from my parents' bedroom furniture. Ahfen's four feet eight frame looked almost comical perched on the edge of the seat, with the tips of her toes barely touching the floor and her torso balanced by her elbows pushing against the sides of the arms to the chair. Yet so gracious, I always felt, because of the green tea gently cupped in her chilblain-swollen hands and poised a few inches above her lap, at the center of her upper body.

I noticed that mostly Ahfen just sat there beaming into the lid of her tea cup, as if she were just as aware and anxious to preserve the symmetry I saw the cup adding to her posture. Or as if she were too busy holding in the joy of seeing the family united and too worried that the joy might evaporate with the steam and bittersweet scent of green at the mere lift of the lid to her cup. At other times, I wonder if she was simply delaying the first sip to prolong the luxury of just sitting there, which she had earned so late in her life and only with the help of a Cultural Revolution. Or maybe, she had simply wanted to avoid the risk of deadening her taste buds with cup after cup of scalding liquid, a hazard of the leisured class she had observed through years of servanting.

Ahfen was not the only one bringing an air of festivity to these afternoons. "A cup of green tea sounds appealing," Mmma had said quietly one afternoon in November when I was putting tea leaves in the cups I had arranged on the window sill, waiting for my sister to bring up the still boiling water. It took even my 84-year-old but sharp as ever grandmother a few extra seconds to register Mmma's request. We were barely getting over the excitement of Mmma's return from her post in front of the window with a cup of hot water in hand to join Papa for coffee and tea. And now she wanted green tea made in an individual cup, all for herself!

With Papa's return, she could once again afford to devote her time and energy to her family rather than providing full daycare to someone else's child. A new Daisy! That was what I saw when I watched Papa, who refused to join in, watch Mmma gently wave the lid of her cup to brush back the floating tea leaves from her lips as she took her sips. I wondered if my mother was silently warning herself that the old Daisy, the one so overwhelmed by her sense of economic dependence on Eddie that she had confined herself to the dictates of his tastes and needs, could not, would not be allowed to return again. She had earned her right to join Haopo and Ahfen over a cup of green tea, working woman to working woman. And she needed that reminder to help her woo Eddie places they had never trod, even in the best of the good old days.

At the same time, I found my own participation in this joyful sight of my three favorite women drinking green tea profoundly disturbing. "Hot water was what you should be drinking instead," I imagined my then-mother-in-law chiding me as I sipped on mine. My then-father-in-law, another connoisseur of Long Jing, never trusted anyone but his wife to make his tea. I knew my mother-in-law liked green tea. I had seen her smile sheepishly when she took a sip from the tea served to a guest who had just left without having touched it. "An evil doing to waste," she'd explain as she savored her drink. But hot water was what she drank from day to day, while she served her husband and had her guests served green tea.

I knew in the eyes of many I was no different from her. Except for the six months at the beginning of the Cultural Revolution when I was being reeducated in a factory, I had never earned a penny. No work available for Society Youth with my family background, the cadre at the lane organization told me whenever I went to ask for a job assignment during Papa's imprisonment. After Papa's rehabilitation, the cadre had to switch to: "Wait for your turn." To remind the cadre of my earnest interest in getting *my turn*, I had been waiting for some time now outside his office for his arrival every Monday morning. No one in my then-husband's family ever asked why I was in such a hurry to leave the house on Monday mornings, assuming that being the pampered daughter, I was rushing to join my parents over the Western breakfasts which had returned with Papa. And I did not volunteer to correct them, knowing that they would not approve of my effort to get a job.

Then I got pregnant. Everyone was thrilled. "A good-fortune child," they predicted, noting how the baby had arrived in sync with the upturn in my parents' life. The Good-Fortune tag made me nervous. I knew that if a job opportunity ever came (which, it turned out, did come soon after my daughter was born), the battle over whether I should take the job assignment would be even tougher now that I had been named the mother of a Good-Fortune child: "Why work when you can afford not to? When the baby needs you?"

The voice of my mother-in-law said: "Virtuous wives make good mothers. Hot water was what you should be drinking."

My body said: "Get up and make yourself another cup of fresh green tea." And I did.

And my mind wondered why I filled myself with cup after cup. Because I was the pampered daughter of Eddie and Daisy? Because the thought of turning into my mother-in-law frightened me? Because I wanted to quench my doubt over my own determination to get and hold a job assignment? Because I wanted to drown my fear of being pulled back by those feet already strong enough to kick me awake in the middle of the night and soon to venture out (before the head, as it happened) and then stand up and walk? And because I wanted to belong where Haopo, Ahfen, and Mmma had finally convened?

"Look at all this." My husband and I were amazed by the tea paraphernalia filling up a whole shelf in the kitchen cabinet in my daughter's studio apartment. I itemized the green, red, and herbal tea, teapots, tea inserts, tea cups from England, Japan, China.

Part of me is convinced that my daughter was born with this unquenchable thirst for tea. This part of me wants to cheer her on: "Drink up, daughter. Don't stop until you've finished all those cups your father's mother never thought to make for herself and your mother's mother never lived to savor." When I listen to this part of myself, I feel confident that the bittersweet scent of this pale green liquid will help my daughter concentrate on where she needs to go to be the kind of working woman she aspires to be.

Another side of me worries about the monster I have created out of my residual guilt, anger, and anxiety from my nonworking pregnant woman days. This other side says: "The voices of thou-shall-thou-shall-not (which Virginia Woolf — a favorite author of Haopo, Mmma, my daughter, and me — had called *the angels in the house*) are not the exact same in my daughter's house and mine." At 50 and after over 15 years of marriage, the angel of my house still chides me for buying green, black, herbal tea — a luxury my husband, the coffee drinker, does not need. I don't want this virtuous wife angel in my daughter's house. At the same time, I also worry that the TV angel in the house where my daughter grew up applauds all attempts to indulge ourselves in the slightest of whims before we have had a chance to sense or find the name for it. There were no hot-water-drinking women in my daughter's life to inject her green tea with the same yearning for release from political, economic and emotional trappings as there were in the household where I conceived her. *A woman not afraid to pamper herself.* In the worlds in which my daughter travels, this could mean irresponsible self-indulgence.

I admire the confidence with which my daughter fuses traditions of tea drinking picked up through me, from TV programs on Japanese tea ceremonies, and while studying abroad in Europe. I don't know how much this confidence will help and how much, hinder, my daughter where she is heading. All I know for certain is that she hears my stories of coffee, tea, and hot water in everything I do, whether I tell them or not. I have to keep on working at these stories, teasing out new details, links and contours as we move on. So she will have her own stories to tell when asked where she is from and whether the Chinese do drink coffee.

Who Was That?

"Who was that?" My daughter and husband asked in 1989, when we were spending a summer in Berkeley and bumped into a young man at an Asian food market.

"Just a student I once had when teaching high school in China," I replied.

"What were you two chatting about?"

"Making arrangments to get together over brunch tomorrow," I announced as casually as I could manage.

"All of us?" My husband wanted to know.

"Yes. The three of us, this student, and his wife, whom I had never met."

To punish me for changing our original plan to spend the morning cruising scenic Highway One, my daughter said that judging from this student's English, I could not have been a very good teacher. "I was his math teacher and only for one term," I explained, "since I was a temporary at the time."

"How could you remember him then, and he, you?" My husband and daughter wanted to know. We had obviously not seen one another since 1975, when this student could not have been more than 15. Besides, at 50 students a class, I had to have encountered at least a thousand such students at the three schools I was assigned to during my five-year history as a high school teacher. Yet I had recognized him as soon as he identified me.

How come? My student and I asked the same of each other during brunch the next day.

I offered the same speculation I had given to my husband and daughter the day before, but this time in Chinese and to my student and his wife: we remembered because we both stood out as obviously not belonging in that classroom.

Yes, yes. My student concurred. We did not have to wait for a dozen some years to meet over brunch in San Francisco to find out about our same — Rotten Nine Category — family background.

We said all this to my student's wife, whom I had just met, because we did not expect my daughter and husband to understand fully. But we knew she would follow how and why my student and I would immediately detect the similarity in our situation from the studied calmness we had both displayed toward the havoc roused by the toughies to intimidate the new female temporary teacher. A demeanor stating to the toughies that we were, in their lingo, *understanding of doctrines.*

The three of us rehearsed what the term had meant: to be understanding of doctrines was to have figured out why the toughies acted tough, how they selected their targets, and how neither to provoke nor be intimidated by their rage. We reminded one another of its meaning. Not because we thought one of us might have forgotten, but because we understood the pleasure of uttering and hearing words we had not needed to use for a long time, because we knew that we were safe from that past in which we had last used them.

His wife reassured us that she could imagine what my student and I also said to ourselves when we maintained our studied calmness: "I needed to hold back all those ugly memories of times when I had been the direct target of toughies. I could not afford to show my fear, so I had better act as if I didn't have any."

In many fewer words than it is taking me now to narrate this conversation, my student and I caught up on the background we had guessed about one another but never talked about. I told about how, when my turn for a job assignment finally came soon after my daughter was born, it was a one-term position teaching biology at a school two hours' bus ride away from where I lived. My student and his wife did not need movies to help them imagine how packed those buses could get, nor what kind of students lived in that district. The cadre at the lane organization had *saved* this assignment for me because he never expected me to last more than a week. After I survived the whole term, the cadre further tested me by reassigning me to a new school which, like the first one, was in a rough neighborhood known for youth gangs. And that was how I became a math teacher for one term to this student.

My student talked about how his parents were moved to the wood shanty in that school district during the Cultural Revolution of 1966. Afterwards, he told of the break from heavy field work he had once gotten from me and had been grateful for ever since. During the month of October, I was assigned to go with his class down to the People's Commune to learn farming. And I had selected him, one of the physically weakest of all 54 students, to be my help around the kitchen. This had been for partially selfish reasons, I quickly assured my student and his wife, since I had figured that I could count on him to give me more help and less trouble than any of the toughies.

My student and I traced the parallels in our Cultural Revolution experiences which we had not dared to talk about, even during the three weeks when we had worked together ten hours daily to keep the stove alive with dried husks and stalks. It only took us a few minutes to cover that past over brunch. We exchanged a few names of the street his or my family had lived on before the Cultural Revolution, of the schools our elders had attended, and of people our families had known. And we let ourselves fill in the rest. No need to restate the pain and shame we could see in one another's eyes.

We did not expect my husband and daughter to follow most of our exchanges, not even if we were to translate our conversation into English for them, as I would have been perfectly willing to. So instead, we got the *two foreigners* more dim sum from the passing cart and filled them in, in English, on the names of the special ingredients we were teaching them to distinguish with their taste buds.

We knew that one had to have been there in that long-ago classroom to understand why I would take time from my hard-earned vacation to catch up, and he on his graduate student stipend would fight for the bill when brunch was over. His wife had not actually been in that classroom, yet she understood as we did that we had not fought to pay for brunch just out of so-called Chinese politeness. Neither merely because, as we say in China, migration makes blood relations out of strangers from one's native land. Rather, it was also the gratification of being reminded that we were no longer there, in that classroom where we first met. This made whatever worries we might have now, over here, worthwhile.

Earlier, during brunch, we had talked about those worries in between our complaints over the impossibility of finding Shanghai-style dim sum in any Chinatown. My student feared that his American professors might not pass his thesis because of his uneven English. His wife worried about choosing the right major, when the two had saved enough tuition dollars for her and after she had picked up more English from the old couple she was taking care of. Were computer programming and MBAs really as hot as everyone had said? Even her parents had heard so in China and, thus, had been pressuring her to go into these fields.

Should he, too, listen to her parents and switch majors?

No job in physics, we agreed, unless he wanted to go into the academy, like me.

Poor pay for academics, we volunteered together.

Yes, tenure-track jobs were few and hard to get, part of the reason my husband and I now lived in the Midwest. Not to mention all the horror stories you hear of people who had been denied tenure after slaving away six years of their life, destined to move from one insitution to another every three years.

"That was why they were called gypsy scholars," I explained.

Yet, even as we spoke, we knew that the *scholar* part would still lure my student on, through his Masters and Ph.D. to a research lab in some university, because his hunger for knowledge had been whetted by years of schooling where teachers were not allowed to teach nor students to learn.

Things would work out, we reassured one another at the end as we waited for the waiter to return with the change. I knew the dazed look on my face from seeing it on my student and his wife. We'd just spent three hours explaining to ourselves what had happened to bring us to this moment. Not the first time, nor the last when we'd run through the same explanations. Yet, in spite of all the stories we'd each learned to repeat to ourselves and others, neither I, my student, nor his wife could forget all these cruel accidents — or the incredible breaks as they often seemed in retrospect — fate had brought us. We knew that without any of those breaks, each of us could have easily ended up still in Shanghai, being a very different person living a very different life. This fortune which had brought us this far, which made us doubt ourselves and fear for its abandonment, was too precarious to be talked about casually over brunch with people we barely knew and might never meet again.

So instead, we said in parting: things would work out.

Meaning: You had to have done something right to have fooled fortune into staying with you this far. So the least you could do was to show gratitude for what you had, which of course always brought me back to my daughter and husband and, I hoped, my student and his wife to one another.

In the car with my family on our way back from brunch, I mused over how close I had felt throughout the little get-together to this student and his wife and also to my husband and daughter. This closeness was all the more stunning because of my apparent inability to capture for my family the past I once shared with that student and his wife, nor for my student and his wife the present I now enjoy with my family.

I suspect it is this very awkwardness which draws me to such get-togethers. It reassures me that I can afford to feel close to this and many other former acquaintances because I know I do not have to live the life I once shared with them. The surge of relief I feel from such a knowledge fires me up for the life I am building with my husband and daughter. But I also know that my husband and daughter only go to these get-togethers for me. Because, as they have both observed, no matter how much I might complain before and after about such occasions, I inevitably get really involved during them. I apparently do not want to miss any of them. It amazes them that I should get all flushed and dazed, brimming with a past I sometimes insist I have no interest in revisiting and over people I often openly admit to having barely known and hardly liked in China.

Who was that?

Just another person I used to know from back home.

I know my husband and daughter have continued to ask the question because they know there is more about this *person* and that *back home* than my answer indicates. There is much more about both than they could gather from either the body language exchanged between me and my acquaintance or from the literal translation of our conversations, which I willingly provide. I think they keep on asking because they know I want them to know more. Because they trust that, if they keep on trying, they might eventually lure me into finding the words to help them know more.

Not all trips down memory lane work the same way. I don't know if either my daughter or husband would remember that other time when we spent Thanksgiving in Chicago and decided to go Chinese since most of the restaurants were closed.

"Do you know this woman?" My daughter asked as she motioned with her eyes to a woman with another party waiting for a table. For some time, the woman had been turning around to steal a look at me. I too had noticed, and had been wondering if she was the person I took her to be and if I should go and talk to her. Then she turned around again. And almost as if we were both responding to the same command, we started walking toward one another, seeking eye contact.

"Who was that?" My husband asked after the woman and I had talked and her party got their table.

"A former classmate of mine from China who now lives in Ohio," I replied.

"A close friend?" My daughter added dutifully.

"I have not talked to this woman for 38 years, since I was 12."

"How come?" both wanted to know.

"Oh, too complicated."

Sensing my reluctance, they gave up.

Too complicated for whom? Neither of them asked. Knowing both, I knew the question could not be far from their minds.

Too complicated for both them and me, I suppose.

To explain how and why this woman (let's call her Neng) and I had stopped talking 38 years ago, I have to go all the way back to 1958 — the winter term of my first year in junior high. I had missed my midterm exams because they were scheduled on the week following Easter Sunday, that time of the year when my family joined Papa's diplomat and banker patients on a vacation by the West Lake in Hangchou. So, a week later, I had to make up my math midterm examination along with several other students who had also been too ill — the official reason for my skipping school — to take the original test and with all the students who, like Neng, had flunked the original exam.

Another week later, instead of getting my grade, I got called into the principal's office. It took me a while to figure out what was going on. The principal questioned me on who was sitting next to me, what I did during the exam, whom I talked to. Then he became more specific. What did I say to Neng, who had sat next to me, towards the end of the exam period? How did she give me the answers? For how many and which of the problems? He assured me that Neng had already told the facts to my homeroom Teacher Xu — in writing! — so he did not really need my confession. He was only giving me the opportunity to come forward on my own, to show my contrition and thus plead leniency for the discipline I was bound to receive.

I don't remember much about the whole conference beyond this sense that I had done something — I didn't know exactly what but it was certainly stupid — to have caused this nightmare. For I realized immediately that no one at school would ever believe my innocence, no matter how I tried to explain. I think I broke down as soon as I got home and saw Ahfen. Then Haopo was brought in and then, Mmma.

Mmma was livid with anger. At me, I felt, for being caught in this ridiculously humiliating situation and for acting so scared when I knew I was innocent. Then she called the principal to demand an appointment, while Haopo kept on reminding her not to assume that the principal was entirely on the side of my homeroom Teacher Xu. I believe the whole episode dragged on for a month, long enough for me to identify the Neng supporters among my classmates who stared, whispered, and sometimes called me names in passing. When Mmma finished her appointment with the principal, Neng supporters escorted her to the school gate while chanting: Old demon woman! Old demon woman! The commotion impressed on me the hopelessness of my situation, of having my innocence defended by a mother who was "decadent enough to be still wearing makeup (!) and pre-revolutionary style clothing."

Nevertheless, the principal stopped harassing me after Mmma's visit. Then, Teacher Xu began to look more and more preoccupied during morning homeroom period. When I got my report card at the end of the term, my midterm grade for Algebra was an A instead of the F it would have been if I had still been accused of cheating. No one from the school ever notified me or my mother why the charge had been dropped in spite of Neng's confession and Teacher Xu's conviction. When I returned to school next fall, we had been assigned a different homeroom teacher who acted, along with all the Neng supporters, as if the incident had indeed been a nightmare I alone had dreamt up. But I noticed that everyone acted as if they expected Neng and me to be enemies from then on and, as the code went at school, completely ignore one another's existence. So we did.

Although I can sketch the events leading to when Neng and I stopped talking to one another, I don't know for certain what had actually happened to have caused and then ended my nightmare. Several people offered different but equally plausible accounts.

One came from my best friend through junior high, a girl I'll refer to as Li Li. Unlike a majority of my classmates, Li Li was five instead of two years older than me. Li Li started school a whole three years later than the norm because her Red Army parents had had to leave her behind with a peasant family in the early 1940s and were not able to relocate her until 1951, after she turned ten. Li Li's younger sister was born into that Western-style mansion ten blocks from my parents' house which the Party had taken over in 1949 from imperialist bankers and assigned to her high revolutionary official parents. Li Li once told me that for months after she arrived in Shanghai, she referred to her new home as *your place* and to her parents as *your parents* when conversing with her younger sister. The first time she was served potato salad, Li Li offered to wash the dressing off, mistaking the dressing for the slimy white residue she had seen on rotting potatoes.

Teacher Xu had assigned Li Li a seat next to me so that this Daughter of the Revolution could help my homeroom teacher keep an eye on my incorrigible bourgeois consciousness. Teacher Xu did not think it right that my father, with his exorbitant income, should qualify as a High-Ranking Intellectual. As a result of this class ranking, Teacher Xu could not legitimately put me where she felt I properly belonged: with students from Capitalist, Landlord, or other Anti-Revolutionary family backgrounds in dire need of political reeducation. To her chagrin, Li Li and I soon became inseparable. Li Li said she liked me because I reminded her of her younger sister: spoilt but warm-hearted. I took to her because she reminded me of Ahfen's adopted daughter Yinyin: the same small but tough build, alert but open to the outside world. Teacher Xu was always saying to Li Li that *we* — meaning, of course, Teacher Xu and Li Li, the Descendants of Revolutionary Classes — should seek solidarity only with people of *our own* class. But Li Li, who had the highest ranking cadre parents in the whole grade, did not have to take the teacher's not-so-subtle warnings against bourgeois me.

As illustrated by the cheating episode, the same obviouly did not hold true for the rest of my classmates. According to Li Li, the whole cheating episode had begun during the week after the make-up exam, when I was again absent from school, this time from a real cold which Ahfen was convinced I had caught from not wearing appropriate clothing when cruising in the cool evening air on West Lake. At a Youth League meeting, several students had reported that they had seen Neng trying to peek at my exam sheet. Under much probing from Teacher Xu, they concluded that I could have been a willing accomplice to Neng since no one had seen me trying to cover up my sheet. Instead, I had acted as if I was not even aware of Neng's attempts.

Teacher Xu was openly ecstatic over the possibility of pinning me down as an accomplice. Neng was in the teacher's office for a whole day. According to busybodies who kept track of its progression by peeping through the windows during the breaks, Teacher Xu became more and more visibly agitated sometime toward the afternoon. Li Li speculated that when Neng failed to yield any evidence of my willing assistance, Teacher Xu began to lead and coerce. By the time Neng was allowed to leave the teacher's office, she had revised her confession enough to have turned herself into a reluctant accomplice to me, the cheater, who was allegedly leaving my exam sheet in her view to indicate to her the problems I had failed to solve and needed help with. In the written confession, which Teacher Xu leaked to her trusted student leaders, it was stated that I had bribed Neng into all this with the promise of an imported pencil box, two tiered, with a rolling-screen lid like the one I had been sporting at school, which would itself be filled with imported pencils with brightly colored plastic baby-doll heads on the tips, pencils I had also been known to give, freely, to corrupt my classmates. With the confession in hand, Teacher Xu had immediately gone to the principal and pressed him to discipline me.

Li Li wasn't sure whether the principal ever believed Teacher Xu. But she assured me that Teacher Xu would never have let the case rest until I had been given a failing grade, if she had not been caught having an affair with the physical education teacher toward the end of the term and consequently been labeled a Rightist during the summer vacation.

Mmma's version corroborated Li Li's story on the source of evil, although Mmma had a different explanation for Teacher Xu's motives. Envy (and an inferiority complex) was Mmma's conclusion when commenting on the antagonism she sensed in my teacher's body language towards *our kind,* which Mmma had detected as early as the fall before, when Teacher Xu had paid us a home visit. And Mmma traced Teacher Xu's inferiority complex to her noticeable country accent, her vulgar gold-filled tooth, her dark, shriveled skin.

Mmma attributed the happy ending to my nightmare to the lack of academic foundation to the allegation. At Haopo's suggestion, Mmma had brought five years' worth of report cards, which she shoved in front of the principal in a manner Haopo would definitely not advise. What kind of grades had the *other girl* — Mmma's name for Neng — been making? A solid A student asking for help from a girl who had failed both her midterm and final the previous term and had just failed again during the midterm? Only a perverse, crazy homeroom teacher like Teacher Xu could actually buy the story from this *other girl.* My mother's reasoning, she told Haopo upon returning home, rendered the principal speechless.

My mother could not get over the perversity of a teacher trying to get at a student out of pure envy. But neither could she live with the idea that I might have owed my deliverance from the ridiculous situation to a communist political movement against the Rightists. So she put her faith in the triumph of reason and facts over petty lunacy.

My elder sister and her friends had their theory on how and why Teacher Xu was out to get me. They believed it was my parents' fault for not properly admonishing Cook whenever he acted snotty toward our school friends and some of Haopo's poor relatives. This Cook treatment, unfortunately for me, was given to Teacher Xu during her very first home visit. To Cook's north-of-the-river ears, there was little difference between my homeroom teacher's Shanghai country accent and the accent Ahfen brought from her south-of-the-river province. Assuming that Teacher Xu was someone from Ahfen's village, he had made her wait in the pantry. Twenty minutes later, when Ahfen finally came back to the pantry and figured out she was talking not to someone who had asked for her but to my homeroom teacher, Ahfen was so flustered that she led Teacher Xu straight to the downstairs parlor instead of the much more modestly furnished upstairs small dining room usually used for government-related visitors. The long wait in the parlor for Mmma to be awakened from her afternoon nap and get dressed probably made things worse, adding insult to the injury rubbed in by the contrast Teacher Xu was sure to have noticed between the pantry and the parlor and the significance of having been initially misplaced in the former.

You are doomed, kiddo, my sister had announced right away.

While I saw a point in all three theories, my own understanding of the whole cheating episode expanded as I became more attuned to the national context of Teacher Xu's frenzy in persecuting me. History books have since taught me to locate the episode within the Anti-Rightists movement of 1956–58, a difficult time for Intellectuals at all ranks, including school teachers and high school students. In 1956, some Intellectuals took seriously the Party's call to "Let a hundred flowers bloom, let the hundred schools of thought contend" and publicly voiced cogent criticisms of several Party policies. To pluck clean the *poisonous flowers* it had lured into blossom, the Party launched an Anti-Rightists movement in 1957. Every work unit was assigned a quota — a specified number of Rightists supposedly lurking among the Intellectuals working within the unit. A recent movie helped me grasp the kind of finger pointing — away from me, please! — resulting from these quotas. The main character returned to a meeting after a brief visit to the bathroom to discover that he had just been named a Rightist by equally frightened colleagues with stronger bladders.

Ironically, the word Rightist took on concrete meanings for me from watching the demise of Teacher Xu. During political education class, we were assigned to study the Big Character Posters strung in neat rows across the gym aimed at Rightist students and teachers. From the posters, my classmates and I learned the "dirty secrets" haunting my former homeroom teacher. It turned out that she was from the country but not the daughter of a Poor Peasant. Instead, she was born into a Rich Peasant family, which put her in an entirely different and not at all pure class ranking. One caricature featured her as a wolf in sheep's clothing, with a gold tooth flashing through her bloody mouth. The sign of vulgarity which had tipped off my mother had now become proof of Teacher Xu's anti-revolutionary heritage. A Big Character Poster exposed another dirty secret: her betrayal of her husband, the son of a Poor Peasant, himself a Working-Class man, by committing adultery with a Bourgeois Intellectual, himself the son of a Landlord!

The posters put me in touch with Teacher Xu's anxiety over being caught passing as a Daughter of the Revolution, which in turn explained the vehemence with which she had impressed upon students like myself the purity of her own (faked) family background in comparison to the corruption of ours. I understood better her anger at my father's ability to pass as a High-Ranking Intellectual and then, to remain exempt from the Anti-Rightist movement targeting Intellectuals of all ranks, a frenzy which she knew coud easily land on her at the slightest hint of her secrets. Her eventual demise during the movement almost made logical her vengeance against my entitlement as the daughter of my specially-stationed father.

It surprised me that I could not derive much joy from her descent even though I felt I should, given the nightmare she had put me through. I found myself feeling sorry for her when seeing her publicly taunted by the same Neng supporters who had earlier called me and my mother names. Every Thursday for the next two terms, Teacher Xu — now sentenced to full time labor-reform — and I had to take orders from the same workers in the school cafeteria, where I was assigned with some of my classmates to learn physical labor. (Others in the class went to factories or worked under the school custodians.) Watching Teacher Xu snap peas across the table from students like myself whom she had formerly so vehemently criticized, I often wondered if she had taken notice of the parallel in her present and my former situation. If she had, I could tell from the dirty looks she continued to give me that she found it much more humiliating to have me than someone like Li Li witness her descent. So I tried to stay clear of her. If she only knew how much fear her looks could still invoke in me!

The national context to Teacher Xu's hatred made me question my own previous conclusions that my elementary school teachers had been more accepting of me because they were more humane, as Haopo would have put it, or because they had more moral integrity, as my mother would put it. I had always been the first to wear a skirt to school and the last to change back to pants. *Little Soviet girl,* the one-legged elementary school principal had always called me when I showed up in my wool pleated skirt and white cotton knee socks in late October. This nickname automatically sealed an approval of my foreign dress code, since all at the elementary school knew of the principal's Revolutionary Glories, which had cost him a leg but earned him this leadership post.

The fact that I took private ballet lessons with a White Russian had not bothered the Chief Instructor of the Red Pioneers in elementary school as it had Teacher Xu. The Chief Instructor had seemed delighted to have me dance the main role in my leather ballet slippers alongside my schoolmates in their black, cotton-soled, homemade shoes. We won all kinds of awards for the school in citywide competitions. And when a news reporter interviewed me and I was modest toward myself and praised instead the achievements of my teammates — as Haopo had always taught me to when playing with my siblings and cousins — the Chief Instructor praised my Socialist Group Spirit on the school intercom during morning period. She had seemed happy to have been invited to my recital, for which my White Russian ballet teacher had rented the best theater (on the opposite corner from the French Club), and my parents had greatly pleased my ballet teacher by buying up several rows of seats during one performance. Papa's patients sent baskets of fresh flowers which the photographer had trouble squeezing into one picture, with me, of course, pivoting in the center, with various beautifully wrapped gifts scattered around. And when I took the photo to school, my Chief Instructor had asked for a copy to keep.

When a flood devastated the countryside north of the river, I cleaned my bookshelf of folk tales I had lost interest in and donated them along with two months' worth of my allowance money to the flood relief organized at school. For my larger-than-most support to our Peasant Brothers and Sisters, I was awarded a special prize at the end of the school year. The fate of Teacher Xu during the Anti-Rightist movement made me wonder how my one-legged elementary school principal and my Chief Instructor of the Red Pioneers had fared through the national frenzy, how they would have treated me if I had been a fourth or fifth grader under their supervision in the midst of that movement.

Seeing Teacher Xu's fate also put a slant on my anger toward Neng, whose father, Li Li later learned from a Youth League member meeting, had also been labeled a Rightist. By that time the word Rightist had taken on other, personal meanings. I had lost one of my best friends at the ballet school to that word. When her Rightist father was sentenced to 15 years in a labor camp in the northeast of China, her family lost its main source of income. I had seen the fear this same word had brought into the eyes of my paternal aunt: a Big Character Poster had appeared at her work unit denouncing an unnamed wife of a bourgeois man, which my aunt knew everyone else would recognize as meaning herself, who had been overheard speaking English on the phone when talking to family members during office hours.

I loved my parents enough to sense what it could have meant for my cousins to see that fear in their mother's eyes. The thought made me wonder how my cousins would have acted if one of them had had to undergo the kind of pressure I knew Teacher Xu had put on Neng, my enemy, during the cheating episode. I wondered after learning about the fate of Neng's father: did Neng cooperate with Teacher Xu out of concern for her and her father's vulnerability? The suspicion was deepened when, years later, I was to realize that Neng had probably suffered through the cheating incident all alone, never mentioning any of it to her parents.

It turned out that Neng's father was in medical school with Papa. A small world indeed. My mother found that out when bumping into Neng's mother in the early 1960s, shocked by how much that woman had aged. During the encounter, Neng's mother mentioned that their daughter had been in the same class with me. They (Neng's parents) had figured it out from the beginning, since there could have been just one *foreign doctor* in Shanghai. I, of course, had always heard my parents mention this doctor friend who happened to have the same last name as Neng, but I never made the connection. I don't think Neng's mother would have mentioned me in connection with Neng if she had been aware of the cheating incident. From the way my mother carried back the information, I did not think she had connected the daughter of Eddie's doctor friend with that *other girl* who had so unfairly wronged me.

I am not quite sure why I never pointed out the connection to my parents either. A part of me probably did not want ever to recall this episode. Part of me might have been worried that my mother's sense of righteousness would push her to announce the fact to Neng's mother when they met again. That would have been embarrassing, given how much Neng's family had already suffered because of her father. So although Neng and I stayed on non-speaking terms, our parents remained clueless. And news of Neng and her family kept on filtering to me through my parents because they assumed I would be interested in *that classmate of yours*. Well, they were right for the wrong reasons.

Through the years, as I moved myself further and further away from this nightmarish scene of my adolescence, I began to see differently my own bourgeois behavior leading to the incident. *Spoilt* was the word my mother and friend Li Li had used to describe my guileless taking-for-granted attitude toward my privileges. I now call it an obnoxious sense of entitlement. I don't condone what Teacher Xu and the Neng supporters had done, because I think they were wrong to resort to political witch hunting to vent their (rightful) irritation at my sense of entitlement. As my friend Li Li had implied, her sister, the daughter of the highest ranking Party Official, could be just as spoilt as me, the daughter of an Imperialist Lackey.

But I have learned to blush for my adolescent insensitivity to the deprivation of others. I have long since shared the irritation of Teacher Xu toward my 11-year-old self wallowing in my own generosity when bringing to school, to share, all this imported stuff — food, school supplies, pocket money — which still remained, almost a decade into socialism, far beyond the reach of most of my classmates with their just as hard-working and capable parents. Here is where I parted ways with Teacher Xu and the Neng supporters. It seemed clearer and clearer to me as I got older that my insensitive behavior had little to do with the class rank assigned by the Party to my parents but everything to do with the kind of lifestyle which my and Li Li's parents were able to buy for their children. Hence my anger at people who, when irritated by such a privileged lifestyle, vented their rage only toward the children of the privileged but less politically favored classes but not toward the children of high government officials.

This much I also learned during the Cultural Revolution, when the family backgrounds of high ranking Party officials were widely exposed through Big Character Posters: the lifestyle linking me and students like Li Li had its base beyond the kind of houses we lived in and the domestic services we were provided. We were also connected by the educational experiences our parents shared. Could it be any wonder that my best friend in elementary school until sixth grade, when boys and girls stopped talking, was also the child of a High-Ranking Party Official?

I'll refer to this elementary school friend as H. H transferred to my school in second grade, when his father had been assigned, directly from the Central Committee in Peking, to literally run Shanghai. My homeroom teacher assigned me to share a desk with H probably because I was considered outgoing (so claimed all my earlier report cards) and a favorite of the one-legged Red Army principal, who had personally escorted H with a bodyguard in Liberation Army uniform to our class. The principal then reminded us of our duty to welcome the son as the city had welcomed the father by doing everything we could to help H adjust to the changes he and his family were making in answer to a call from the Party.

So I put out my warm-hearted best, and H and I became inseparable at school. I have a lot of fond memories of this schoolmate. Imagine, a sunny late autumn afternoon, H and I kicking up the fallen leaves on the pavement as we chased one another down the five blocks to that intersection where we had to part ways to return to our Western-style family houses, his even more grandiose than mine. His bodyguard walked steadily but silently about three paces behind us while Ahma and the pedicab man teased one another and me and H as they followed, the pedicab man peddling Ahma along.

This scene came to mind during the Cultural Revolution, when the Red Guards publicly paraded H's father right in front of the municipal building wearing a lead-laden tall hat with the characters "Capitalist Roader" running vertically across it. I learned from the newspaper about the father's family background, which I at seven and eight had probably intuited from H's manners. A small world, indeed. H's father was the son of a Good Family like my mother's people, except they made their fortune in Tianjin, the most Westernized city in the North. Both his parents were, like my father, products of American missionary schools.

I remember thinking when reading the article during the Cultural Revolution: how much of my friendship with H was built on the possibility that our parents had shared the same enlightenment values but believed in different routes for realizing them? H's parents chose Marx;

mine, Darwin. Yet both, it seemed, were good enough at their chosen paths to buy their children (until 1966) the privileged life denied to the Teacher Xus and the Neng supporters of the world. It struck me as ironic that during the Cultural Revolution, at a point in my life when I had the most reason to be nostalgic toward those lost privileges, I was also most convinced of the unfairness of it all.

Maybe because the Cultural Revolution had finally put me at the bottom of the other side, I also began to wonder how Neng's father might have talked about the fortune of my father and his practice with Western diplomats and bankers during the height of the Anti-Rightist movement. How had Neng felt about my imported pencil box and pencils when I took them to school, when she had just spent the previous evening trying to figure out what had put that fear into the eyes of her less fortunate but equally skilled and more hard-working doctor father? And I wondered how long I would be able to resist cooperating with the authorities if I had been Neng, finding myself caught in such a vulnerable family and personal situation.

I realized that Teacher Xu's call to draw a clear class line from students like myself would not, could not, mean the same to students with as different family privileges as my best friends Li Li or H, my enemies Neng, and some of the Neng supporters from truly working-class families. Later on, when I learned of the suicide of my junior high principal, whose impure family background had come under attack during the Cultural Revolution, I wondered too if he recognized me as someone brought up with the same notions of honesty, diligence, and study habits he had instilled in his children. How much had his impure background affected how he had heard Teacher Xu's accusations and Mmma's defense and consequently, how he had taken care of my fate?

Predictably, since coming to the States and until I ran into Neng in Chicago that Thanksgiving, I never thought about this cheating incident at all except after I was experiencing shock and anger at the guileless sense of entitlement I noticed in my daughter, the children of some of our relatives and friends, and some of my students. "So spoilt," I say when making a mental checklist of the stuff — gadgets, vacations, clothing, lessons — so eagerly showered upon and casually accepted, and then carelessly dispensed with by these youngsters. Watching these kids, I often wonder how many of my observations on their personality traits — lazy, unmotivated, confused, spoilt — have to do with my anger at the fundamentally unfair distribution of wealth among equally hard-working and deserving parents on both sides of the Pacific. And I try to remind myself of my own adolescent warm-hearted idealism as well as my guileless sense of entitlement. And I ask: "What kind of words and action from a teacher and elder would have best benefitted youngsters like my adolescent self?" If I too had been granted the authority to hand out grades, educational futures, political privileges based purely on the government-assigned class ranks of the parents of such spoilt but warm-hearted youngsters, would I be as fair-minded as my 11-year-old self had hoped her teachers to be? I would like to be able to say that such thoughts have made a better teacher and elder of me. I don't know that I can.

When Neng and I finally talked to one another that Thanksgiving in Chicago while waiting for our tables, we did not once mention that incident, almost 40 years earlier, instrumental in turning us into nonspeaking enemies. Instead, we talked about what each had heard about the fate of the other's father during the Cultural Revolution. Then we talked about the relatives, my mother's sister and her father's brother, who had sponsored me and her to leave China — our way of reassuring each other that we had both realized long since that the ugly memories surrounding the winter term of 1958 were not the only thread linking us. Through the years when we were not-talking, we had been rehearsing in our minds the other links we were only just now finally establishing, face to face on Thanksgiving day in Chicago. And our awareness of these links had long since changed our understanding of what we did (and did not do) in junior high from the understanding we had back then.

With the old business out of the way, Neng and I caught up on the present. She expressed surprise at news of my being an English professor, reminding me of the fact that I was one of the few to have been admitted to the most prestigious science-oriented high school in Shanghai — her way of acknowledging my command over math and the ludicrousness of accusing me of cheating?

I wanted to tell her that I never did realize I was so interested in science until that incident, which put my mastery of the subject in question. "Show them," Li Li had whispered to me going into the classroom for our finals that winter term, when my fate was still uncertain. I had studied and studied, as I never had, worried that I might let down people who had banked their trust in my innocence. I was determined to get that straight A they believed I deserved. I studied so hard that I discovered a love for these subjects, which I had up till then only learned because I had to.

But I decided not to mention any of that to Neng, since I could not figure out how to say it without referring to the incident and thus risk embarrassing her. Instead, I asked her what she did. A computer analyst. I told her that I was not surprised, indicating my knowledge that she made better than passing grades in math after the incident. I had often speculated that the incident and her father's downfall had somehow jarred her out of her complacency and made Neng, as Mmma would have said, want to learn, and in ways she never had before.

But I didn't say any of that aloud either. We talked about children, husbands, and former schoolmates. I wonder if she, too, had not mentioned most of the Neng supporters simply because she did not have any good news of them. I myself had noticed that almost all the classmates from High-Ranking Party Official families and Capitalist or Intellectual families were either abroad or doing extremely well in China's *new, open market*. I had heard talk of the dire lives of ordinary people as a result of China's Great Leap Westward. And I wondered if most of the Neng supporters had again fallen between the cracks of China's ever-changing government policies because of their continued lack of cultural capital. My guess was, most of them had been, as they say in China, let down from their positions. Meaning, put on pensions by their bankrupt state-owned work unit, pensions which were worth about one quarter of the income earned by workers with jobs at private enterprises. But there was no time to get into any of that. The hostess came by to let Neng's party know their table was ready.

We were lucky, Neng and I reassured one another on parting. Maybe not enough in comparison to those above us but certainly abundantly in comparison to those below us.

"Who was that?" My daughter and my husband asked as we followed the hostess to our table.

"A former classmate I have not talked to since junior high," I replied.

I wanted to add: "I once sat next to this woman when taking a makeup midterm math exam 38 years ago. And I don't know if I would have become me and she, her, if I had not done that."

But I did not. I did not think I could make my husband and daughter understand all this I have just written down.

I think my husband and daughter keep asking questions about my past because they know I want them to know more and because they trust me to eventually find the words to help them know more. But I will only be able to tell more if I learn to seize the help they offer with their questions and trust their willingness to hear more. From now on, I'll have to try harder. They deserve more for their questions.

No more missed opportunities.

New questions and new revisions, as we prod one another backwards to move forward.

Why Couldn't You Be More Like That?

I have a fifth cousin who never tires of reminding my sisters and me that he was sent to medical school at St. John's University in Shanghai during the late 1940s because his father had been inspired by what Haopo had done for Papa.

A few years ago, this cousin, whom I will call Dr. Wong, took early retirement from his position in a major hospital in Shanghai to help his son study for the MCAT in the States. He had better English than his son, thanks to his having been sent to the *best* missionary schools. When his son was accepted by a medical program, Dr. Wong accompanied his son to a university town in the South. And this is what Dr. Wong does in his son's studio apartment (across the Pacific from his wife, to whom he plans to return after his son passes the board examinations): he cleans and cooks so that the son will not be distracted from his studies. Then he goes over the lecture notes provided by the program for the courses his son is taking, putting Chinese translations by the side of concepts which his son may already know through biology training in China but must now re-learn in English. At night, Dr. Wong goes over the lecture notes with his son, this time to explain the concepts which his son does not yet have enough English to fully grasp.

No matter which of my relatives is telling this story and for what purpose, I am overwhelmed by the parental devotion this father demonstrates toward his children. Stories like this one remind me that I am the world's most unnatural and therefore, most undeserving mother. I left my daughter at the tender age of eight. Worse yet, I had hesitated to bring her out when, a few months afterwards, the Chinese and U.S. governments reached an agreement to let family members of Chinese students accompany them when they studied abroad.

When relatives suggested that I take advantage of this unprecedented opening in U.S./Chinese diplomacy, I was the mother who had said: "I don't know if I can handle it."

I longed to have my little girl with me. But I couldn't decide which was better for her: the life of "a princess" under the love of two doting grandparents with the wealth to hire servants and grant all her material needs or life with "a single mother" struggling to keep the grade average necessary for retaining a graduate assistantship and thus, a foreign student visa to remain in the U.S.? I was not sure I could trust love alone to sustain us through the hurdles of immigration, divorce, graduate school, and financial strain.

I was the mother who could not say in good conscience that she would have promptly started the application procedure if her relatives had not taken matters in hand. They literally pushed me into immediate action by promising and then promptly mailing to me the necessary application forms. A relative of a relative volunteered to chaperone my daughter during the 19-hour flight when she herself would return to the Midwest after she had paid her annual visit to her aging parents in Shanghai. Another relative living in the same midwestern town offered to keep my daughter for a whole month, to buy me time to find a place close enough to the university that did not have a no-pets-no-children policy and which I could afford with my $500 per month teaching assistant stipend. During the day, this relative took my daughter with her to her clinic, where a friend from church, her receptionist, and nurse took turns babysitting. Then, this relative personally dropped my daughter in the eastern city where I lived while insisting that *it was no trouble at all* — merely on her way to another relative's for the Christmas break.

I was the mother who did not know for certain if she would have filled out the necessary forms for getting her daughter out of China if she had not also known that she could always count on more promises to help out with money, time, and love, promises made without words and before she even knew to ask. I knew what to expect because we had been there before: I would never have been able to handle my job assignment back home if my sisters had not taken turns looking after my infant daughter, as they waited for their own job assignments. No need for words because that was what family did. Sure enough, all my expectations were as promptly met this second time around as they had been back in China. The ones who lived close by took my daughter in during spring and fall breaks whenever the holidays interfered with my work schedule. Those living further away helped with the bus or air fare. All sent her home to me afterward with clothes, toys, pocket money, and the precious knowledge that she was loved and worthy of being loved by men and women so different that they could not agree on what made her a good girl, why she was so good, nor what was best for her.

Worse yet, I was the mother who, on the very first day she got her daughter back, had told her daughter to entertain herself with a paper construction kit. How do you explain to an eight-year-old daughter you had walked out on a year earlier why you had to type up this term paper and hand it in before five in the afternoon, just because you had to? No matter how I tossed the words around — foreign student visa, graduate assistantship, rent and grocery money, . . ., all pending on the completion of this paper — I knew I was practically telling my child that I had made her come all this way so that she could be neglected by me.

My daughter, however, was very understanding and played quietly with the kit by my side. Around noon time, she asked: Mom, do we eat lunch at this place of yours?

The word *yours* brought back the image of Li Li referring to her new home with her parents as *your house.* Tears welled up (as they do now, at the memory of my daughter's young voice). So much to be done to make this place *ours* yet so little time between noon and the five o'clock deadline.

Seeing my agitation, my daughter announced proudly that Granny Ahfen had taught her to make fried rice with eggs and leftovers.

So I had to say *not now,* and give her juice and crackers instead.

I don't know if she still remembers that we did make fried rice that evening, after I had dragged her out into the December snow around

4:30 to hand in the term paper. We walked the 25 minutes each way to save bus fare. Our first family outing in the U.S. Afterward, I stood her on a chair in front of the stove and pretended to follow her instructions. Never tasted better, I assured her, and meant every word of it. I was so happy to have her back that I shuddered at the thought that, were it not for my relatives, my daughter could still be in China and I could still be wondering if I would be able to "handle it all."

Because I know all this about myself, I am always acting weird around my daughter. I say mean things to her about relatives and friends whose parenting styles I worry might make me look bad. Yet I elaborate and defend the point of view of these relatives and friends whenever she expresses the slightest hint that they appear nosy and controlling to her increasingly standardized American eyes. Deafened by guilt, I can only imagine one intent and function for all the good parent stories my relatives are always passing around: as set recipes for judging what all parents should do — what I failed to do when my daughter was eight.

But my daughter is no longer eight, nor I the woman I was. Nowadays, my daughter comes home with new recipes she has developed from all sorts of cuisines. And I don't pretend to follow her instructions all the time. I work on them instead, knowing that she trusts, expects me, to substitute an ingredient here and alter a measurement there, as she herself has done to all the recipes I have gleaned from my relatives back home and over here. Sometimes, between the two of us, we come up with so many improvisations that we lose track of the original recipe. And we laugh when we realize that. We tell each other that this is probably what cooks do, anyway.

I want to involve my daughter in doing the same with the good parent stories my relatives are always passing around, to play with new, different ways of hearing, telling, and using these stories. Knowing her, I would not be surprised that she has long been improvising on these stories. To get her to share with me where she has been taking these stories, I have been working on a few possibilities, rough cuts on how I might break my habit of clinging to the refrain of "Why can't you be more like . . ." when consuming my relatives' stories and their story-telling efforts.

Cut One: Collective Prompting

The story of how I got my daughter back is more than a story of my hesitation to start the application procedure. It can also be told as a story of the good fortune of having relatives not afraid to repeat to me the many good parenting stories they felt I should not be allowed to forget — stories (they knew?) I would never want to forget. And it can be told as the story of those relatives not being afraid to remind me of these stories at a time when I was most likely to have trouble remembering. So many mothers willing to help before I even knew to ask. All of them have stories of themselves and others suffering the pain and guilt of long separations from their children, of emotional gaps which took years, often without much success, to mend. All are brimming with memories of broken hearts, of the confusion and anger of young children who had to be told, often by themselves — the children's mothers — that a father who had gone abroad to study had abandoned them for another woman, over there. All have tried and seen others struggling to preserve with carefully chosen words and actions the conviction that children come first.

A side of me will always believe that when recalling these stories, my relatives often wonder why I could not be more like the good ones than the bad ones. But another side of me also knows that they could have used these stories to arrive at very different actions: taken meas-ures to pressure me to either go back to my first husband or delay my doctoral work, all in the name of "children come first." Both reso-lutions would have been familiar, had been previously pressed upon them or their friends and relatives. Many of my relatives had indeed done so: both stayed with the marriage and delayed their graduate education for the sake of the children. But, when trying to help me, my relatives relied on neither of those solutions. Instead, they came up with offers that prompted me to seek actions which tested my heart and will in the new setting I aspired to move toward.

My relatives had not taken steps to turn my life into a replica of the characters populating their good parenting stories. Rather, they took action to create a situation, one in which my daughter would remain a central character in my waking life as well as in my dreamscape while I coped with my divorce and graduate work. They offered advice and promised help, but did not prescribe a standard setting, nor set roles, for either my daughter or me. It seems that they had recalled these stories to figure out not only the similarities (which I had assumed to be their sole purpose) but also the differences between then and now, back there and over here, those parents/children and this daughter/mother. They had used these stories to figure out what they could do to help, in ways others had earlier failed to do for them. They took my daughter in during school breaks to buy me the time to prepare for my comprehensive exams. They received "the 11-years-younger foreigner" I later married with the same graciousness and seriousness as they would the husband of any other relative.

Without their input, my daughter and husband would not have a story about those Thursday evenings in 1982, when I was taking a graduate seminar required for my degree: he in his apron cooking over the stove and she, standing on a chair placed eight steps away — a distance which had taken them weeks of fighting to settle on — so that she could see what he was doing and offer unsolicited criticisms without crowding his space, while he followed the instructions I'd earlier scribbled on a piece of paper to make her the dish of her choice. She knew what "stir until done" meant from growing up in a household where, being the "little princess," she was always welcome to hang around the kitchen and sample the food as it was being cooked. He came from a household where "stay away" was what kids do when Mother prepares dinner, and where food was cooked according to oven temperature and timing. They both loved food. They both had strong opinions on what the other should or should not do. There were no sit-coms or movies

telling them how to live with each other and with me. So they improvised on the rules of conduct as Thursday evenings came along.

Twelve years later, she brought home, after a semester in Paris, a
cookbook with a recipe for *Coq au vin* which took her two days to prepare for him on Father's Day. After the meal, she claimed with equal
pride and taunting that, terrible cook as he was, he nevertheless owed
all his pitiful skills to her coaching during those Thursdays. He concurred by mimicking her consternation when he threatened to serve
her his famous baked chicken and her "bratty shriek" when he was a
mere second too slow in removing the wok from the fire.

Without my relatives' collective prompting, we would not have our
story of Thursday evening cooking lessons. Distributing guilt is not the
only reason my relatives collect and pass around good parenting stories. Theirs is a storytelling tradition which prompts tellers and listeners
to rework old scripts in new settings. In helping to make my daughter
a central part of my life in the U.S., they have offered the three of us an
opportunity to be a part of this tradition. How to stay in touch with this
tradition is the question I'm learning to focus my energy on when listening to and recounting my relatives' good parenting stories.

Cut Two: In Search of New Metaphors

To find more constructive uses for the stories my relatives like to
tell is also to grasp the cultural war these stories often invoke within
me. Someone repeats the story of Dr. Wong's devotion to his son. I
immediately imagine him chiding: "I wonder how your daughter is
doing!" "You must try to be more like I am toward my son, who is just
like your daughter." "Why can't you be more like your Haopo, who was
famous for her devotion to her children?"

I remember I don't deserve to have this daughter who seems to be
managing quite well, all on her own. I fear that she will never be as
close to me as the son of my cousin is to him. I say and do things which

make my daughter feel I am only repeating the story of my cousin to ask why she couldn't be more like that good son of my cousin. Then I fear that she will see me as even more like that Domineering (Chinese, Jewish, . . .) Mother with which comedians are always having such a field day. That makes me angry, bringing back the many times my daughter had asked, as she did in third grade after a sleepover at her new best friend Phoebe's: Why can't you be more like her mother?

An All-American Parent is all kisses, hugs, and sweethearts. I composed this alter ego from studying the differences between the parental figures my daughter finds appealing and the style passed down from my mother and my relatives' good parenting stories. My All-American Parent is soft-spoken, positive, and patient, like Mister Rogers in his neighborhood, a show my daughter watched religiously when she first came to the States. This parent was never in a rush to catch that bus which would transfer my daughter and me to the one that stopped by the university because most affordable housing around the campus was strictly No pets, No children. This parent always teaches through gentle emphasis on the harmony between *you* and *me*, through the *we*. This parent never says: Stop this!

Or: Never do that again!

Only: Can you do what I am doing? That's right!

As I had often told my daughter after she asked her "why can't you" — when she was still young enough to say the words aloud — I would not drug my child with that litany of *I think you are unique and special and therefore beautiful and wonderful no matter what the rest of the world says.* I had to prepare my daughter for the neighborhood I was responsible for having moved her into, where *you* meant foreign and poor, *me* stood for native born, and where doing the same things gently prompted by Mr. Rogers or her best buddy's mother seldom accrued the same responses and rewards for *you* and *me*. Besides, I believed in my mother's dictum: self-improvement is a human responsibility.

But I also knew from the secret joy I got from watching my daughter storm out of the room that I could no more be like my All-Chinese

Parent than like my All-American Parent. I would not call my child *ugly* and *bad* to impress on her the need to be stronger, more motivated, more conscientious, and to better brace herself against the world. The worst products of both parenting styles appeared strangely alike to me. *Injured Souls*, I called them. People so scared of, or oblivious to, the opinions of the world that they can never be weaned from reliance on the positive voice, nor from angry rebellion against the negative voice. However, after 20-some years of fumbling my way through parenthood, I still find myself at the mercy of a tug-of-war between that All-Chinese Parent and this All-American Parent.

One says: Why can't you be more sincere with your daughter? That is what family is for, to be honest with each other about things others do not care enough about you to tell to your face but have no qualms in holding on to and against you when dealing with you.

The other takes me aside and whispers softly: We would not want anyone to feel hurt, would we? Can you do what I am doing? That's right! Let's put more trust in the power of positive reinforcement. Let's offer words of comfort and encouragement which the world is often too critical and mean to yield.

Leave me alone, I tell both even as I want to listen, a little bit, to both. I've seen both work for some children. I like the self-confidence occasionally resulting from the All-American style, and I respect the vigilance toward one's own and society's need for improvement some-times enabled by the All-Chinese style. I want to help my daughter and to have her help me develop both potentials. Unfortunately, most of the time, I am so busy fighting off the pressure to strictly follow one or the other parental script that I trap myself in the guilt that I am falling short by both standards, and I am overwhelmed by my fear over the dire consequences my daughter and I might have to suffer as a result.

It seems that the chances of either Parental Voice ever leaving me alone are zero. I have been playing with the wrong metaphor: instead of visualizing a tug-of-war pulling me apart, I might more aptly perceive the two voices as forces pulling at a tightrope on which I have chosen to walk. Instead of being paralyzed by my inability to become more like the All-American or All-Chinese Parent, I have been trying to put my energy on making both forces work for me: keeping the rope taut. I am learning to put my energy on finding new ways of walking this tightrope. To break the monotony of "why can't you be more like . . .," I try out different questions when listening to and recounting the good parenting stories from both camps.

I begin with the question of whether the child wants what the parent wants for the child. A different register emerges as I tally the stories I have heard filial sons and daughters tell about how much they hate their work, of only being in medicine because it is a family tradition their parents are devoted to and because their parents had reassured them this is the best way to make a living — and the only way for them. My father had wanted to be a writer. One uncle fantasized about being a saxophone player in a nightclub band. A cousin cared more about buying and selling stocks than treating allergies. Yet another preferred being a mathematician to having to deal with patients. My father left many tales illustrating the burden of being the bearer of one's family's dreams and shouldering his neverending debt to the labor Haopo devoted to his education. I remind myself to use the story of Dr. Wong's devotion to his son not only to probe what I should do to help my daughter in her medical career but also, what my daughter wants from me and from her career.

What has she made of her mother's and stepfather's insistence that she attend a liberal arts college to make sure that "medicine is really what she wants" — that "her heart is in it?" How is she interpreting our daily, bitter complaints about the discepancy between what we earn (from doing what we want to do) and what various MD relatives and friends make (from doing what they claim to hate and to have been forced into by their parents)? When I report the unsolicited advice of relatives upon learning her decision to enter medical school and then, specialize in obstetrics and gynecology — "There is no money in medicine any more!" "Long hours and high insurance for obstetricians.

Tell her to go into . . .!" — does she sense my fear that my little girl might someday regret her decisions, which I dutifully attempt to hide behind my open exasperation toward my relatives' refusal to accept my defense (more often in silence than words and in her name but for whom?) that "not everyone sees money and job security as the only criteria for career choices!"? When my daughter hears the story of my cousin's devotion, how does she perceive the differences and similarities between herself and my cousin's son, between me and my cousin? How would she like me to — how might she help me to — work through my fears, worries, ambitions, and excitements over her life so that we don't lock ourselves into the devotion-obligation-debt triangle embroiling other parents and children? I tune myself to these questions when listening to and recounting the story of Dr. Wong's devotion. But I am still new at it, more questions than answers.

To the question of what the child wants, I add the question of what else the parent might be after besides aiming to contract filial obligations. When I take seriously my cousin's claim that he is modeling himself after Haopo, I detect in his devotion to his son an endeavor to pool his resources — English, his medical knowledge, and his housekeeping skills — with his son's resources — youthful energy and enthusiasm. I see an *immigrant* ingenuity common among people having to cope with the demands of new crossings. My cousin's story reminds me of another: the story of a friend of a relative I will call Mrs. M — a mother known to have enlisted the husband of the friend of her own mother at the retirement center to drive her 40 miles to her son's campus to deliver the medication she had a relative bring from China at one tenth of the cost in the States, the medicine her son needs for his asthma but cannot afford. On the one hand, it is easy for me to define the motives of Mrs. M and Dr. Wong strictly in terms of the famous Chinese saying — *Raise a son to safeguard one against old age.* Accordingly, their devotion can be construed as attempts at conscripting their children into filial serfdom. On the other hand, I notice in the perseverance and ingenuity of both parental acts a conscientious rebuttal to that all-consuming anxiety among many U.S. parents and children over one another's so-called independence.

Such parental acts remind me of the many other times I have watched other relatives and friends, certified MDs or laymen, swap information on the Chinese names of a medication someone has been prescribed but could not afford in the U.S. I have lost count of the hours relatives and friends spent to figure out a route for bringing from China something someone needs but cannot get in the U.S. through the help of a friend of a relative of a friend of . . . living on both sides of the Pacific. I have seen the same spirit at work when people pooled together their equally scant command of English to help a newcomer prepare for driver's license tests, green card interviews, or mortgage loan applications.

The vitality of these exchanges often seems to reside less in the act of giving or receiving help in the form of language skills, bits of cultural information, car rides, medication, or home cooking than in the act of reassuring one another that one is in the company of *immigrants* interested in mobilizing resources that might be used to *yi* — move or fuse, diffuse, confuse — regulations and procedures "back home" and "over here." Heard side by side with these exchanges, the story of Mrs. M or Dr. Wong becomes also the story of one immigrant — the parent — trying to remind one's self and other immigrants — including the child — of the many possibilities opened up between friends, relatives, parents and children as they learn to face rather than deny their inter-dependence on one another. Their devotion carries a reminder that denial of our inter-dependence to one another is not a viable option for people having to move away from settings and ways of life they have previously grown accustomed to. Such denial is not a viable option for people hoping to bring changes to settings and ways of life they are now taking part in. It sends an invitation to the child to participate in a creative scavenge for resources and for innovative ways of employing these resources in circumstances they were not intended for. It is a story of reciprocal giving and receiving: in offering help to the child, the parent receives an opportunity to test his or her desire and ability to cope with life's new crossings.

This is the register my relatives and I are having the most difficulty bringing forward when recounting our stories of parental devotion. Knowing it by heart through the little things we see one another do from day to day, we seldom see any need to talk about it among ourselves. Anxious to spare our children the pain of exile, we often let our own need to reassure ourselves and our children that we've done everything possible to ease their crossings dominate our conversations with them. Instead of using our rightful skepticism toward the Mr. Rogers Parental voice to come up with new ways of representing our intentions and efforts, we have also often, out of frustration toward the appeal of Mr. Rogers for our children, retreated back to the rhetoric of filial contracts in spite of our realization that this rhetoric, too, fails to do justice to the stories we pass around. We have thus often been more eloquent in recounting our devotion to our children than in recounting the immigrant attempts we try to make through our devotion.

I am looking for opportunities to go over some parental devotion stories with my daughter: immigrant to immigrant and child to parent rather than merely parent to child. Knowing how much she loves fusion cooking, I believe she will find the image of our developing new steps for walking a tightrope far more appealing than the image of our being torn apart by a tug-of-war between an All-Chinese faith in parental devotion-filial obligation and an All-American anxiety toward maintaining absolute independence. She can help me if I learn to ask for her help. I try without much success most of the time. I will try again.

Cut Three: Listening to the Unspoken

I have also been re-collecting the many virtuous wife tales my relatives like to tell. There is an old saying given in China to women married to less than ideal husbands: "Married to the chicken, stick with the chicken. Married to the dog, stick with the dog." Virtuous wives make good mothers! One does not need much knowledge in pop psychology to understand why I am an avid collector of tales of female piety in marriage.

There is a woman known (and admired) for handling her husband's extramarital affairs "maturely." One of the affairs allegedly involved a younger woman who loved to wash his feet. "An excellent therapy," they say with equal sarcasm and empathy toward the husband's need for ego-boosting. All praise the wife for being so understanding of the stress facing immigrant men: mortgage payments on their $400,000 American-dream house in the suburbs, not to mention dealings with foreigner clients to whom one could just never get close, no matter how much golf or tennis one played with them. They call her wise for knowing that he will come back, always has, after his ego-tripping/stress-releasing affairs: he dotes on his children, a son and a daughter. They admire her ability to keep one eye closed and the other, open and focused on the children.

And then there is another woman who puts up with her husband's public displays of temper, which could erupt with her slightest reluctance to make that phone call to inquire for him after that newspaper ad about a Lincoln Townhouse in mint condition. Some think it makes sense that he is always berating her terrible cooking, her watermelon-shaped body, the spotty cleaning job she does around the house. So humiliating for a man when his wife, a former schoolteacher, is making more money working at a bank than he, a former electrical engineer, now packaging wonton wrappings in a Chinatown factory. All because her English is better.

She picked up more English and faster because she spent more time with the son, whose English had been sped up and fine-tuned by school pressure and TV. Besides, she was the one designated to deal with the foreigners, since he was always so worried about losing face. My conclusion: a vicious circle. But people are always reminding one another that in their late 40s he is still so much better looking than she. I guess I am supposed to see that as another reason she should put up with his verbal abuse. Yet another reason was of course their son, so good-looking and talented with the piano. At 11, the boy is already winning all sorts of scholarships.

For the children, my female relatives and friends are always saying after telling of the compromises they or some others have to make. I mostly sit and fume. I sometimes think they like telling me these stories because they expect from me the comfort only a fallen woman could provide. They can assume my sympathy toward the anger and pain brought by their (to me) insane sacrifices. And they come looking for proof of my failure to give my daughter whatever presumably was ensured to children of unbroken marriages, so afterward they can console themselves with the wisdom of sticking to their *chickens or dogs.*

It angers me to see women I care about suffer like that. I have personal and book knowledge that lead me to believe that children do not benefit from parents who stick together out of fear, greed, obligation, or tradition rather than love. Love, however, is the sticking point for me. I know my own need to see these marriages as dysfunctional and to believe that these women are the guileless victims of traditional teaching. That is my way of compensating for the guilt I feel when their actions bring out the divorcee in me. As a result, it has always been easier for me to assume a parallel in their situations and the situation leading to my divorce. It has been much more taxing for me to hear the love resonating from the bass when the trumpet flirts with the familiar tune of female piety in marriage.

At this point in my life, love is the ingredient I am most interested in extracting from these stories on how to survive and thrive the grinder of immigration. Yet, love between a couple is also that pinch of salt my relatives seldom bother to mention when telling stories of their own lives or the lives of others. It is something we have learned not to call by its name but to assume that anyone who has tasted the stuff our stories are made of would immediately know to treat as a main ingredient.

One of my favorite good wife stories concerns a couple I used to know in China. They met in medical school. Upon graduation, she was assigned to become a radiologist, and he, a surgeon, in a city in the northwest of China. They were in their early 40s when the U.S. government let them in as the married children of her naturalized father. She, not the husband, had enough English to study and probably pass the medical board. But instead, she took a job as a lab assistant so that he, too, could function (with little English) as an assistant in the same lab. And there they have stayed.

"Making so little and living in this cheap neighborhood," the relatives tell me.

"She has been a good wife to him," they add.

"Married to a chicken, stick to the chicken." All agree, some nodding and others, shaking their heads.

A familiar story until I go in search of more. This couple has developed a hobby in glass etchings, which they often send as wedding or Christmas gifts. When I expressed an interest in seeing more of that glasswork, I found a home full of surprises. There were glass objects of all shapes and sizes, with swans, lotus flowers, boats, pagodas etched at the center. None of them would appear tasteful to most of my friends, but each, when you care to ask about the history of its making, could arouse this couple in ways I would never have known to expect.

He designed the pattern for this one, building in seven, eight layers to give the etching depth.

That one? It had so many sharp corners that only she could handle the precision it demanded.

The ones sitting on the piano were more recent, made after their uncle, the dentist, had updated his office and passed his old drills to the couple.

The window panel took them months to finish. Still more time to figure out a way to hang. . . .

I sensed the thrill in their voices, eyes, necks, as they traced the pattern with forefingers so eager that they often got into one another's

way. I saw more in their house — an old upright piano they had bought
from a garage sale and stripped and varnished. Neither of them played,
they told me. But he had always wanted to have one when growing up.
And she liked the look of it. Her grandmother had one just like that,
she and I said simultaneously. So there it stood, proudly, out of tune,
in the corner of their living room.

Then I noticed thick, hardback books with pieces of notes sticking
out, piled on the dining room table. I, being the nosy one, wanted to
know if they were medical books. Yes, indeed. He explained that they
were trying to develop this complex procedure that the lab director
had asked them to perform on one of the animals. They take turns
assisting one another during the operations, he added. She reminded
me that she had always been interested in surgery but was not given
the choice back in China, where everyone was assigned a specialization
upon graduation. Being small and fragile looking, she had been assigned to the radiology deparment. He cut in to reassure me that there
were things she could do in their lab now that neither he nor any other
surgeon he had ever worked with would even try. Lots of practice from
the glasswork, she joked.

Of course, she pointed out, where they work, they operate only
on animals.

That remark reminded all three of us of the fundamental unfairness of fate.

A long pause.

I noticed there was no scrambling to get over the pause with the
usual strategies: no jokes at the expense of the foreigners, nor any
philosophical explanations couched in old Chinese sayings. This was a
new kind of silence I had never experienced before. There was a matter
of factness in the air, almost as if a long time ago, these two had agreed
to practice this silence, deliberately, whenever they were reminded of
this unfairness.

It was a silence which said, let us take a moment to face the
facts. Fact one: the two of them were each making about $30,000 a

year assisting a team of (American) certified MDs whose funding and achievements depended entirely on the couple's surgical skills which, with the proper certification, could be used to save real, human lives in dire need of such assistance and probably bring in at least ten times what they were being paid by the lab. Fact two: she could have taken the board exams, passed them and then gotten into one of those less competitive specializations with shorter residencies which my relatives are always advising recent arrivals from China to look into but which, like radiology, she had no interest in. He could have gotten a job involving neither language, nor surgical skills. But their combined income would end up being significantly larger than what they were currently earning. Fact three: they had decided otherwise. Fact four: because of that decision, they would always wonder, the world would make sure they did, if they had made the wrong decision. A tension in their marital relationship which had impact on everything they did or did not do.

The way they let me into that silence suggested that they had agreed never to cover up the hurt they experienced whenever they were reminded of these facts. They knew the labels others (including myself) had been quick to pile on them: victims of exploitative lab directors and unfair gatekeeping certification rituals, virtuous wife, domineering husband, lack of self-motivation, fear of failure, naive commitment to science, impractical bookworms. Yet, in letting the silence ride, it was almost as if they were saying to me and one another: we could, as others had, use a few of these labels as a shield to fend off the assault of other labels. But we were not going to do that. We would, instead, focus our hearts on helping one another become more than just a label.

I don't, of course, really know what that silence meant to each of them. I know only it felt different to me, that day, from how others and myself usually acted on similar occasions. And I was grateful to them for having let me into this new way of dealing with a familiar roller coaster of emotions. Perhaps similar openings had been offered to me by others previous to that day. But, if they had, I had not seemed ready to take advantage of any. To notice such openings, I had to become more interested in learning about how to make a marriage work at all odds than in justifying why some have to be broken.

Looking back, I realize that I have often heard this couple use the expression *married to a chicken and stick with it* to describe their commitment to one another, both before and after my visit to their house. But that afternoon, what name they gave to this commitment stopped being important to me. I found myself caring only about what they were able to make from it. I was in their house and I had heard them talk about each other and their life. And I, who had lived my whole life in rebellion against the same teaching they claimed to have followed, saw things I could use. I saw other things that afternoon I could dwell on when telling about this couple. But somehow, these details appeared stale. I already knew how to talk about them, too well, and repeating that talk had not seemed helpful for me and, as a result, for the people I love.

No more stories on who did the right or wrong thing, nor on the comment such action makes on my divorce. For the time being at least, I am going for details which can teach us how to live with our compulsory and voluntary crossings.

These rough cuts, I am afraid, are the best I can come up with right now. A beginning, I hope, for my husband and daughter to add on to and revise. Some of my lecturing mode will never go away. I am, after all, someone who makes a living producing words from the words of others.

I always think that if there is a purgatory similar to the one Dante described, my life after death will go something like this: I am strapped in a lecture hall chair. A line of people who have been forced to hear and read my words when I was alive files continuously past me to give me my words back. My husband and daughter, because I love them the most and because they have had to suffer me the longest, reappear the most frequently in that line. I want to convince them that everything they have made of what I had once said to them is the opposite of what I was really trying to say. I want to remind them that, for everything they say I had once said, I had found different things to say on other occasions. But I have no vocal cords.

That would be my purgatory, for all the things I have said and did not say. I think I prefer this to some versions of heaven I hear floating around. For in my purgatory, I will still feel anger, fear, guilt, hunger, desire, hope, ... So will they. Without any of these feelings, I don't know if the three of us can go on making love as we fight, with or without vocal cords.

A Few More Words to My Daughter

One of the professional hazards of immigrants — people with the yearning to *yi* — is the impulse to annotate all how-to books, instruction manuals, recipe books, or family legends. To keep track of which of the tips have worked and which have not worked for us at which of life's crossings, we are constantly rewriting our own as well as others' notes, mentally or orally if not always in writing. We cross out a word here, insert a line there, use expressions coined out of the languages of our past, present, and future lives, expressions we fully expect to supplement with new and different ones as life moves on.

The minute a group of us get together, we will begin to argue over any passing remark one of us might make on a new gadget someone has just bought, a new dish another person has just tried out, a dead relative no one seems to have been close to, a smell only people born and raised in Shanghai would know to miss, or a university scholarship, major, or first job the child of a relative of a relative is always hoping to get. We treat all such remarks as how-to tips on what to do or not do in certain situations, tips to be analyzed, accessed, and often countered with a story of how someone else — one's self, another relative, or an acquaintance — has acted in similar or different situations. *Yimins* — immigrants — like myself can never stop tipping and tipping off one another not because we are pushy, controlling, and stubborn about our set ways of doing things (though we often appear to be exactly so to nonimmigrants), but because we are in the habit of weighing each tip against the many others we've been compelled to follow or been forbidden to try out on both sides of the Pacific. We offer questions, reservations, and countertips to every tip offered, because we have learned not to expect ourselves and others to live in situations which these tips were originally meant for or in situations where we would have access to all the necessary resources. We hope for our conversations to anticipate new crossings and provoke new improvisations.

This is the spirit in which I imagine my family stories should be heard. Not as tips on what you should do, but as stories waiting for you to annotate, as you move on. I trust you to read these stories with skepticism. Check them out. Talk, whenever you can, to the people featured in them and bring me back your notes. Test my notations to see which work for you when, to what extent, how. Jot down your improvisations, not just for yourself and those who come afterward. But, I hope, also for me.